# EDMUND BURKE

and the

## CRITIQUE

of

## POLITICAL RADICALISM

# EDMUND BURKE
### and the
# CRITIQUE
### of
# POLITICAL RADICALISM

## MICHAEL FREEMAN

THE UNIVERSITY OF CHICAGO PRESS

The University of Chicago Press, Chicago 60637
Basil Blackwell, Oxford

*Library of Congress Cataloging in Publication Data*

Freeman, Michael, 1936.
  Edmund Burke and the critique of political
  radicalism.
  Includes index.
    1. Burke, Edmund, 1729?–1797 — Political science.
2. Radicalism. I. Title.
JC176.B83F73  1981      320.5'2'0924      80–16266
ISBN 0-226-26175-1

Printed in Great Britain

# CONTENTS

# 1

# The Problem of Political Radicalism

To a person living in the late twentieth century, concerned about contemporary politics, few phenomena are as scientifically puzzling or morally perplexing as revolutions. The twentieth century did not invent revolutions, but it did spread them. The revolutionary struggles in Russia in the early years of the century have cast a shadow over much that has followed them. The period between the two world wars was dominated in Europe by the conflict between revolution and counter-revolution. Since 1945, revolution has run like a prairie fire through the so-called Third World. In the 1960s, the spirit of revolution even paid a brief return visit to its countries of origin, England, America and France. Revolutionary and counter-revolutionary ideology has played no small part in the concerns, concepts, methods and achievements of the social sciences.

Revolution is high moral drama. Good contends with Evil, though the spectators are not always sure who is which. Revolutionaries denounce oppression and proclaim the fight for freedom. Counter-revolutionaries celebrate civilized order and call upon on all persons of goodwill to resist the bringers of anarchy. Oppression and freedom; order and anarchy; good and evil – these antinomies lie at the heart of political theory.

Barrington Moore has expressed very well the problems posed by revolutions.

The contradiction between politics and morality, never far below the surface in so-called normal times, reasserts itself with particular vehemence in times of revolutionary change. Why is it that revolutionaries sooner or later adopt, and sometimes intensify, the cruelties of the regimes against which they fight? Why is it that revolutionaries begin with camaraderie and end with fratricide? Why do revolutions start by proclaiming the brotherhood of man, the end of lies, deceit, and secrecy, and culminate in tyranny whose victims are overwhelmingly the little people for whom the revolution was proclaimed as the advent of a happier life? To raise these questions is not to deny that revolutions have been among the most significant ways in which modern men – and in many crucial situations modern women – have managed to sweep aside some of the institutional causes of human suffering. But an impartial outlook and the plain facts of revolutionary change compel the raising of these questions as well.[1]

Some will say that no outlook is impartial and no facts are plain. None the less, revolutions do compel the raising of these questions by all those who choose not to protect themselves from reality by dogma or self-deception.

Political theorists seek general truths, general principles, general laws. Barrington Moore's questions are general, and they presuppose certain general truths, such as 'revolutionaries sooner or later adopt . . . the cruelties of the regimes against which they fight'. But are there such general truths to be found? Do such questions have answers that are both general and true?

Every revolution can be viewed as an example of a general type of political phenomenon, revolution. Every revolution can also be viewed as a unique event with a unique place in the history of revolution. Historians generally agree that there is a type of revolution, which we may call the 'modern' revolution, which appeared in history at approximately the same time as the modern state, modern social and economic forms, and modern thought, that is, in the seventeenth and eighteenth centuries. There is some disagreement as to which was the first modern revolution: the American War of Independence, the English Civil War and the Netherlands Revolt all have their partisans. But few would disagree that the revolution that broke out in France in 1789 was the first unequivocally modern revolution and that its image has permeated revolutionary and counter-revolutionary thought ever since.

There is a certain continuity in the image of revolution from

1789 to the present. Of what does this image consist? Of an old order, its defenders, their challengers; of conflict – usually violent – between them; of victory by the challengers (if the revolution is 'successful'); of hopes for a new and better social order; of problems, disappointments, disillusion and even failure in the revolutionary enterprise. This generalized revolutionary challenger to established order I shall call the radical. The radical believes that the problems of the old order cannot be solved, its evils not cured, within the framework of that order. He concludes that a fundamentally new order is required and is prepared to use extreme political means to the end of bringing it about. The radical has an opponent: the generalized conservative. The conservative believes that societies should be thought of as having been built through centuries of human endeavour; that any actual society will be imperfect, containing a mixture of good and evil; that the good should be carefully conserved and the evil carefully remedied; that radicals do not recognize the good that exists and, in their impatience to cure the evil, destroy the good without replacing it with the better. To the conservative, the radical is mistaken about the old order, the revolution and the new order. He does not appreciate the first; he overestimates what the second can achieve; and he does not realize the 'speculative' or 'illusory' character of the third. To the radical, the conservative is at best complacent about the evils of the old order, at worst an apologist for oppression.

The continuity of the debate between radicals and conservatives can be stated more specifically. As the quotation from Barrington Moore suggests, old regimes, seen from the radical viewpoint, are not simply 'evil', but cruel, socially divided, deceitful, tyrannical, and miserable for most of their people. From the conservative standpoint, radicals, through their revolutions, increase rather than diminish these evils. There is one political value not mentioned by Moore which has been at the centre of the dispute between radicals and conservatives: freedom. Modern revolutions have all been fought for something called 'freedom' or something rather like it, such as 'liberation' or 'emancipation'. Conservatives claim that the type of freedom radicals fight for is either unattainable or undesirable or both. They claim, too, that revolutions achieve freedom in no sense, but tyranny.

Radicals at any one time hold varying views. Even that important sub-type of radicals known as 'Marxists' vary greatly. Radicals at one time vary from those at another. The political theories of Thomas Paine, Karl Marx and Mao Tse-tung were quite different. But they were all radicals. They all prescribed and participated in revolutionary movements. What they had in common as radicals is important.

If the French Revolution of 1789 was the first unequivocally modern revolution, Edmund Burke was undeniably its first great critic. Burke was an eighteenth-century political activist, rhetorician, pamphleteer and thinker. He was passionately concerned about the issues of his day, though, in this, he was not different from the other acknowledged masters of political thought. Burke attacked political radicalism. His chief enemies were the revolutionaries of France and the radicals of England. The ideas he attacked were the ideas of these particular radicals at this time and in these places – or, rather, the ideas he attributed to them. But, although Burke believed the French Revolution to be wholly unprecedented, he believed its ideas to be generalizable. Indeed, the chief force behind his violent polemics against the Revolution was his fear that they would be generalized.

The main thesis of the present book is that Edmund Burke, in the face of a particular revolution which he detested and feared, proposed a general conservative theory of revolution and of political radicalism in order to combat and refute the general radical ideas he believed the revolutionaries to hold. It is not important to my purpose to inquire whether Burke correctly characterized the ideas or actions of his opponents. The historian of radical ideas can easily show us that he did not. It is not the particular and distinctive ideas of these particular radicals that concern me. It is the general features of radicalism that Burke identified and criticized. The former are of great interest to the historian. The latter are of greater importance to the political theorist.

If Burke put forward a general conservative theory in order to criticize a general radical theory (which is an abstraction from all particular radical theories), his importance to the late twentieth century is clear. We are still experiencing modern revolutions. Some persons living today wish to promote more of them. Others oppose this project. Both sides assume certain general truths. Our experience of revolution in the twentieth century has been highly problematic. As the first great critic of the first great modern revolution, Burke's theory should at least state the conservative case clearly and forcefully and, in so far as the conservative case has merit, it may also throw light on the perplexities which modern revolutions produce in us.

Any political thinker can be examined and interpreted in different ways from different viewpoints. Here is this man. He lived in this time and this place. He lived in this situation. He faced these problems. He offered these solutions. His ideas were an attempt to change his situation in these ways. This may be called a 'situational' or 'contextual' approach to interpretation.

But no political thinker produces his thought at a blow. His life extends through time. His situation changes. So do his problems. His ideas change. They have a history. This view may lead us to a developmental approach to the ideas of a political thinker.

However, political thinkers do not respond to situations and problems from nothing. They have some knowledge of past political thought. They draw on this to formulate the solutions to their problems. Some past political thought they may take for granted. It may lie beneath the surface of their texts. They may not make it explicit because they think it obvious and that their audience will take it for granted too. Thus, the under-standing of political ideas requires in part the understanding of the intellectual influences upon it.

All these considerations enter into the historical reconstruc-tion of the thinker and his thought. It is the historian's task to reconstruct the thinker in his time and in relation to his past. But to the political theorist, as to the concerned citizen, the relation of the thinker to his future and our present is also important. Here is this man. This is what he thought. What is it to us? His thought drew upon thinkers before him. Can ours usefully draw upon his? The political theorist, concerned with his situation and the problems it raises, moves from this present to that past. The historian, *qua* historian, moves straight to the past and its past and is less concerned with the future of that past. If he is too concerned with the future of the past, he may interpret the past anachronistically, that is, in a way that would not make sense to those whose thoughts and actions were being interpreted.

My ultimate aim, therefore, is to contribute to the solution of the scientific and moral problems raised by modern revolutions. My present aim is to set forth systematically, to some extent to reinterpret, and to assess the important and, I believe, underrated contribution made by Edmund Burke to this enterprise. These aims, and the methods by which I have sought to achieve them, are open to certain philosophical objections. The best statement of these objections has been made in a well-known series of papers by Quentin Skinner.[2] I shall state and argue against certain of his contentions, not to expound nor to refute his general methodological position, but to clarify my own and to defend it against certain plausible objections.

The introduction of Skinner's writings for this purpose immediately poses a dilemma. Skinner is concerned to establish a correct method for understanding texts. He opposes several methods commonly used by scholars and proposes an alternative of his own. By what method are we to understand the texts of Skinner? By his own or by some other? The dilemma is that, in order to *understand* Skinner, we seem obliged to settle the issues he raises. But, to settle these, we must understand his position. A bad case of chicken and egg.

This problem is worse than it looks at first sight because Skinner's method (unless I have misunderstood him) rules out the simplest solution: to get at his meaning by reading what he wrote very carefully. Skinner vigorously attacks the view that a text can be adequately understood merely by reading it with care. It is true that his remarks are addressed to the historian of ideas seeking to understand classic texts. But Skinner's ideas are part of the history of ideas and it is an open question whether his texts are classics. In any case, none of his prescriptions for understanding texts depends on the texts being classics.

We might apply to Quentin Skinner's method, which is 'first of all, to delineate the whole range of communications which could have been conventionally performed on the given occasion by the utterance of the given utterance, and, next, to trace the relations between the given utterance and this wider *linguistic* context as a means of decoding the actual intention of the given writer'.[3] This is rather a tall order, especially if we consider that every text which we seek to understand in order to understand Skinner must be understood by this same demanding method. It is clear that we shall be propelled into a regress which, if not infinite, will certainly be unmanageably long.

Fortunately, Skinner does offer us a solution. In practice, though not in theory, he considers it sufficient, in understanding texts written by his contemporaries, to confine himself to what they have written and to abstain from going beyond their texts to the wider linguistic context. I shall therefore consider it proper to interpret his writings with the method he uses to interpret those of the scholars he criticizes. Even if this method should unfortunately lead me to misunderstand Skinner, it should be remembered that my chief purpose is not to recover the meaning of his works but to raise certain objections to my own.

Skinner identifies what he considers to be a number of common but erroneous methods in the history of political ideas. The first may be called the Myth of Perennial Ideas. The mistake here, according to Skinner, lies not merely in looking for the 'essential meaning' of a political idea as something which must necessarily remain 'the same', but even of thinking of an 'essential meaning', to which individual writers 'contribute', at all.[4] The persistence of certain expressions, such as the 'idea' of utopia, tells us nothing reliable at all about the persistence of the questions which the expressions may have been used to answer.[5] The classic texts cannot be concerned with our questions and answers, but only with their own. There simply are no perennial problems in philosophy: there are only individual answers to individual questions, with as many different answers as there are questions, and as many different questions as there are questioners.[6]

I hold this view to be quite mistaken. There simply are perennial problems in political philosophy. One perennial problem is this: do revolutions tend to bring about extremely authoritarian forms of government even when their stated aims are extremely libertarian? The statement of this perennial problem does not entail a belief that ideas such as 'revolution', 'liberty' and 'authoritarianism' have an 'essential meaning'. It assumes only that the problem is raised by different revolutions taking place in quite different places and times – such as the French, the Russian and the Cuban revolutions. When Burke puzzled over the relation of liberty and tyranny in the French Revolution, and Trotsky sought to explain the 'betrayal' of the Russian Revolution, and Barrington Moore worries about the cruelties committed by those in revolt against cruelty, we have indeed individual questioners asking individual questions; but there seems sufficient intuitive similarity between the questions (why do revolutionary achievements so often contradict revolutionary aspirations?) to justify exploration of the possibility that the answers given by one questioner to his questions may be relevant to similar questions asked in different situations. Skinner's doctrine that the classic texts cannot be concerned with our questions and answers is obviously true (Burke was not concerned with the Cuban Revolution), but the attack on the idea of perennial problems suggests that Burke's answers are irrelevant to our questions. I do not think that he establishes that nor that it is true, as I hope this book will demonstrate.

A second erroneous method in the history of political ideas identified by Skinner may be called the Myth of Coherence. This error consists in mistaking scattered remarks by a classic theorist for his 'doctrine' on a subject about which in reality he held no doctrine. The converse of this mistake is to criticize a theorist for failing to produce a doctrine on a subject the interpreter believes he should have treated.[7]

It may be (and indeed it very often happens) that a given classic writer is not altogether consistent, or even that he fails altogether to give any systematic account of his beliefs. If the basic paradigm for the conduct of the historical investigation has been conceived as the elaboration of each classic writer's doctrines on each of the themes most characteristic of the subject, it will become dangerously easy for the historian to conceive it as his task to supply or find in each of these texts the coherence which they may appear to lack.

This procedure gives the thoughts of various classic writers a coherence, and an air generally of a closed system, which they may never have attained or ever meant to attain.[8]

In all such cases, the coherence or lack of it which is thus discovered very readily ceases to be an historical account of any thoughts which were ever actually thought. The history thus written becomes a history not of ideas at all, but of abstractions: a history of thoughts which no one ever actually succeeded in thinking, at a level of coherence which no one ever actually attained.[9]

In his principal formulation of the Myth of Coherence, Skinner attacked 'the astonishing, but not unusual, assumption that it may be quite proper, in the interests of extracting a message of higher coherence from an author's work, to discount the statements of intention which the author himself may have made about what he was doing', but, in a later essay, he conceded that an author's statement of his intentions were not conclusive proof of what those intentions really were.[10] None the less, it is, he argues, surely a fact about many people that they may consciously adopt incompatible ideals and beliefs in different moods and at different times. Even if there have been thinkers whose ideals and beliefs remained in a more or less steady state, their attempts to synthesize their views are likely to reveal conceptual disorder as much as coherent doctrines.[11]

Skinner complains that 'even Burke' has been subjected to this treatment. It has been assumed that he never essentially contradicted himself nor changed his mind, but that a coherent moral philosophy underlies everything he wrote and that the corpus of his published writings may therefore be considered as a single body of thought.[12] It is certainly not true that Burke never contradicted himself. He was also expressly opposed to systematic political theory and never set out a 'system' of his thought. However, he did, in his *Appeal from the New to the Old Whigs*, claim consistency of principles throughout his active political life, so that, if we begin our search for his political thought with his own statement of his intentions, we may, even in Burke, look for some of the coherence of which Skinner is so scornful.

Skinner summarizes his own prescription and his objection to the Myth of Coherence as follows:

[I]f a given statement or other action has been performed by an agent at will, and has a meaning for him, it follows that any plausible account of what the agent meant must necessarily fall under, and make use of, the range of descriptions which the agent himself could at least in principle have applied to describe and classify what he was doing. Otherwise the resulting account, however compelling, cannot be an account of *his* statement or action. It will be evident by now that it is precisely this consideration which is so readily ignored whenever a given classic writer is criticized by an historian of ideas for failing to enunciate his doctrines in a coherent fashion, or for failing to enunciate a doctrine on one of the allegedly perennial issues. . . . And if such historical studies are not to be studies of what genuine historical agents did think (or at least could have thought), then they might as well be turned into fiction by intention, for they must certainly be fiction by attainment.[13]

Skinner concludes that the essential question which we confront, in studying any given text, is what its author, in writing at the time he did write for the audience he intended to address, could in practice have been intending to communicate by the utterance of this given utterance.[14]

There is a third myth, according to this doctrine, the Myth of Prolepsis. The characteristic of this myth is the conflation of the necessary asymmetry between the significance an observer may justifiably claim to find in a given statement or other action, and the meaning of that action itself.[15] This distinction is important and it is an important defect of Skinner's methodological polemic that he does not explore it adequately. One thing here distinguished is a justifiable claim by an observer to have found 'significance' in a given statement or action. What this is distinguished from is the 'meaning' of statements or actions. Skinner prescribes a method for understanding the latter. He does not discuss the correct method for the former. Thus, his methodological polemics do not touch those who are justifiably engaged in the former activity. Ironically (though not surprisingly since he does not consider their intentions), Skinner misunderstands the point of some of the texts he criticizes.

It is not Skinner's conclusion that the history of ideas has no philosophical value. For him, it is the very fact that the classic texts are concerned with their own quite alien problems which provides the key to the value of studying them. The classic texts of political and moral theory help to reveal 'the essential variety of viable moral assumptions and political commitments'.

To recognize, moreover, that our own society is no different from any other in having its own local beliefs and arrangements of social and political life is already to have reached a quite different and, I should wish to argue, a very much more salutary point of vantage. A knowledge of the history of such ideas can then serve to show the extent to which those features of our own arrangements which we may be disposed to accept as traditional or even 'timeless' truths may in fact be the merest contingencies of our peculiar history and social structure. To discover from the history of thought that there are in fact no such timeless concepts, but only the various different concepts which have gone with various different societies, is to discover a general truth not merely about the past but about ourselves as well.

To demand from the history of thought a solution to our own immediate problems is thus to commit not merely a methodological fallacy, but something like a moral error.[16] In view of the fact that he regards the doctrine of perennial ideas as 'something like' a moral as well as a methodological error, it is a pity that Skinner never explained his distinction between 'general truths' which may apply both to the past and the present, one of which he claims to have discovered himself, and 'timeless truths', which he claims do not exist.

There are no perennial problems, but there may be apparently perennial questions, 'if these are sufficiently abstractly framed'. But whenever it is claimed that the point of the historical study of such questions is that we may learn directly from the *answers*, it will be found that what *counts* as an answer will usually look, in a different culture or period, so different in itself that it can hardly be in the least useful even to go on thinking of the relevant question as being 'the same' in the required sense after all. More crudely: we must learn to do our own thinking for ourselves.

This *is* crude and, consequently, unhelpful. How should we think for ourselves? What is the correct method? Skinner says what is not but not what is. He attacks those who have used the method of seeking help from the great thinkers of the past, but offers no alternative method. Yet all these thinkers, whose greatness Skinner never disputes, looked to the great thinkers of their past for help. Why should this method, which served them well enough, be methodologically and morally forbidden for us?

Skinner concedes that the history of philosophy must be conceived in terms of our own philosophical criteria and interests. 'Whose else?', he asks rhetorically.[17] He also concedes that, if the observer is to communicate successfully his understanding of an unfamiliar conceptual scheme within his own culture, it is inescapable, though also dangerous, that he should apply his own familiar criteria of classification and discrimination.[18] He has, further, in a later article, made a distinction, similar to one we have already noted as implicit in his 'classic' paper, between the meaning of a text for its writer and its meaning for the reader.[19] Finally, in a reply to his critics, he has vigorously denied that his methodology rules out the study of *genres* and traditions of discourse.[20]

Cumulatively, these concessions seem to grant a great deal to the 'mythological' doctrines Skinner opposes. There are traditions of political discourse. We may conceive of them in terms of our own philosophical interests. We may write about them with our own concepts. In that somewhat revised version of his position, Skinner introduces an idea which is both unfortunate and helpful. 'We can hardly claim to be concerned with the history of political theory', he writes, 'unless we are prepared to write it as real history – that is, as the record of an actual activity, and in particular as the history of ideologies.'[21] It is unfortunate to claim that the 'real history' of political theory is the history of ideologies without providing any justification for treating 'theories' and 'ideologies' as synonymous in contradiction of the common view that they are not. The remark is helpful because it makes clear what is at issue between Skinner and his critics. By emphasizing what a political theorist, 'in writing at the time he did write for the audience he intended to address', intended to communicate, Skinner tends to downgrade classic political theory to mere ideology. His opponents, by refusing to treat theory as synonymous with ideology, emphasize the lasting, and therefore most interesting elements in it.

In his reply to his critics, Skinner states that he never sought to deny that a classic political theorist may have had the intention to speak 'transhistorically'.[22] He also says that we must be prepared to make some crucial decisions at the outset about what deserves to be studied and what is best ignored. The decisions we have to make about what to study must be our own decisions, arrived at by applying our own criteria for judging what is rational and significant.[23] It does not seem unreasonable to jdge as significant precisely what is 'transhistorical' in the political theory of the past. Such a judgement is the basis of the present study.

*Pace* Skinner, therefore, and, to some extent, *pace* Burke, this is a study of Burke's system of ideas. It is neither fiction nor a study of what Burke thought. It is a systematic reconstruction of what Burke said. It does not entail the belief that Burke was always consistent, for he was not and such a belief is indeed absurd. It seeks to demonstrate that, within the various texts Burke wrote for various purposes on various occasions, there is a fairly coherent body of thought with considerable interest for us. The criterion for judging what is significant is provided by the problem of radicalism which, if not perennial, is certainly common. But, in order to understand what Burke thought about this problem and why, we must examine his fundamental ideas. In order to do this in a way that is both systematic and revealing, we must use certain modern criteria of classification: we shall examine, in sequence, his metaphysics, his epistemology, his moral theory, his theory of society, his theory of government and his theory of political change. Fortunately (from a Skinnerian point of view), these criteria would not have seemed very alien to Burke, though he would not have liked to have his thought thus systematized. But the decision to do that is mine, not his, and I must be judged by its consequences.

Because Burke criticized certain general radical ideas from a deep philosophical position, the study of his thought helps to expose some important assumptions and implications of embarking upon any radical political project. Because Burke relied on certain general conservative ideas, the criticism of his thought helps to weaken the criticism of radical projects.

The central general thesis of Burke's critique of political radicalism was this: there is a law of nature which states that revolution, which is the pure practical implementation of radical political theory, leads necessarily via anarchy to tyranny. The thesis is important because, if it is true, political radicalism rests upon a false theory. If political radicalism is to be rendered plausible, Burke's critique must be overcome.

NOTES

1.   Barrington Moore, Jr., *Reflections on the Causes of Human Misery* (London: Allen Lane, The Penguin Press, 1972), p. 38.
2.   See 'Political Thought and Political Action: A Symposium on Quentin Skinner', *Political Theory*, 2 (1974), pp. 251–303, for a discussion of Skinner's ideas and references to the literature.
3.   Quentin Skinner, 'Meaning and Understanding in the History of Ideas', *History and Theory*, VIII (1969), p. 49.
4.   Ibid., p. 37.
5.   Ibid., p. 39.
6.   Ibid., p. 50.
7.   Ibid., pp. 7 *et seq.*
8.   Ibid., p. 17.
9.   Ibid., p. 18.
10.   Quentin Skinner, 'Motives, Intentions and the Interpretation of Texts', *New Literary History*, III (1972), p. 405.
11.   'Meaning and Understanding', p. 30.

12.  Ibid., p. 17.
13.  Ibid., p. 29.
14.  Ibid., pp. 48–9.
15.  Ibid., p. 23.
16.  Ibid., pp. 52–3.
17.  Ibid., p. 6, especially footnote 16.
18.  Ibid., p. 24.
19.  'Motives, Intentions and the Interpretation of Texts', pp. 404, 405.
20.  Quentin Skinner, 'Some Problems in the Analysis of Political Thought and Action', *Political Theory*, 2 (1974), p. 287.
21.  Ibid., p. 280.
22.  Ibid., p. 286.
23.  Ibid., p. 281.

# 2

# The Nature of Things

For, gentlemen, it is not your fond desires or mine that can alter
the nature of things; by contending against which , what have
we got, or shall ever get, but defeat and shame?

Edmund Burke
*Speech at Bristol previous to the Election*, 1780.

Two opposing views about Burke's philosophy dominate the
scholarly commentaries. Both are partly right and partly misleading. The first says that Burke was a philosopher and that
his philosophy was the basis of his political theory.[1] The
second is represented by Dr Conor Cruise O'Brien's view that
'the various systems called "Burke's philosophy" which ped-
ants have constructed, out of the hollower components of his
rhetoric and the commonplaces of his education, are sad,
boring objects, not worth consideration'.[2]

The first view is right to insist that Burke's political theory
had a philosophical basis, but is too concerned to celebrate and
too little concerned to criticize it. The second view rightly
judges that Burke's philosophy was neither original nor subtle,
but underestimates its importance to his politics.

Burke declared himself hostile to abstract speculation.[3]
Theory, he considered, often obstructed, or even corrupted,
political action. A few rather obvious moral principles and a
comprehensive understanding of the situation before you
were generally sufficient.

But Burke's hostility to abstract thought was not absolute.
What he really objected to, when he spoke disparagingly of
'metaphysics', was the direct application of a few, simple,
abstract ideas to politial problems without consideration of

complex circumstance. The inevitable result, he thought, was extremism.

Burke was a metaphysician in that he believed in a superior reality lying behind the flux of events and that some knowledge of this reality was essential for right action. Father Canavan is exactly right when he says of Burke:

Despite his constant denunciations of 'metaphysics', his thought had unmistakable metaphysical foundations and his understanding of the structure of the state and society was based on certain definite assumptions about the nature of the Universe.[4]

Burke's distaste for abstraction extended to theology, which he thought best left to theologians. Non-theologians would do well to stay with the religion in which they were brought up. Where religious issues entered into politics, they should be settled on political, not theological grounds. The end of politics was not religious orthodoxy, but good order and morality.

Perhaps [religious] truth may be far better [than social peace]. But as we have scarcely ever the same certainty in the one that we have in the other, I would, unless the truth were evident indeed, hold fast to peace, which has in her company charity, the highest of virtues.[5]

Despite Burke's impatience with theology and his tendency to place political before religious goals, it is an error to regard him as an essentially secular thinker. He had a deep attachment to religion while being tolerant of sectarian differences. Atheism was one of the chief sins of the French revolutionaries as religion was one of the chief glories of British society: 'Better this island should be sunk to the bottom of the sea, than that (so far as human infirmity admits) it should not be a country of religion and morals.' For religion was 'the vital principle of the physical, the moral, and the political world'.[6]

However, although Burke's commitment to religion was strong, he did emphasize its social utility much more than its truth. Religion was the basis of social life; it gave dignity to human existence; it was the source of human happiness; it offered consolation in time of misfortune.[7] Yet the social advantages of religion touched such fundamental aspects of human existence that they constituted, for him, proof of its truth. Burke was concerned, above all, to defend a certain conception of civilization. He believed so strongly that religion was vital to this civilization that the idea that it might yet be false was almost unthinkable.

The foundation of Burke's political theory was, therefore, Christian metaphysics. 'I love order', he wrote, ' . . . for the Universe is order.'[8] God is 'the awful Author of our being' and 'the Author of our place in the order of existence'. That order 'is made to us, and we are made to it'. God has appointed us to our country and to our station within that country.[9] We are all bound by the law that God has prescribed for us. This 'great immutable, pre-existent law' connects us with the 'eternal frame of the Universe'. We are part of nature and subject to nature's laws. This eternal law also gives to our conventions and compacts 'all the force and sanction they can have'. The dominion of man over man is ruled by it. It controls the rights and duties of governors and governed.[10]

Burke's concept of a moral law which existed prior to human life is no longer plausible, at least to the secular mind, but its interest lies not in the idea itself, but in the use to which Burke put it. For he tended to invoke eternal law in defence of those he saw as oppressed peoples, such as the Catholics of Ireland and the natives of India, against abuse of power by their rulers. The problem of finding a sure philosophical basis for identifying and condemning outrageous acts of oppression remains as perplexing as it is urgent. Burke wished to ground his most important political judgements in 'the eternal frame of the Universe'. If this ground were defensible, it would have the appropriate depth and grandeur. It enabled Burke to speak of important matters with a suitable rhetoric. Notwithstanding its philosophical weakness, and even banality, his position has some of the right properties of the solution to what is certainly a real and important philosophical problem.

God, Burke held, was the author of civil sociey. He willed the state because it is the necessary means by which our nature is perfected by our virtue. Civil society is a realm of reason and order. Civil society is thus part of the nature of things. It is a state of nature.[11]

This metaphysical view provides a foundation for political conservatism. God wills order. He is the benevolent ruler of the Universe and restrains us only for our own good. The law of our nature requires us to trust our earthly rulers with power to restrain us for our own good.[12]

The foundation is not solid, however. For the concept of 'order' is ambiguous. It might mean 'stability' or it might mean merely 'pattern'. An orderly universe might be one that was harmonious or one characterized by regular turbulence. The complex structure of Burke's political theory lies upon this metaphysical fault. It will lead him to wonder whether the French Revolution is contrary to nature, because disorderly, or an inscrutable part of the nature of things.

There is a more specific link between Burke's metaphysics and his politics. It is not just social order which is part of the nature of things, but *the* social order, that is, the traditional social order of Europe.[13]

Burke was a traditionalist. But did he hold that traditional institutions were good because traditional or good because they were in harmony with the nature of things?

The relation between tradition and nature is treated in the following passage.

By a constitutional policy, working after the pattern of nature, we receive, we hold, we transmit our government and privileges, in the same manner in which we enjoy and transmit our property and our lives.[14]

The 'pattern of nature' is here identified with the 'manner in which we enjoy and transmit our property and our lives'. Now, the manner in which we enjoy and transmit our property is a matter of law and tradition. In justifying British constitutional traditions by reference to property, Burke is justifying one tradition by another, thereby begging the question as to whether tradition as such has any moral authority. He disguises the vacuity of the argument by arbitrarily calling English property law 'the pattern of nature'.

But the manner in which we transmit our lives is biological, not traditional. Burke is here seeking to justify political tradition by reference to nature. Whatever the value of what he calls the 'philosophic analogy' between hereditary political institutions and genetic inheritance, this appeal to nature is not vacuous.

The question can be further clarified by another example. Writing of possible trading relations between revolutionary France and the rest of Europe, Burke wrote:

Why should these nations of commerce and economy enter into any pecuniary dealings with a people who attempt to reverse the very nature of things; amongst whom they see the debtor prescribing, at the point of the bayonet, the medium of his solvency to the creditor; discharging one of his engagements with another; turning his very penury into his resource; and paying his interest with his rags?[15]

This might be considered an example of Burke's vacuous method of justifying tradition. The revolutionaries are condemned as unnatural because they reject financial tradition. The appeal to the nature of things (it might be thought) is superfluous, as in the case of English property law.

If the passage were considered in isolation, this interpretation would be plausible. But, if it is set in the context of Burke's belief in natural law; of the content of traditional natural law; and of Burke's familiarity with that content; then it is clear that he deprecated revolutionary financial practice because he thought it violated the law of nature. For debtors to prescribe the medium of their solvency to their creditors at the point of the bayonet is so obviously a violation of Burke's conception of natural law that we must assume this to be the true ground of his objection. This method of paying debts was no doubt contrary to French financial tradition. But the tradition was good because it was in accord with nature.

Thus, Burke respected the traditional European social order because he thought that it was, on the whole, in harmony with the nature of things. But he also held that natural law teaches us to respect tradition as such. There is a natural-law basis to his well-known doctrine of prescription.

I see the national assembly openly reprobate the doctrine of prescription, which one of the greatest of their own lawyers tells us, with great truth, is a part of the law of nature.[16]

Here prescription is to be respected, not just because it is traditional (as in the case of English property law), nor because the content of a particular precriptive claim happens to be in accord with natural law (as in the case of traditional French financial institutions), but because natural law has issued a general command to respect prescription.

Nature is hierarchical.

For, in all things whatever, the mind is the most valuable and the most important; and in this scale the whole of agriculture is in a natural and just order; the beast is as an informing principle to the plough and cart, the labourer is as reason to the beast; and the farmer is as a thinking and presiding principle to the labourer.[17]

Thus, an orderly society is naturally divided into ranks. To attempt to make society more equal is to go against nature, and that is both wicked and foolish.

Believe me, Sir, those who attempt to level, never equalise. In all societies, consisting of various descriptions of citizens, some description must be uppermost. The levellers therefore only change and pervert the natural order of things; they load the edifice of society, by setting up in the air what the solidity of the structure requires to be on the ground. The associations of tailors and carpenters, of which the republic (of Paris, for instance) is composed, cannot be equal to the situation, into which, by the worst of usurpations, an usurpation on the prerogatives of nature, you attempt to force them.[18]

Political equality is, therefore, against nature. Social equality is against nature. Economic equality is against nature. The idea of equality is subversive of order.

Good order is the foundation of all good things. To be enabled to acquire, the people, without being servile, must be tractable and obedient. The magistrate must have his reverence, the laws their authority. The body of the people must not find the principles of natural subordination by art rooted out of their minds. They must respect that property of which they cannot partake.

Mot men are destined to 'travel in the obscure walk of laborious life'. The idea of equality is a 'monstrous fiction' which raises expectations that can never be realized. Poverty and inequality are part of the nature of things.[19]

Burke's philosophy is under considerable strain here, since the idea of inevitable poverty appears incompatible with that of a just and benevolent God. Burke tries to patch up the crumbling structure.

The idea of forcing every thing to an artificial equality, has something at first view very captivating in it. It has all the appearance imaginable of justice and good order; and very many persons, without any sort of partial purposes, have been led to adopt such schemes, and pursue them with great earnestness and warmth. . . . I am, for one, entirely satisfied that the inequality which grows out of the nature of things by time, custom, succession, accumulation, permutation, and improvement of property, is much nearer that true equality, which is the foundation of equity and just policy, than anything that can be contrived by the tricks and devices of human skill.

Natural inequality is therefore something like true equality, which is the foundation of justice. Inequality is not only just. It is also good for you. For happiness is to be found by virtue in all conditions, and in this consists 'the true moral equality of mankind'. Inequality is not only irremediable, it is established by the order of civil life 'as much for the benefit of those whom it must leave in a humble state, as those whom it is able to exalt to a condition more splendid, but not more happy'.[20]

This presents too easy a target as a piece of reactionary ideology, implausibly parading as social science and Christian morality, to warrant elaborate refutation. Two points will suffice. First: Burke makes no serious attempt to show that the distribution of wealth in eighteenth-century England or France met even traditional natural-law or Christian criteria of justice, nor that the virtuous poor were happy. Second: Burke *did not believe* that the inequality in his time was just nor that the poor were happy. The evidence for this comes from one of his most anti-egalitarian tracts, the *Reflections on the Revolution in France*. On justice, he says the following.

The body of the people . . . must labour to obtain what by labour can be obtained; and when they find, as they commonly do, *the success disproportioned to the endeavour*, they must be taught their consolation in the final proportions of eternal justice.[21]

If they find injustice, as they commonly do, then let them say prayers.

Edmund Burke on the happiness of the virtuous poor.

The monks [of France] . . . are as usefully employed as if they worked from dawn to dark in the innumerable servile, degrading, unseemly, unmanly, and often most unwholesome and pestiferous occupations, to which by the social economy so many wretches are inevitably doomed.[22]

It is Adam Smith who comes to the rescue of beleaguered natural law. The 'benign and wise disposer of all things' obliges men, whether they will or not, in pursuing their own selfish interests, 'to connect the general good with their own individual success'. The laws of commerce 'are the laws of nature, and consequently the laws of God'. But the ideological intention makes this bad theory. Burke places in his Universe of reason and order a God who is just and unjust, a multitude of poor who are happy and miserable, and most of the time he ignores the realities of eighteenth-century life.[23]

God made the world for us and us for the world. He made an orderly world. He gave us an appropriate nature.

We fear God; we look up with awe to kings; with affection to parliaments; with duty to magistrates; with reverence to priests; and with respect to nobility. Why? Because when such ideas are brought before our minds, it is *natural* to be affected; because all other feelings are false and spurious. . . .[24]

This is the Universe of order in which all people have their place with the feelings proper to that place. What place is there in such a universe for revolution?

With respect to the French Revolution, Burke's answer was forthright. It was 'a wild attempt to methodise anarchy; to perpetuate and fix disorder'. It was 'a foul, impious, monstrous thing, wholly out of the course of moral nature'. It was a revolt against God, against nature, against order, against 'a mild and lawful monarch', against property and rational liberty.[25]

How is it that such an evil event can occur within an order of things created by an omnipotent and benevolent God? Burke's answer is in part the conventional Christian one – God made Man free to choose good or evil – but in part it significantly deviates from it.

It may be natural to be good, and to look up with awe to kings, etc., but some men (and the French revolutionaries are such men) are criminals by nature. Such men dupe the multitude, whose nature it is to be easily duped. When Burke attributes the evildoing of revolutionaries to their evil 'nature', he does not mean to say that their actions are unavoidable. Actions may be from necessity or from choice. The first are not to be blamed. The second, if evil is chosen, are.

It is the first and supreme necessity only, a necessity that is not chosen but chooses, a necessity paramount to deliberation, that admits no discussion, and demands no evidence, which alone can justify a resort to anarchy. This necessity is no exception to the rule; because this necessity itself is a part too of that moral and physical disposition of things to which man must be obedient by consent or force; but if that which is only submission to necessity should be made the object of choice, the law is broken, nature is disobeyed, and the rebellious are outlawed, cast forth, and exiled, from this world of reason, and order, and peace, and virtue, and fruitful penitence, into the antagonist world of madness, discord, vice, confusion, and unavailing sorrow.[26]

Thus, Nature takes her revenge on those who *choose* to break her laws. Men cannot achieve anything they happen to desire. Politics has to respect the laws of nature, including those of human nature. 'For, gentlemen, it is not your fond desires or mine that can alter the nature of things; by contending against which what have we got, or shall ever get, but defeat and shame?' Defeat and shame. The laws of nature bind us empirically and morally. Going against nature is both futile and immoral.[27]

In particular, Nature teaches the lesson of moderation. Peace and happiness depend on the control of our passions. Providence has decreed vexation to violence and it is ordained in the eternal constitution of things that men of intemperate minds cannot be free. The revolutionaries of France disobeyed nature and met the fate due to such unnatural rebels.

They have found their punishment in their success. Laws over-turned; tribunals subverted; industry without vigour; commerce expiring; the revenue unpaid, yet the people impoverished; a church pillaged, and a state not relieved; civil and military anarchy made the constitution of the kingdom; every thing human and divine sac-rificed to the idol of public credit, and national bankruptcy the consequence. . . .[28]

Burke here teaches the Christian view that freely chosen evil leads necessarily to appropriate punishment. But he also advances three parallel sociological theses: (1) there are laws of human nature and society; (2) revolutionaries try to push through policies in defiance of these laws; and (3) the conse-quence is disaster.

Burke's deviation from Christian orthodoxy consists in the idea that the resort to anarchy may be justified by necessity. Burke makes little of this because it threatens to subvert his whole attack on the French Revolution. What if the French were driven to revolution by necessity? Can he prove that they were not? He claimed, of course, that the old regime in France was not such as to justify revolution.[29] But, on this point, he is vulnerable to refutation on the facts – dangerous ground for a man who admitted, shortly before writing his masterwork on the Revolution, that he was very imperfectly acquainted with French politics.[30]

The French Revolution put Burke's doctrine that the nature of things was order under enormous strain. As early as January 1791, only two months after the publication of the *Reflections*, he was conceding that the Revolution was prospering in its defiance of nature.[31] How could God allow such things to happen? And was vengeful nature sleeping?

Burke's metaphysics collapsed under the impact of the French Revolution as did the social order he sought to defend.

As the Revolution refused to fail, he came to believe that, despite its monstrous nature, God might, for some inscrutable purpose of His own, be behind it.

If a great change is to be made in human affairs, the minds of men will be fitted to it; the general opinions and feelings will draw that way. Every fear, every hope, will forward it; and then they, who persist in opposing this mighty current in human affairs, will appear rather to resist the decrees of Providence itself, than the mere designs of men. They will not be resolute and firm, but perverse and obstinate.[32]

The concept of God as revolutionary was not an invention of Burke's despairing old age. It can be found in his early *Abridgement of English History* (1757), in which he wrote that 'we are in a manner compelled to acknowledge the hand of God in those immense revolutions by which at certain periods He so signally asserts His supreme dominion and brings about that great system of change, which is, perhaps, as necessary to the moral as it is found to be in the natural world'. And in the *Reflections* itself he wrote of kings 'hurl'd from their thrones by the Supreme Director of this great drama, and become the objects of insult to the base, and of pity to the good'.[33]

The theory does collapse. The God of order is also the God of revolution. The benevolent God, the 'awful Author of our being', the God who made the world to us and us to the world will 'complete our ruin'.

Faced with the problem presented to his metaphysical theory by the French Revolution, Burke responds also with an epistemological doctrine.

. . . [We] behold such disasters in the moral, as we should behold a miracle in the physical order of things. We are alarmed into reflexion; our minds . . . are purified by terror and pity; our weak unthinking pride is humbled, under the dispensations of a mysterious wisdom.[34]

Revolutions, therefore, are moral miracles. We should not expect to understand them fully, for they are manifestations of God's wisdom, which is mysterious.

It is often impossible in these political inquiries, to find any proportion between the apparent force of any moral causes we may assign and their known operation. We are therefore obliged to deliver up that operation to mere chance, or, more piously, (perhaps more rationally), to the occasional interposition and irresistible hand of the Great Disposer.[35]

Chance cannot be excluded from political explanation. Complete, deterministic theories are rarely, if ever, to be had. There certainly can be a sociology of revolution, but we must learn to live with uncertainty and inadequate data. Nevertheless, we can, on the basis of existing empirical knowledge, distinguish between a sensible and a foolish political programme. We can, and should, stick to the rules of prudence 'which are formed upon the known march of the ordinary providence of God'.[36]

Burke was sceptical about extreme claims for a social science modelled on physics. It is a mistake, however, to regard him simply as an 'irrationalist'. In order to show the epistemological links between his metaphysics and his social theory, we must examine his views about the value of reason, experience and 'prejudice' as instruments of knowledge.

'I do not vilify theory and speculation – no, because that would be to vilify reason itself.' In his *Letter to a Noble Lord* he wrote: 'I have ever abhorred, since the first dawn of my understanding to this its obscure twilight, all the operations of opinion, fancy, inclination, and will, in the affairs of government, where only a sovereign reason, paramount to all forms of legislation and administration, should dictate.'[37]

Politics requires good minds. In the *Reflections* he says that 'to form a *free government*; that is, to temper together these opposite elements of liberty and restraint in one consistent work, requires much thought, deep reflection, a sagacious, powerful, and combining mind.' There is a role for the speculative philosopher in politics. His job is to 'mark the proper ends of government'. The job of the politician, 'who is the philosopher in action', is to discover proper means for those ends. But even the politician needs 'large and liberal ideas', a 'connected view' of society, and some kind of 'system' to his policies.[38]

In such passages, Burke seems to hold a view of political philosophy and political practice as equal partners, each complementing the other. But what of the Burke we all know, the scourge of the French vice, speculative political theory?

He exists of course. The propensity of the people to resort to political theory is one sure symptom of an ill-conducted state. Indeed, it shakes the foundations even of 'the best governments that have ever been constituted by human wisdom'. And it has been the 'bane of France'.[39]

How are we to distinguish between the speculative political philosopher dutifully marking the proper ends of government and the speculative subversive shaking its foundations? 'I do not vilify theory and speculation. . . . No; whenever I speak against theory, I mean always a weak, erroneous, fallacious, unfounded, or imperfect theory; and one of the ways of discovering, that it is a false theory is by comparing it with practice.' The speculative theorists errs when he does not know his place. Theory is useless unless applied in practice, but its application in practice will lead to disaster unless carried out by the *experienced* politician. 'The science of government being therefore so practical in itself, and intended for such practical purposes, [is] a matter which requires experience.'[40]

The French revolutionaries were, at best, '*only* men of theory'. France was being crucified on the cross of '*untried* speculations'. Those who tried to implement general ideas without taking into account the infinite variety of actual circumstances were not in error, they were 'stark mad . . . metaphysically mad'.[41]

Reason was sovereign but reason divorced from experience was very dangerous. Reason is the law of nature; experience is our chief means of learning nature's laws.[42]

This is, however, not the whole story. If reason is sovereign, then experience plays the role of House of Commons, ensuring that the sovereign does not abuse his power. In the event of conflict, though reason is formally the superior partner, experience is the ultimate court of appeal. Thus, though Burke's metaphysics are in the rationalist natural-law tradition, his epistemology is strongly empiricist.

Human testimony is the strongest proof we can have of anything; and leaves no doubt when it is very strong. That there is such a city as Rome, is a proposition of which we can doubt less than that the square of the hypotenuse is equal to the squares of the other two sides, even when the latter is demonstrated. The highest degree of testimony leaves less doubt than demonstration.[43]

This preference for human testimony over abstract reason is immensely strengthened when the testimony can be characterized as 'the ancient permanent sense of mankind' and the reason is that of an individual or dissident group. Nowhere does Burke stand more squarely against the Englightenment than in his mistrust of individual reason.

A man is never in greater danger of being wholly wrong than when he advances far in the road of refinement; nor have I ever that diffidence and suspicion of my reasonings as when they seem to be most curious, exact and conclusive.

Each individual's stock of reason is small. But the 'general bank and capital of nations, and of ages' is, by comparison, vast. 'The individual is foolish. The multitude, for the moment, is foolish, when they act without deliberation; but the species is wise, and when time is given to it, as a species it almost always acts right.'[44]

Thus we reach Burke's traditionalism. Three points may be made here. Firstly, it is an epistemological as well as a political doctrine: Burke prefers tradition to reason because he believes it to embody more reliable knowledge. Secondly, although Burke's traditionalism is assuredly anti-Enlightenment in its epistemological rationale, it shares an Enlightenment belief in progress. Tradition is to be respected because it represents the 'progressive experience' of mankind. Finally, the wisdom of tradition is the wisdom of God working through human experience in the course of human history.[45]

Tradition connects nature and wisdom. To follow nature is 'wisdom without reflection' because we naturally respect tradition, which contains the wisdom of the ages. This wisdom is embodied in custom, which should therefore be regarded with deference, and even in 'popular notions', which are not always to be laughed at.[46]

Burke's empiricism leads through traditionalism to a kind of epistemological populism and an apparent leaning towards irrationalism. If the wisdom of the ages is embodied in custom and popular notions, then 'feeling' may be a more reliable source of knowledge than reason. '[When] our feelings contradict our theories . . . the feelings are true, and the theory is false.'[47] This epistemology of feeling is closely associated with political conservatism.

You see, Sir, that in this enlightened age I am bold enough to confess, that we are generally men of untaught feelings; we cherish them to a very considerable degree, and, to take more shame to ourselves, we cherish them because they are prejudices; and the longer they have lasted, and the more generally they have prevailed, the more we cherish them.[48]

Two important aspects of Burke's doctrine of prejudice save him from the charge of irrationalism. The first is that he makes it quite clear that he values prejudice because he believes it embodies reason.

Many of our men of speculation, instead of exploding general prejudices, employ their sagacity to discover the latent wisdom which prevails in them. If they find what they seek, and they seldom fail, they think it more wise to continue the prejudice, with the reason involved, than to cast away the coat of prejudice, and to leave nothing but the naked reason; because prejudice, with its reason, has a motive to give action to that reason, and an affection which will give it permanence.

Secondly, Burke often uses the term 'prejudice' in its usual sense, to mean ideas (typically, popular ones) that are foolish are wicked. There are good and bad prejudices. And reason tells us which is which.[49]

These doctrines raise two serious problems for Burke. The first is that epistemological populism might be thought to imply political democracy, since both commonly rest upon a belief in the wisdom of the people. Burke was politically opposed to democracy, partly because he did not hold such a belief about the political capacity of the people. Was he here involved in a contradiction? Notwithstanding his populistic tendencies, he did not hesitate to claim the authority of reason when he disliked popular prejudices. The appeal from 'popular notions' to 'reason' is generally a political appeal from the masses to an élite. Burke is acquitted of contradiction only because he does not make clear the relation between prejudice and reason.

The second problem raised by Burke's traditionalism arises from the common-sense objection that there are bad traditions. There are two varieties of this objection. The first is that some traditions, valid at one time, become invalidated by changing circumstances. The second is that some traditions are unjust and are maintained, not by consensus, but by coercion, overt or covert, of the victims by the beneficiaries of the injustice.

Burke acknowledged these problems. He believed, for example, that, because the French Revolution posed an unprecedented challenge to the traditional social order of Europe, it required an unprecedented response.

The world of contingency and political combination is much larger than we are apt to imagine. We never can say what may, or may not happen, without a view to all the actual circumstances. Experience, upon other data than those, is of all things the most delusive. Prudence in new cases can do nothing on grounds of retrospect. . . . The physician that let blood, and by blood-letting cured one kind of plague, in the next added to its ravages.[50]

Burke is here using the concept of 'novelty' for conservative purposes: he is saying that a new situation requires new methods to preserve old institutions. But the epistemological point – that novel circumstances can render traditional wisdom obsolete – opens the door to the political argument that new circumstances require new institutions. Such arguments become more plausible in times of rapid social change. Since Burke lived in such a time, his traditionalism and his realism tended to conflict.

In assessing the second objection to Burke's traditionalism – that it was a defence of injustice – we must consider his view of progress. Burke believed that the concept of 'progress' had meaning and that progress could be observed in history. He believed that eighteenth-century England was superior to earlier England. But, if the present was superior to the past, why should we revere the past? Surely, from the standpoint of the present, even the recent past contains much injustice? Burke did not idealize the past.

> History consists, for the greater part, of the miseries brought upon the world by pride, ambition, avarice, revenge, lust, sedition, hypocrisy, ungoverned zeal, and all the train of disorderly appetites, which shake the public with the same
>
> > – troublous storms that toss
> > The private state, and render life unsweet.

In speaking of the Reformation, 'one of the greatest periods of human improvement', he refers also to the 'vast structure of superstition and tyranny, which had been for ages in rearing, and which was combined with the interest of the great and the many, which was moulded into the laws, the manners, and civil institutions of nations, and blended with the frame and policy of states'. This vast structure could not be brought to the ground without 'a fearful struggle' and 'a violent concussion of itself and all about it.'[51]

Thus, Burke did concede that the past contained evils which could sometimes be removed only by revolution. Consequently, his appeal to ancestral wisdom as a defence against the ideology of the French Revolution seems fragile. Once again, he must resort to the argument that the old regime in France was not in fact tyrannical and did not in fact require a revolution to improve it.

Burke believed that bad epistemology led to bad politics. In particular, a mistaken methodology of social analysis, because it embodied a mistaken view of human nature, led to fundamental mistakes about society and social change. Social knowledge is inevitably uncertain. It follows that the correction of injustice should be cautious and that the choice of revolution is usually irrational.[52]

A further mistake about social knowledge was the belief that it could employ the same concepts and methods as the physical sciences. 'These philosophers consider men in their experiments, no more than they do mice in an air pump, or in a recipient of mephitic gas. . . . It is remarkable, that, in a great arrangement of mankind, not one reference whatsoever is to be found to anything moral or anything politic; nothing that relates to the concerns, the actions, the passions, the interests of men.'[53]

Burke implicitly distinguishes three types of person: (1) civilized persons, whose nature has been cultivated by rational, that is, traditional social institutions; (2) natural, uncivilized persons, in whom barbarism is mixed with a certain instinctive humanity and sociality; (3) 'scientized' men, whose distinctively human features have been repressed for the purposes both of 'scientific', that is materialist philosophy, and for tyranny. This last type had been created by the revolutionaries of France.

> Endeavouring to persuade the people that they are no better than beasts, the whole body of their institutions tends to make them beasts of prey, furious and savage. For this purpose the active part of them is disciplined into a ferocity which has no parallel. To this ferocity there is joined not one of the rude, unfashioned virtues, which accompany the vices, where the whole are left to grow up together in the rankness of uncultivated nature. But nothing is left to nature in their systems.[54]

The task of the philosopher is to show how the second type of person becomes the first, what social institutions sustain this achievement, and to expose the fallacies and dangers of the third view. System and scientism are the epistemological and political errors of this view.

Burke held that rational politics required a knowledge of the nature of things and that this knowledge required a certain epistemological method. I have shown how his view of the metaphysical nature of things was of a conventional natural-law kind and how his view of epistemological method tended towards empiricism. I have also shown how both the metaphysics and the epistemology are impregnated with conservative assumptions which provide him both with a philosophical basis for his political theory and with unresolved theoretical problems. These problems arise because, although the philosophy can be rendered compatible with conservative politics, it does not entail conservative conclusions. Thus, we must conclude that Burke's philosophy is important for those who wish to understand his political theory, and that it fails.

## NOTES

1.   See, for example, Peter J. Stanlis, *Edmund Burke and the Natural Law* (Ann Arbor: The University of Michigan Press, 1965); Francis P. Canavan, *The Political Reason of Edmund Burke* (Durham, North Carolina: Duke University Press, 1960); Charles Parkin, *The Moral Basis of Burke's Political Thought* (Cambridge: Cambridge University Press, 1956); Burleigh Taylor Wilkins, *The Problem of Burke's political Philosophy* (Oxford: Clarendon Press, 1967).

2.   Conor Cruise O'Brien, 'Introduction' to his edition of Edmund Burke, *Reflections on the Revolution in France* (Harmondsworth: Pelican Books, 1968), p. 70.

3.   Edmund Burke, *Works and Correspondence* (London : Rivington, 1852), vol. IV, p. 407; *Reflections*, p. 153.

4.   Canavan, p. 19.

5.   Thomas H. D. Mahoney, *Edmund Burke and Ireland* (Cambridge, Massachusetts: Harvard University Press, 1960), p. 98; *Works and Correspondence*, vol. VI, pp. 75–6; Carl B. Cone, *Burke and the Nature of Politics: The Age of the American Revolution* (Lexington: University of Kentucky Press, 1957), p. 220.

6.   *Works and Correspondence*, vol. V, pp. 39, 489.

7.   Ibid., pp. 297, 481.

8.   *The Correspondence of Edmund Burke* (Chicago and Cambridge University Presses, 1958–70), vol. VI, p. 460.

9.   John C. Weston, Jr., 'Edmund Burke's View of History', *The Review of Politics,* 23, 1961, p. 208; *The Works of the Right Honourable Edmund Burke,* (London: Rivington, 1812–1815) vol. 10, pp. 104–5; *Works and Correspondence*, vol. VI, p. 75.

10.   Canavan, p. 21.

11.   *Reflections*, pp. 196, 195; *Works and Correspondence* vol. III, p. 441; vol. IV, p. 466; vol. V, p. 324.

12.   *Works and Correspondence*, vol. IV, pp. 363, 582.

13. *Reflections*, pp. 120, 142–3.

14. Ibid., p. 120.

15. Ibid., p. 359.

16. Ibid., p. 260.

17. *Works and Correspondence*, vol. V, p. 193.

18. *Reflections*, p. 138.

19. Ibid., pp. 372, 124, 271.

20. Thomas W. Copeland, *Our Eminent Friend Edmund Burke* (New Haven: Yale University Press, 1949), p. 166; *Reflections*, p. 124.

21. *Reflections*, p. 372 (emphasis mine).

22. Ibid., p. 271.

23. *Works and Correspondence*, vol. V, p. 360; C. B. Macpherson, 'Edmund Burke', *Transactions of the Royal Society of Canada*, LII, 1959, pp. 19–26; *Works and Correspondence*, pp. 194, 203–4.

24. *Reflections*, p. 182 (emphasis Burke's).

25. *Reflections*, pp. 92, 359, 126, 141–2; *Works and Correspondence*, vol. I, p. 596; vol. V, pp. 462, 21; vol. IV, p. 401.

26. *Works and Correspondence*, vol. IV, pp. 372, 578; *Reflections*, p. 195.

27. H. V. F. Somerset, ed., *A Notebook of Edmund Burke* (Cambridge: Cambridge University Press, 1957), p. 68; *Works and Correspondence*, vol. IV, p. 384.

28. *Works and Correspondence*, vol. V, p. 401; vol. III, p. 271; vol. IV, p. 389; *Reflections*, pp. 195, 282, 126; *Works and Correspondence*, vol. IV, pp. 363, 582.

29. *Reflections*, 231 et seq.

30. *Works and Correspondence*, vol. I, p. 557.

31. Ibid, p., 596.

32. *Works and Correspondence*, vol. IV, p. 591.

33. *Works and Correspondence*, vol. VI, p. 216; *Reflections*, p. 175.

34. *Correspondence*, vol. VIII, p. 35; vol. IX, p. 307; Weston, p. 228; *Works and Correspondence*, vol. I, p. 607; *Reflections* p. 175.

35. *Works and Correspondence*, vol. V, p. 254.

36. Weston, p. 212; *Works and Correspondence*, vol. V, pp. 324, 342.

37. *Works*, vol. 10, p. 99; *Works and Correspondence*, vol. V, p. 225.

38. *Reflections*, p. 374 (emphasis Burke's); *Works and Correspondence*, vol. III, pp. 170, 183.

39. *Works and Correspondence*, vol. III, pp. 322, 79; vol. I, p. 598.

40. *Works*, vol. 10, p. 99; *Reflections*, p. 152.

41. *Reflections*, pp. 128, 277 (emphasis mine); *Works*, vol. 10, pp. 41–2.

42. *The Speeches of the Right Honourable Edmund Burke* (London:

Longman, Hurst, Rees, &c., 1816), vol. IV, p. 23; *Works and Correspondence*, vol. III, pp. 372, 222.

43.   Somerset, p. 74.

44.   *Reflections*, pp. 275, 183; Somerset, p. 90; *Works*, vol. 10, p. 97.

45.   *Works and Correspondence*, vol. IV, p. 388; Weston, p. 218; Canavan, p. 78.

46.   *Reflections*, pp. 119, 121; *Works and Correspondence*, vol. V, p. 360; Somerset, p. 90.

47.   *Works and Correspondence*, vol. IV, p. 406.

48.   *Reflections*, p. 183.

49.   *Reflections*, p. 183; *Works and Correspondence*, vol. III, pp. 204, 377; vol. V, pp. 562, 563, 564, 237.

50.   *Works and Correspondence*, vol. IV, p. 574.

51.   *Reflections*, pp. 247–8; *Works and Correspondence*, vol. III, p. 423.

52.   *Works and Correspondence*, vol. V, pp. 254, 342; vol. I, p. 564; *The Writings and Speeches of Edmund Burke* (1898–9), vol. III, p. 215; *Correspondence*, vol. VI, p. 109.

53.   C. P. Courtney, *Montesquieu and Burke* (Oxford: Blackwell, 1963), pp. 152–3; *Reflections*, p. 297.

54.   *Works and Correspondence*, vol. V, p. 304.

# 3

# Man and Morality

'The principles of true politics', said Burke, 'are those of morality enlarged.' These principles are 'moulded into the nature
and essence of things'. They are thus part of the divine order,
which is universal and eternal.[1]

What did Burke mean by the claim that there are moral
principles which are universal and eternal? Did he mean that
there are some moral principles which are in fact recognized
by all persons everywhere and always? If so, the claim is rather
implausible. Further, it would make the task of articulating
fundamental moral disagreements rather difficult, for such a
task presupposes that there are fundamental moral principles
that are not empirically universal. And Burke did want to say
that the moral disagreements between himself and the French
revolutionaries were fundamental.

His alternative is to claim that universal and eternal moral
principles exist in 'the nature and essence of things' even
though they are not acknowledged by everyone everywhere.
This places on Burke the burden of proving the existence of
these principles and of showing how he can see them while
others cannot. This is not an easy task.

At the metaphysical level, Burke believed in universal moral
principles without equivocation.[2] At the mundane level, he
vacillated. On the one hand, he held that 'the laws of morality
are the same everywhere'.[3] On the other, he maintained that
'nothing universal can be rationally affirmed on any moral, or
any political subject.'[4]

This is not the sort of question on which one should expect
Burke to be systematic or precise – or even consistent. He did
not value these qualities very highly anyway. 'The lines of

morality are not like ideal lines of mathematics.'[5] He was apt to appeal to a strong, simple, universal moral principle when he wanted to thump hard what he regarded as outrageous behaviour, such as that of Warren Hastings in India, but liked to hedge his bets by pulling back now and again from complete universality, in case such a principle should exceptionally produce an undesired result. Burke implies some hierarchy of moral principles such that, the higher the principle, the stronger the burden on those who wished to show that particular circumstances warranted an exception to it.[6]

The source of morality, according to Burke, is 'the nature and essence of things'. By 'the nature and essence of *things*' he meant principally 'the nature and essence of *humanity*'. If Burke did believe in universal moral principles, it was because he believed in a universal human nature. But did he believe in this?

The answer to this last question appears to be an unequivocal affirmative. But his view of human nature helps to explain his equivocation about the universality of moral principles. Certain properties, he believed, were intrinsic to human nature and were thus possessed by all men. But he also believed that these fundamental properties were few and that humanity's observable nature was complicated and varied by the various customs of different times and places.[7] The common nature of humanity suggested certain universal moral principles, while the diversity of custom suggested great caution in applying these universals to specific situations without qualification. This explains how Burke could both be attached to simple moral universals and yet denounce the French revolutionaries for applying simple moral principles directly to politics.

The ultimate ground of morality, for Burke, was God's will. The laws of God and the natural moral laws were synonymous. This was because God had created Man, placed upon him the obligation to obey the will of his maker, and placed within him a natural tendency and capacity for moral feeling and action.[8] Thus, when Burke speaks of 'natural' morality, he is always making two references: one to God's will and the other to human nature. This raises two questions.

If the moral law accords with human nature, how can human beings do evil? And if empirical human beings can do good and evil, how does the concept of 'natural' morality help to distinguish between the two?

Burke held that human beings in fact vary greatly in their degree of virtue. The best of men are sinners, but the best of men are a great deal more virtuous than the worst of men.[9] But are men good or evil by nature? Burke vacillates. At times he suggests that men are 'naturally' savages who are brought to virtue only by the restraints of social institutions.[10] At others, he seems to believe that men are naturally good, but corruptible.[11] Paradoxically, both views can support his traditionalism. For, if men are by nature savage, they must be controlled by society, but Burke sees the most effective control, not, as Hobbes did, in naked power (though he holds this to be a necessary supplementary instrument), but in the psychological force of traditional morality embodied in traditional social institutions. But Burke can also accept that men are naturally good and rely on their traditional moral beliefs as the basis of his conservative politics.

Burke's view as to the source of evil in the world is obscure. He believed that men have the free will to choose between good and evil.[12] But why do some choose good and others evil? Are some good by nature, and others evil? Why should this be, if it is so? How could such a hypothesis be reconciled with that of the divine creation of man and his moral nature? Or, are all men good by nature, but some corrupted and some not? If this is so, why should it be? How did the corrupters come to be corrupters? Burke cannot answer such questions satisfactorily. This weakness derives from the fact that he wished to provide morality and politics with a religious basis but could not overcome his distaste for the theological theorizing necessary to make this basis rationally intelligible.

The second fundamental question for Burke's moral philosophy is how we distinguish evil from good. According to Burke, there are two principal means: natural feeling and reason.

We have seen in the previous chapter that Burke sometimes

places feeling higher than reason as a reliable source of moral knowledge.[13] The moral reliability of these natural feelings derives from the fact that they have been implanted in us by God.[14]

Some of these natural feelings are very general, non-controversial and without definite political implications. For instance, a 'kind Providence', according to Burke, 'has placed in our breasts a hatred of the unjust and cruel'. The same benevolent donor has given us 'the natural taste and relish of equity and justice'.[15]

But Burke goes on to claim that there are much more specific natural feelings. It is natural to fear God, revere priests, look up with awe to kings, defer to the aristocracy, feel affection for parliaments, respect magistrates, admire the British constitution, prefer the wisdom of the past to that of the present, and feel sorrow at the fall of the prosperous and great.[16] In short, it is natural to be conservative, unnatural to be radical.

There is an obvious objection to all this. When Burke seeks to justify conservative attitudes on the ground that they are 'natural', he is merely applying an emotive label, not presenting an argument. An opponent could label these attitudes 'servile' and would stand in exactly as strong, and as weak, a logical position.

But, as political psychology rather than moral philosophy, Burke's view is more substantial. It may not be 'natural', but it is quite common for many people to fear God, revere priests, look up with awe to kings, defer to the upper classes, respect magistrates, admire the constitution under which they live, and sympathize with the sorrows of the great, even when it appears to be against their interest to do so. One cannot move logically from the frequency of such feelings to their propriety. And they are neither universal nor immutable. But they are stubborn facts of political life.

For Burke to hold that we feel and act justly whenever we feel naturally, he must hold that our natural feelings are necessarily good. But we have seen that he does not hold this view. He holds, on the contrary, that we have a natural propensity for evil.[17] His doctrine that natural feeling reliably distinguishes between good and evil appears, therefore, to be quite ill-founded.

This is Burke's solution to this difficult problem. God made man imperfect. For that very reason, we should not be greatly ashamed of our weaknesses. 'There is no part of our condition, but we ought to submit to with cheerfulness. Why should I desire to be more than man? I have too much reverence for our nature to wish myself divested even of the weak parts of it.' And, more strongly: 'He censures God who quarrels with the imperfections of man.'[18]

This tolerance of moral weakness has important political implications. Men who hate vice too much, says Burke, love men too little. Men of excessive virtue may take excessive measures to bring ordinary men into the path of virtue. In the womb of moral puritanism lies the seed of political authoritarianism. Fanaticism, even if altruistic, perhaps especially when altruistic, poses a greater threat to freedom and humanity than ordinary selfishness. Paradoxically, extreme virtue turns into extreme vice.[19]

Is it consistent of Burke to advocate toleration of moral weakness as he defends the moral law of God? He tells us that our duty to God, to our fellow-men, and to our country, are all greater than our duty to ourselves. Self-denial is one of the pillars of morality. Self-interest is one of the vices of men. If excessive virtue may lead to tyranny, so may the selfish desire of the powerful to use their power for their own profit. And excessive self-love is often part of the revolutionary's intellectual and moral arrogance.[20]

Thus, even if moral weakness is tolerated and excessive virtue suspect, virtue remains virtue, self-denial is virtue and self-seeking vice. The exception to this set of Christian platitudes is the pursuit of economic self-interest, which, Burke tells us, has the blessing of God. It is a law of nature that those who pursue their economic interests necessarily promote the general good. 'The love of lucre, though sometimes carried to a ridiculous, sometimes to a vicious excess, is the grand cause of prosperity to all states.' Even if an employer is excessively avaricious, he will be all the more concerned, according to Burke, to further the wel-

fare of those upon whose labour his gains must principally
depend.[21]

Burke does not here justify moral weakness as an unavoidable evil which must be tolerated. He celebrates the
pursuit of self-interest both because it is part of the nature of
things and because it promotes the good of all. We must
conclude that the Christian morality of self-denial and the
bourgeois morality of self-interest are in contradiction here.
Christian metaphysics provides the dress to beautify the most
unchristian greed for material gain. To the poor Burke
preaches resignation; to the bourgeoisie he justifies avarice.

However, the contradiction is not as straightforward as it
appears. Burke distinguishes sharply between economic and
political life. The first is the sphere of flawed man, where the
pursuit of self-interest is not only tolerable, but beneficial. The
second is a higher sphere, where higher moral standards are
needed and thus may be expected. Burke makes this distinction very clear in one of the most famous passages in the
*Reflections*.

> Society is indeed a contract. *Subordinate* contracts for objects of mere
> occasional interest may be dissolved at pleasure – but the *state* ought
> not be to considered as nothing better than a partnership agreement
> in a trade of pepper and coffee, callico or tobacco, or some other such
> *low* concern, to be taken up for a little temporary interest, and to be
> dissolved by the fancy of the parties. *It is to be looked on with other
> reverence*; because it is not a partnership in things subservient only to
> the *gross animal existence* of a temporary and perishable nature. It is a
> partnership in all science; a partnership in all art; *a partnership in every
> virtue, and in all perfection.*[22]

For these reasons, a much higher standard of virtue is required
of the rulers than of the ruled, and, while the natural moral law
is universal, it must be applied syrictly to the powerful, with
more latitude to the ordinary person.[23]

Karl Marx considered Burke to be a vulgar bourgeois
ideologist. And, even though Burke demanded strict standards of virtuous self-denial from the ruling class, while justifying bourgeois egoism, his distinction between political and
economic morality does not enable him to escape the grasp of

Marxist analysis. For the Marxist would hold the distinction itself to be ideological. The state, he would claim, necessarily reflects its economic base, so that, where the latter is characterized by bourgeois egoism, the former will be a bourgeois state.

This Marxist analysis of Burke's treatment of the relation between state and civil society itself encounters a difficulty in Burke's moral and political ambivalence towards the commercial bourgeoisie. On the one hand, he both provided a theoretical defence of bourgeois egoism and defended in practice the commercial interests of his Bristol constituents. On the other hand, he opposed further extension of the franchise to the middle classes: the 'solid interests' of his Bristol constituents became the 'sordid mercenary' occupations of the trading class when their right to further participation in government came into question.[24] And, of course, he violently opposed the French Revolution which both he and Marx considered to be a bourgeois revolution.

Does Burke's ambivalence towards the bourgeoisie lead him into theoretical contradiction? Burke was defending the English *status quo*: government largely in the hands of the landed aristocracy; commerce in the hands of an entrepreneurial bourgeoisie; and for the poor, the consolations of religion. Thus, he prescribed Christian resignation for the poor, to keep them in their place; avarice for the bourgeoisie, to create wealth; and Christian duty for the ruling class, to legitimize the whole system. Burke was, therefore, the ideologist, not simply of a bourgeois society, but of the particular form of bourgeois–aristocratic alliance that characterized eighteenth-century England. This does not mean that he was hypocritical in his demand that the ruling class be subject to the natural moral law. His denunciations of government policy towards Ireland, America and India were genuine. But Burke's political ideal was an idealized version of contemporary society. And his political ideology conditioned his moral philosophy. At the philosophical level, he could not reconcile self-denial and avarice. This reflected his political support for a combination of benevolent aristocracy and *laissez-faire* economy.

Burke's doctrine that we should submit with cheerfulness even to the less attractive parts of the nature that God has given us does not justify moral complacency. We ought to 'make the best of our condition; and improve our very necessities, our wants, and imperfections, into elegancies; – if possible, into virtues'.[25]

Two points are significant in this passage. First, we have a *moral* duty to improve our *moral* defects into *elegancies*. Second, elegance is an improvement on moral imperfection, but is second best to virtue. Social manners are, therefore, important as an intermediate stage between vice and virtue. And the aesthetic dimension of social manners – their 'elegancies' – has a definite moral significance.

Burke believed there to be an intimate connection between the aesthetic and the moral. 'For the mind when it is entertained with high fancies, elegant and polite sentiments, beautiful language, and harmonious sounds, is modelled insensibly into a disposition to elegance and humanity.' Vices that are 'polished' are thereby mitigated and morally far superior to the 'debauches and bacchanals' of, for example, the French revolutionaries.[26]

That Burke's aesthetic morality is associated with his political conservatism can be clearly seen in the famous 'age of chivalry' passage in the *Reflections*.

But the age of chivalry is gone. That of sophisters, economists, and calculators, has succeeded; and the glory of Europe is extinguished for ever. Never, never more, shall we behold that generous loyalty to rank and sex, that proud submission, that dignified obedience, that subordination of the heart, which kept alive, even in servitude itself, the spirit of an exalted freedom. The unbought grace of life, the cheap defence of nations, the nurse of manly sentiment and heroic enterprise is gone! It is gone, that sensibility of principle, that chastity of honour, which felt a stain like a wound, which inspired courage whilst it mitigated ferocity, which ennobled whatever it touched, and under which vice itself lost half its evil, by losing all its grossness. . . . But now all is to be changed. All the pleasing illusions, which made power gentle, and obedience liberal, which harmonised the different shades of life, and which, by a bland assimilation, incorporated into politics the sentiments which beautify and soften private society, are to be dissolved by this new conquering empire of light and reason.[27]

Conservative politics ('loyalty to rank'), morality ('chastity of honour') and social aesthetics ('unbought grace of life') are all here in close association.

The social aestheticism which Burke represents is not necessarily conservative, however. It is a romantic protest against a utilitarian society. Such protest can, of course, come from the political left. Phrases such as 'unbought grace of life' and 'sentiments which beautify and soften private society' would not seem alien to adherents of the counter-culture. Linguistic philosophers, quantitative social scientists and technocratic administrators are the modern equivalent of the hated sophisters, economists and calculators.

We have seen that certain obvious facts about natural vice raise problems for Burke's morality of natural feelings. But, if moral weakness and bourgeois egoism cause some uneasiness, there is sheer philosophical terror in store. For Burke acknowledges as natural several feelings that may be conducive to political radicalism. If innocent men are unjustly accused, he says, the accusation 'naturally excites indignation and abhorrence in mankind'. Men provoked, he says elsewhere, give way to 'natural feelings in hot language' and cannot be much blamed for doing so. It is natural for men 'to shrink from pain, and poverty, and disease'. It is natural for the poor to resent extravagance which is founded on their poverty. It is even natural, he states in contradiction to his view of 'natural' deference, for people to rejoice at the overthrow of the high and the mighty. And it is natural for the numerous poor and idle of great cities to be 'mutinous'.[28]

Burke's attempt to distinguish both between good and evil, and between 'deferentials' and 'radicals', by use of the concept of 'natural feelings' is, therefore, unsuccessful. Conservative and radical sentiments are equally natural.

Burke uses the term 'natural feeling' in two senses, which are not clearly distinct in his mind, but may be in ours. One is 'feeling that accords with the natural law'. The other is 'the general feelings of men' or 'the general sense of mankind', which are phrases he often uses.[29] This idea in Burke's moral philosophy is closely related to the 'epistemological populism' noted in the last chapter. The prejudices of the people are often truer and the feelings of the people more virtuous than the theories of intellectuals. Burke even inclines to the view that majority opinion is the safest criterion of right and wrong.[30]

This conception of 'natural feeling' raises more problems. Not only does majoritarian morality imply political democracy, to which, as we have seen, Burke was opposed, but it threatens the whole structure of his thought. If Burke should find himself at odds with 'the general sense of mankind', he has put forward a doctrine to support his enemies. If there was one thing against which Burke railed more than anything else, it was the individual who set his own opinion against that of the community.[31] Yet his most strongly held political views, including those on the French Revolution, were often not supported by the general sense of mankind, nor even by the general sense of Englishmen. As his metaphysics were thrown into disorder by the apparent success of the French Revolution, so was his moral philosophy by the hostility of public opinion. For the man who put his trust in the general feelings of men had to admit, at the very end of his life, that he had a 'number of enemies greater than probably ever man had and that with a degree of rancour and bitterness hitherto unexampled'.[32]

However, natural feeling is only one of the two chief sources of moral knowledge, the other being reason. It is true that Burke sometimes suggests that feeling is the superior of the two.[33] But, elsewhere, reason seems to be the master. Men frequently feel right, he says, and argue wrong. Instinct is always in the right – provided that it is 'under the direction of reason'.[34]

Rationality in morals and politics means, for Burke, pragmatism. No moral questions, he says, are ever abstract questions, and he will not judge any abstract proposition unless it is embodied in circumstances. Circumstances are what 'render every civil and political scheme beneficial or noxious to mankind'.

Circumstances are infinite, and infinitely combined; are variable and transient; he, who does not take them into consideration is not erroneous, but stark mad. . . . A statesman, never losing sight of

principles, is to be guided by circumstances; and judging contrary to
the exigencies of the moment he may ruin his country for ever.[35]

Burke's doctrine of circumstance is platitudinous, but this
platitude, like many others, is true and often forgotten, and
therefore bears repetition, especially when the repetition is as
vigorous as this.

I must see with my own eyes, I must, in a manner, touch with my
own hands, not only the fixed, but the momentary circumstances,
before I could venture to suggest any political project whatsoever.
. . . I must see all the aids, and all the obstacles. I must see the means of
correcting the plan, where correctives would be wanted. I must see
the things; I must see the men.[36]

Burke did not always practise what he preached about taking
all the circumstances into consideration. He was well-
informed neither about France nor about England.[37] He often
stood by principle in defiance of the facts. Ironically, his
speculative theories have outlasted his accounts of political
circumstance.

The doctrine of circumstances has many important implications. The first is that abstract principles, however appealing,
cannot be applied directly to solve real political problems. Any
attempt to do so will have futile or harmful results.[38] There is
no such thing as a political principle which is good in itself, but
not practicable. If it is not practicable, it is not good, for
practicability is the test of fitness for a political idea.[39] If a
principle works, it cannot be wrong, even if it offends some
abstract standard of right.[40]

Thus Burke begins with the rather innocuous idea that
principles should be applied with due regard to circumstances
and ends with the more incisive notion that right may be
rendered wrong, and wrong rendered right, by circumstance.

Neglecting circumstances may lead to disaster. The rightness
or wrongness of a principle is to be judged by the consequences
of applying it in a particular situation. Thus the doctrine of
circumstances has utilitarian implications. 'Old establishments are tried by their effects. If the people are happy,
united, wealthy, and powerful, we presume the rest.' And still

more clearly, in his *Letter to a Member of the National Assembly*:
'You never go into the country, soberly and dispassionately to
observe the effect of your measures on their objects. You
cannot feel distinctly how far the people are rendered better
and improved, or more miserable and depraved, by what you
have done.[41]

We saw in the previous chapter that Burke was a religious
utilitarian: the social utility of religion was more important
than its truth. Similarly, he was more concerned with moral
utility than truth in politics.

The practical consequences of any political tenet go a great way in
deciding upon its value. Political problems do not primarily concern
truth or falsehood. They relate to good or evil. What in the result is
likely to produce evil, is politically false: that which is productive of
good politically true.[42]

It is not clear whether Burke meant here that questions of truth
are of secondary importance in politics compared with questions of good and evil consequences, or whether he meant that
good consequences define the truth of political ideas as bad
consequences define falsehood. The second and third sen-
tences of the quotation suggest the first interpretation, while
the last sentence suggests the second.

On another occasion Burke made the following complaint
of Charles Fox.

It is not easy to state for what end, at a time like this, when the
foundations of all ancient and prescriptive governments, such as ours
. . . , are undermined by perilous theories, that Mr. Fox should be
fond of referring to those theories, upon all occasions, even though
speculatively they might be true, which God forbid they should![43]

Here Burke clearly seems to be advocating the suppression of
theories which may be (speculatively) true on the ground of
(fundamental) social utility. The appeal to God to forbid that
they be true hardly affects this point, since Burke does not
indicate how God might comply with this injunction.

Burke's consequentialism leads him to an important suggestion for the evaluation of political principles. 'Proceeding,

therefore, as we are obliged to proceed, that is upon an hypothesis that we address rational men, can false political principles be more effectually exposed, than by demonstrating that they lead to consequences directly inconsistent with, and subversive of, the arrangements grounded upon them?'[44] Here Burke has stated a principle it seems impossible rationally to deny. If a person holds a political principle which, if implemented, would achieve results opposite to those posited by the principle, the principle is self-denying and it is therefore irrational to hold it.

Burke's consequentalism also leads to a moral puzzle. Suppose that we are utilitarians and favour policy P because it will produce happy consequences H – or would produce them were it not for the intervention of evil persons who will cause P to have disastrous consequences D. Burke gives a more concrete example: '[I]s there any reason, because thieves break in and steal, and thus bring detriment to you, and draw ruin on themselves, that I am to be sorry that you are in possession of shops, and of warehouses, and of wholesome laws to protect them?'[45]

The strict utilitarian answer seems to be that P is a bad policy because it has in fact consequence D, which is a bad consequence. Burke rejects this answer. In the situation posited, P should not be abandoned, the evil men should be restrained. He raises this dilemma, and proposes this solution, in considering Ireland. P was a measure to relieve Catholics. The evil persons were Protestant bigots.

Burke's consequentialist morality generally has conservative political implications. Men are highly fallible. They may easily mistake the consequences of their policies. Thus caution is necessary. 'If circumspection and caution are a part of wisdom, when we work only upon inanimate matter, surely they become a part of duty too, when the subject of our demolition and construction is not brick and timber, but sentient beings, by the sudden alteration of whose state, condition, and habits, multitudes may be rendered miserable.'[46]

Burke held that political policies must be cautiously designed, not only to minimize the risk of undesired consequences, but also, since such consequences can never be completely eliminated, to maximize the chance that errors can be detected and corrected.

I have never yet seen any plan which has not been mended by the observations of those who were much inferior in understanding to the person who took the lead in the business. By a slow but well-sustained progress, the effect of each step is watched; the good or ill success of the first, gives light to us in the second; and so, from light to light, we are conducted with safety through the whole series. . . . The evils latent in the most promising contrivances are provided for as they arise.[47]

Revolutionaries, in seeking the rapid and total transformation of society, defy the natural principle of human fallibility and the consequent principle of cautious social experiment.[48]

If the morality of an act is determined by its consequences, apparently evil acts may be justified by their good consequences. It may seem that, under this doctrine, ends justify means. But Burke does not take this view. Because all belief is fallible, the consequences of any act are uncertain. The means, however, being more immediate, are more certain. It is always morally dubious, therefore, to justify evil means by claiming that they will bring great benefits in the future.[49]

Revolutions cause great disorder and suffering. Revolutionaries justify this by the great ends being served. But, says Burke, the suffering is certain, the attainment of the fine ends doubtful. 'I confess to you that I have no great opinion of that sublime abstract, metaphysic reversionary, contingent humanity, which in *cold blood* can subject the *present time*, and those whom we *daily see and converse with*, to *immediate* calamities in favour of the *future and uncertain* benefit of persons who *only exist in idea.*'[50]

Not only is it doubtful whether evil means will lead to good ends, evil means tend to perpetuate themselves and thereby poison the ends. Violence and deceit are the characteristic means of revolutionary subversion. If they are successful, precisely because they are successful they will remain the means of revolutionary government.[51]

Burke, like many critics of radicalism after him, accused revolutionaries of Manichaenism, the belief that the world is divided between the forces of Good and Evil. He wrote of the French revolutionaries:

When all the frauds, impostures, violences, rapines, burnings, murders, confiscations, compulsory paper currencies, and every description of tyranny and cruelty employed to bring about and to uphold this revolution, have their natural effect, that is, to shock the moral sentiments of all virtuous and sober minds, the abettors of this philosophic system immediately strain their throats in a declamation against the old monarchical government of France. When they have rendered that deposed power sufficiently black, they then proceed in argument, as if all those who disapprove of their new abuses, must of course be partisans of the old; that those who reprobate their crude and violent schemes of liberty ought to be treated as advocates for servitude.[52]

Anti-revolutionaries often criticize revolutionaries for justifying violent revolution with the false argument that it is the only alternative to violent despotism.

If Manichaeanism be a fault, however, Burke committed it. He described the war against the revolutionary government of France as 'a war between the partisans of the ancient, civil, moral, and political order of Europe against a sect of fanatical and ambitious atheists which means to change them all'. Elsewhere, he wrote: 'In a cause like this, and in a time like the present, there is no neutrality. They who are not actively, and with decision and energy, against Jacobinism, are its partisans.' The revolutionaries say: if you are not for our kind of freedom, you are for tyranny. This, says Burke, is specious. But Burke says too: if you are not for my form of freedom, you are for tyranny.


## NOTES

1. *The Correspondence of Edmund Burke* (Cambridge and Chicago University Presses, 1958–70), vol. II, p. 282; *The Works and Correspondence of Edmund Burke* (London: Rivington, 1852), vol. III, pp. 348, 441; Francis Canavan, *The Political Reason of Edmund Burke* (Durham, North Carolina: Duke University Press, 1960), p. 21;

Burleigh Taylor Wilkins, *The Problem of Burke's Political Philosophy* (Oxford: Clarendon Press, 1967), p. 43.

2.   *Works and Correspondence*, vol. III, p. 441.

3.   Peter J. Stanlis, *Edmund Burke and the Natural Law* (Ann Arbor: University of Michigan Press, 1965), p. 63.

4.   *Works and Correspondence*, vol. IV, p. 407.

5.   Ibid.

6.   *Works and Correspondence*, vol. VI, p. 19; Wilkins, pp. 36 *et seq.*; Canavan, p. 18.

7.   *Works and Correspondence*, vol. IV, p. 516; vol. VI, p. 17; vol. III, p. 325; Wilkins, p. 95; *Reflections on the Revolution in France* (Harmondsworth: Penguin Books, 1968), p. 299.

8.   *Works and Correspondence*, vol. IV, p. 520; Canavan, pp. 54, 55; Stanlis, p. 188.

9.   *Works and Correspondence*, vol. III, p. 411; Carl B. Cone, *Burke and the Nature of Politics; The Age of the American Revolution* (Lexington: University of Kentucky Press, 1957), p. 4; Stanlis, pp. 177, 185–6.

10.   *Works and Correspondence*, vol. IV, pp. 372, 389; Canavan, p. 58.

11.   *Works and Correspondence*, vol. III, p. 424; vol. V, p. 542; Canavan, p. 57.

12.   *Reflections*, p. 189; Stanlis, p. 188.

13.   Supra, pp. 30f.

14.   *Reflections*, p. 182; *Works and Correspondence*, vol. IV, p. 406; vol. V, p. 475; Canavan, p. 55.

15.   *Works and Correspondence*, vol. V, p. 475; Canavan, p. 55.

16.   *Reflections*, pp. 175, 182; *Works and Correspondence*, vol. IV, pp. 487–8; vol. VI, p. 26.

17.   Supra, p. 39.

18.   *Works and Correspondence*, vol. III, p. 411; H. V. F. Somerset, ed, *A Notebook of Edmund Burke* (Cambridge: Cambridge University Press, 1957), p. 92.

19.   *Works and Correspondence*, vol. V, p. 241; Stanlis, p. 178.

20.   *Reflections*, p. 119; *Correspondence*, vol. VI, p. 140; vol. IX, p. 168; *Works and Correspondence*, vol. VI, p. 60; Wilkins, p. 42; Somerset, pp. 72, 73, 74.

21.   *Works and Correspondence*, vol. V, pp. 194, 390, 391, 200; vol. VI, p. 35; vol. III, p. 420.

22.   *Reflections*, p. 194 (emphasis mine).

23.   *Reflections*, pp. 131, 139, 189, 191–2, 281; Stanlis, p. 63.

24.   *Reflections*, p. 139.

25.   Somerset, p. 92.

26.   Somerset, p. 88; *Works and Correspondence*, vol. V, p. 485.

27.   *Reflections*, pp. 170–1.

28.   *Works and Correspondence*, vol. VI, p. 60; vol. V, pp. 203, 237; vol. III, p. 351; vol. IV, pp. 405–6; *Correspondence*, vol. VIII, p. 247.

29.   *Works and Correspondence*, vol. III, pp. 302, 185; *Reflections*, p. 175; *Correspondence*, vol. IV, p. 408.

30.   *Works and Correspondence*, vol. IV, p. 534.

31.   *Works and Correspondence*, vol. II, p. 516.

32.   *Correspondence*, vol. VIII, p. 438.

33.   Supra, p. 30.

34.   *Works and Correspondence*, vol. III, p. 376; vol. V, p. 237.

35.   *Reflections*, pp. 90, 193; *Works and Correspondence*, vol. V, pp. 192–3; vol. IV, p. 510.

36.   *Works and Correspondence*, vol. IV, p. 384.

37.   Thomas W. Copeland, *Our Eminent Friend Edmund Burke* (New Haven: Yale University Press, 1949), pp. 164–5; Carl B. Cone, *Burke and the Nature of Politics; The Age of the French Revolution* (Lexington: University of Kentucky Press, 1964), p. 52; Wilkins, p. 203.

38.   *Correspondence,* vol. II, p. 150; *Works and Correspondence*, vol. III, p. 246; vol. V, p. 307.

39.   *Works and Correspondence*, vol. III, p. 401.

40.   *Reflections*, pp. 303–4.

41.   *Works and Correspondence*, vol. IV, pp. 386, 391, 424; *Reflections*, p. 285.

42.   *Works and Correspondence*, vol. IV, p. 462.

43.   *Works and Correspondence*, vol. V, p. 125.

44.   *Works and Correspondence*, vol. IV, p. 361.

45.   *Works and Correspondence*, vol. III, p. 442.

46.   *Reflections*, pp. 376, 125–6, 280–1; *Works and Correspondence*, vol. III, p. 322.

47.   *Reflections*, p. 281.

48.   Ibid., p. 152.

49.   *Works and Correspondence*, vol. I, p. 564.

50.   *Correspondence*, vol. VI, p. 109 (emphasis Burke's).

51.   *Reflections*, p. 176.

52.   Ibid., p. 227.

# 4

# The Sociology of Conservatism

Burke's sociology has been neglected. This is partly his own fault. He was a blatant ideologist. He was a self-conscious rhetorician. Today we tend to think ideology and rhetoric incompatible with sociology. This explains the neglect of Burke's sociology. The neglect is none the less unfortunate.

It is also surprising. A well-known thesis in the history of sociology says that the great nineteenth-century tradition grew, in large part, out of conservative critiques of the French Revolution.[1] R. A. Nisbet has suggested that major ideas in the social sciences 'invariably have roots in moral aspiration'[2] and has noted the connection between Burke's moral thought and some central ideas in social theory which were developed in the century after his death. However, even he has had little to say about Burke's own sociology.

Burke's metaphysics provide the foundation for his theory of society. God created an ordered universe. This universe is governed by eternal laws. These laws are, to a large extent, knowable by human understanding and confront it as necessity.[3]

But God's ways are also mysterious. He is, therefore, the source of an ineluctable uncertainty. There are miracles in the social world.[4] Chance, accident and the caprice of men also contribute to social outcomes.[5]

The complex way in which circumstances combine also makes social knowledge uncertain. We saw in Chapter 2 that Burke opposed the facile application of generalizataions based on past experience to new situations.[6] At times, he seems to contradict this view. The wise and learned, he tells us, 'look back upon experience and history, and reason from things past about events to come'.[7] We may reconcile the two views by imputing to Burke the belief that practical generalizations can be derived from history, but they should be applied to new situations with great caution and with sensitivity to possible combinations wholly new and unlooked for.

Burke was also opposed to the importation of materialistic determinism from the physical into the social sciences.

Individuals are physical beings subject to laws universal and invariable. . . . But commonwealths are not physical but moral essences. They are artificial combinations, and, in their proximate efficient cause, the arbitrary productions of the human mind.

Social laws may exist, but, in so far as they relate to the stability of society, we do not know what they are, and perhaps we never shall. To believe that societies are material entities subject to deterministic laws is to commit both an epistemological and a moral error, for it is to mistake the nature of society and to provide an excuse for inaction where action is a duty.[8]

This part of Burke's thought is easy to misunderstand for he does not always express himself clearly or consistently. Two careful commentators – John C. Weston, Jr. and C. P. Courtney – have been led into misleading formulations. Weston maintains that Burke held deterministic social laws to be undiscoverable, while Courtney says that, according to Burke, inductive laws of human behaviour are not yet known to us.[9]

Both these judgements are inaccurate. For one thing, there are the grand eternal laws governing social life, for instance. 'It is ordained in the eternal constitution of things, that men of intemperate minds cannot be free.' For another thing, there are the rules of prudence which 'are formed upon the known march of the ordinary providence of God' and which are 'as sure as the laws of material nature'. Indeed, Burke does at times talk like a materialistic determinist. On one occasion, for instance, he spoke of 'the laws of physical and political gravitation'.[10]

Thus Burke believed not only that social life was law-governed, but that we are able to derive highly reliable generalizations from experience. These generalizations, he further held, may be true of different societies, especially if they are culturally alike, as he believed eighteenth-century England and pre-revolutionary France to be. And, despite his view that the glory of Europe had been extinguished by sophisters, economists, and calculators, he believed that a rigorous science of economics was both possible and desirable.[11]

How is Burke the social scientist to be reconciled with Burke of the uncertainty principle? He provides us with the following guidelines for the perilous passage between determinism and chaos.

1. 'There are some fundamental points in which nature never changes – but they are few and obvious, and belong rather to morals than to politics.'
2. All generalizations have exceptions. 'But as human affairs and human actions are not of a metaphysical nature, but the subject is concrete, complex, and moral, they cannot be subjected (without exceptions which reduce it almost to nothing) to any certain rule.'
3. There are certain great events affecting the stability and disintegration of states whose causes are obscure.

Burke's philosophy permitted him to construct a general sociological theory while rejecting excessively scientistic claims for such an enterprise.

A further cause of Burke's doubts about the possibilities of social science was the complexity of social life. This complexity was both a methodological problem – how could it be tamed by theory? – and a basic fact.

The nature of man is intricate; the objects of society are of the greatest possible complexity; and therefore no simple disposition or direction of power can be suitable either to man's nature, or to the quality of his affairs.[12]

Burke draws conservative conclusions from this complexity. The British constitution, he says,

. . . is the result of the thoughts of many minds, in many ages.

It is no simple, no superficial thing, nor to be estimated by superficial understandings. An ignorant man, who is not fool enough to meddle with his clock, is, however, sufficiently confident to think he can safely take to pieces, and put together at his pleasure, a moral machine of another guise, importance, and complexity, composed of far other wheels, and springs, and balances, and counteracting and co-operating powers.[13]

But, in addition to this complexity-argument, Burke has a simplicity-argument, which he also uses in his polemic against the French revolutionaries. The British constitution may be 'no simple, no superficial thing', but, he tells us, it has emanated from 'the simplicity of our national character'. For simplicity of heart is 'an healing and cementing principle' and plain good intention is 'of no mean force in the government of mankind'.[14]

Does the simplicity-argument contradict the complexity-argument? How can such a complex constitution have emanated from such simple hearts? And is Burke's charge against the revolutionaries that they are too simple or not simple enough?

A clue to Burke's answer to such questions lies in a sentence just quoted. The British constitution 'is the result of the thoughts of many minds, in many ages'. Each individual mind may be quite simple, but the product of many minds over many generations is extremely complex. To understand this complex constitution requires 'wise and reflecting minds'. But the 'less inquiring' will 'recognise it in their feelings and their experience'.[15] The revolutionary mind is literally mediocre: too clever to accept the constitution as the simple-hearted do, too simple-minded to understand it as do the wise.

Thus Burke seeks to reconcile simple hearts and complex constitutions, and, at the same time, epistemological populism and political élitism. The simple feelings of the less inquiring are sufficient for their place in society, requiring as it does only obedience and loyalty. But government requires wise and reflecting minds. It is the men in the middle, the half-wise, who are dangerous.

This is not quite the whole story, for Burke clearly believes that, in face of the complex constitution, a simple heart and plain good intention are still virtues in rulers. When he speaks of moral principles, simple feeling seems to be sufficient. When he speaks of factual circumstances, refined analysis is necessary. This distinction is important for, notwithstanding his fallibilism and his doctrine of the simple heart, he not only believes that society can, and should be rationally understood, but that it must be understood as a complex whole.[16]

Society, for Burke, is not merely complex, it is mysterious. Like 'complexity', 'mystery' is both a methodological and a substantive concept. Mystery limits the possibilities of knowledge and mystery is a property of society. Each part of every society, and each social whole, partake of the mystery and dignity of eternal society.[17] Society is natural, but not merely natural. Thus Burke combines a natural science of society – not to be confused with a physical science of society – with a supra-scientific metaphysics.

The idea that society is natural is a necessary premise for an adequate empirical sociology. This may seem obvious today, but in Burke this was somewhat original. Hobbes, Locke and Rousseau had all portrayed man as by nature asocial. For Burke there was no asocial man. The only man of whom we could have knowledge was man in society.

The state of civil society . . . is a state of nature; and much more truly so than a savage and incoherent mode of life. For man is by nature reasonable; and he is never perfectly in his natural state, but when he is placed where reason may be best cultivated, and most predominates.[18]

Despite this fundamental difference, Burke does share one important idea each with Hobbes and Rousseau. Like Hobbes, he believed that, without society, man was little better than a wild beast. Like Rousseau, he held that society, if rationally organized, would perfect man's nature.[19]

But surely this contradicts the view that Burke rejected the concept of a pre-social human nature? Is it not a contradiction to say both that man without society is a beast and that there is no man without society? The answer to these questions is that

Burke believed men to have a non-social, but not pre-social, nature, which might be good or bad; but social institutions were necessary to control the bad and develop the good.[20] These institutions must therefore be treated with reverence. Any wholesale attack on them, as in revolution, would bring down civilization with them.

It is illuminating to contrast Burke with Locke on this point. For Locke, the purpose of social institutions was to protect the rights men had in nature. Their task was therefore defensive and static. For Burke, society *improves* man and man's condition; its task is creative and dynamic. Society is the source of wealth, knowledge and morality.[21]

But it is important to the understanding of Burke's sociology to realize that it has a Hobbesian base. Social life requires that 'the inclinations of men should frequently be thwarted, their will controlled, and their passions brought into subjection'. But, unlike Hobbes, Burke sees force as a pathological rather than a normal way of achieving this. Mature men, men fit for freedom, place *moral* chains on their appetites. Only if they fail to do so must society restrain them by force.[22]

Morality is the cement of society. Men are by nature social. They depend on each other. Their actions affect others. They are productive and creative through co-operation. This co-operation requires rules and mutual trust. Over time men develop the rules they need through interaction, mutual accommodation, and adaptation to their environment. Thus they create a common language and common principles which form the basis of a stable society.[23]

Society is then a 'moral essence', a system of mutual expectations, duties and (social, not natural) rights. Revolution, in Burke's view, by *its* very essence, frustrates these expectations. The result is the dissolution of social order.[24]

Burke's theory of moral consensus links his epistemology to his sociology. 'Prejudice' is both a source of knowledge ('wisdom without reflection') and a chief basis of social order. It is rational morality become habit. This morality arises from and governs social relationships. Prejudice gives these relationships stability.[25]

Although Burke believed that morality derived from the

needs of, and transactions between individuals, he did not regard men as rational egoists simply making bargains and rules in their own self-interest. Morality was prior to contract and was a necessary condition for its validity and effectiveness. Individuals are the actors in Burke's society. But individuals always act in a rule-governed situation which has been established for them by social institutions.[26]

It is important to consider here Burke's attitude to 'individualism'. The conventional view is that conservatives are anti-individualistic, giving priority to some 'whole' larger than the individual, such as the nation. Indeed, if conservatism is not tempered by a good deal of liberal individualism, as it usually is nowadays, it is not ideologically distant from those forms of fascism in which the individual is subordinated to a rather mystical state, nation or race. Since Burke is widely (and, on the whole, correctly) regarded as the chief theorist of British conservatism, it is particularly important to articulate as accurately as possible his view of this matter.

Society is divinely ordained, permanent, the source of morality and civilization, the repository of wisdom, the bulwark against chaos and barbarism. The individual is morally and intellectually fallible, transient, and, without society, no more than a wild beast. The doctrine of individual rights is subversive of order, society, morality and civilization.[27]

Yet Burke insists that only individuals are real. 'By *nature* there is no such thing as politic or corporate personality; all these things are fictions of law, they are creatures of voluntary institution; men as men are individuals, and nothing else.' Society is ordained by God for the good of men, that is, individual men. Burke opposed the abstract concept of the rights of man, but defended the rights of Englishmen, which were individual rights, as well as rights of estates and corporations. The rights of corporate bodies were themselves valuable, in part, because they were protectors of individual rights.[28]

Was Burke an individualist? The question has a complex answer. Ontologically, he was: only individuals were real. Morally, he was inclined not to be: morality derives from society and history. Politically, he held that both rulers and ruled should subordinate their individual wills to the general good. In the economic sphere, the pursuit of individual self-interest was not only tolerable, it was highly desirable. Intellectually, individualism was dangerous, unless restrained by humility. None the less, the proper end of government was the protection of true individual rights and liberties. Rights and liberties were true if subject to the moral law, balanced by a sense of duty, and embedded in ancient social traditions.

In so far as Burke related the state to the divine order, he attributed to it a somewhat mystical claim on the loyalty of the individual. But, to him, the doctrine of the rights of man was abstract and unrelated to real individuals. Real individuals were not abstract 'men', but Englishmen, Frenchmen, Irish Catholics, Indians and Americans. These real men lived in and through specific social institutions. Of these institutions he considered the family to be among the most important.

We begin our public affections in our families. No cold relation is a zealous citizen. We pass on to our neighbourhoods, and our habitual provincial connections. These are inns and resting-places. Such divisions of our country as have been formed by habit, and not by a sudden jerk of authority, were so many little images of the great country in which the heart found something which it could fill. The love to the whole is not extinguished by this subordinate partiality. Perhaps it is a sort of elemental training to those higher and more large regards, by which men alone come to be affected, as with their own concern, in the prosperity of a kingdom so extensive as that of France.

Men become attached to their country by a transference of 'natural' family affections through various intermediate bodies to the state. As a consequence, the relationship between the individual and the state in a well-ordered society is one of mutual *love*. As politics is morality enlarged, so the state is the family enlarged.[29]

The thesis that family and other localized ties are a chief source of loyalty to the state and its political institutions has often been proposed by modern political sociologists. There is, however, one strong theoretical objection to it. Family affection will only produce patriotism if the family is patriotic. If the family is 'deviant', strong family ties, far from providing a foundation for loyalty to the state, will provide a foundation for deviance. Burke's inns and resting-places may be dens of subversion.

Children should love and trust their parents. Subjects should love and trust their rulers. This Burke believed – on the whole. He also held somewhat contradictory ideas. Rulers sometimes betray the trust of their people. Rulers are sometimes stupid and ignorant. Rulers are sometimes tyrants. And, although the 'true lawgiver ought to have an heart full of sensibility' and 'ought to love and respect his kind', he should not interfere with the market to help the poor.[30]

Burke's inns and resting-places – 'neighbourhoods and provincial connections' – do not serve only as bases of loyalty to the state. They are barriers which protect individuals from state tyranny. In addition, they prevent society from dissolving into a chaos of isolated individuals, a situation conducive to the rise of tyranny.[31]

The institutions to which Burke looks for protection from tyranny are traditional ones. They are the estates and corporations 'left over' from the Middle Ages rather than the voluntary associations which Tocqueville discovered in the New World of America. Burke was a pluralist, but a conservative one. The institutions to which he attached these social and political functions were not those of the free-enterprise capitalism he also championed. Indeed, it is clear that the former were threatened by the latter.[32]

Burke was also a pluralist in his acknowledgement that society is inevitably characterized by 'conflict caused by the diversity of interests'. This diversity, he believed, is a guarantor of liberty, for each interest is organized to protect itself from domination by others. It is also a guarantor of moderation and a 'salutary check to all precipitate resolutions'. The state creates unity out of this diversity, preserves order and the national interest.[33]

Society consisted, in Burke's view, of a complex, though unified, system of social relations and institutions. Such a view raises the question whether some one institution or sector of society is fundamental, so that it shapes, conditions or determines all the others.

Theories about fundamental social factors must rest upon theories about human nature. For Burke, man was 'by his constitution' a religious animal.[34] He held that, if men were deprived of their habitual religion, they would need and seek another. More specifically, if Christianity were overthrown, some 'uncouth, pernicious, and degrading superstition' would arise to take its place.[35]

Yet, although Burke held that mind or spirit was morally superior to physical appetite, he did not deny that physical needs were (literally) vital. Man cannot live by bread alone, but, without bread, he cannot live at all. Sometimes, indeed, he wrote as if he thought material needs more fundamental than ideas. In the *Reflections*, for example, he declared that 'prattling about the rights of men will not be accepted in payment for a biscuit or a pound of gunpowder'. The context is his attack on the ideology of the French Revolution. But it is important to note that the pragmatic and utilitarian critique of revolutionary 'metaphysics' carries some materialist implications. Burke is not on very solid ground, however, for what he had to offer the poor was religious speculation and not bread.[36]

Burke's view of human nature, therefore, provides a foundation both for the exceptional causal importance of religion and for that of material need. How does this view manifest itself in his sociology?

At times he writes as if he believed religion to be the foundation of society.

We know, and what is better we feel inwardly, that religion is the basis of civil society, and the source of all good and of all comfort.

And, again:

On [the Christian] religion, according to our mode, all our laws and institutions stand as upon their base. That scheme is supposed in every transaction of life; and if that were done away, every thing else, as in France, must be changed along with it.[37]

Burke also attributed great, sometimes earth-shaking, causal importance to ideas, good and bad.

The meditations of the closet have infected senates with a subtle frenzy, and inflamed armies with the brands of the Furies. The cure might come from the same source with the distemper.

Compare the force attributed to 'spirit' in the following.

It is the spirit of the English constitution, which, infused through the mighty mass, pervades, feeds, unites, invigorates, vivifies every part of the empire, even down to the minutest member.

He also suggests that changes in 'manners' lead to changes in laws and in the forms of government.[38]

Since religion, manners and the *spirit* of the constitution form the foundations of society, they are to be especially revered. All were undermined by the Enlightenment and attacked by the French Revolution. It is, above all, in his critique of these that Burke shows the fundamental sociological importance he attaches to ideas. Voltaire and Rousseau are his targets much more than Robespierre.

Yet Burke also acknowledges the fundamental importance of economic factors. 'The revenue of the state is the state. In effect all depends upon it, whether for support or for reformation.' The revenue is 'the spring of all power'. Nothing illuminates the manners of the people, or the form and powers of their government, more than the analysis of state revenue.

The state is/depends on its revenue. The source of its revenue is property. Property, therefore, naturally brings power. Property is the basis of law, politics, morality and the arts. It is the foundation of society.[39]

Burke believed not only that the state conformed to the 'condition of property' in a country, but that it ought to do so. It was natural that property should govern. It was desirable, even necessary, that government should act in the interest of property, for only thus could it serve the general interest.[40]

Religion and property are the twin foundations of society. If society is to be defended, they must be defended. Those who attack either are enemies of society. The French Revolution attacked both. The war against the Revolution was, therefore, literally a religious war. It was also a war for property. It was a war, in Burke's view, for the two chief principles of civilization.[41]

Although there is textual support for the view that Burke held this twin-foundation theory of society, there is also reason to believe that, of religion and property, he held the former to be more fundamental. His Christian metaphysics suggests this. God is the author of society and has instilled in us the ideas and feelings necessary to make society work. These ideas and feelings, which are religious in character, are the foundation of property. Burke also suggests a sociological basis for the priority of religion. For religion functions socially to encourage commerce and to protect property.[42]

These are the foundations of society. But how do they work? In other words, what is the specific content of Burke's sociology of religion and sociology of property?

Religion is not only metaphysically and epistemologically, but also sociologically the source of morals. It is therefore 'one of the great bonds of human society', the 'grand prejudice, and that which holds all the other prejudices together'.[43]

Religion consecrates the state. The state is metaphysically sacred because willed by God. It is sociologically sacred because it is endowed by religion with moral legitimacy. When the state is united with religion (in the institutional form of the church), it is both sanctioned by morality and gives its sanction to morality throughout society.[44]

Thus, Burke believes, 'in a Christian Commonwealth the Church and the State are one and the same thing, being different integral parts of the same whole'. This political sociology of religion is related to a sociology of freedom and a sociology of revolution. For power without moral restraint is tyranny. Morality without religion is insecure. Secular revolutionaries spurn religion and moral restraint. When such revolutionaries gain power, therefore, they cannot but institute tyranny.[45]

Religion controls the politics of the top and the politics of the bottom. Religion is a sort of opium for the people. Society,

Burke admits, is often unjust. Religion teaches the victims of injustice to accept their lot in the expectation of reward in heaven.[46]

It is illuminating to compare the famous passage of Marx.

> Religion is the sigh of the oppressed creature, the feeling of a heartless world and the soul of soulless circumstances. It is the opium of the people. . . . Criticism has plucked the imaginary flowers from the chains not so that man may bear chains without any imagination or comfort, but so that he may throw away the chains and pluck living flowers. The criticism of religion disillusions man so that he may think, act and fashion his own reality. . . .[47]

Burke and Marx agree that religion provides consolation for the sorrows of earthly life. The difference between the two is not about the sociological function of religion, but about the proper political response to it. Marx exhorts men to throw away their chains and fashion their own reality. 'The demand to give up the illusions about their condition is a demand to give up a condition that requires illusion.' Burke believes that it is the radical emancipatory promise that is illusory. The radical critic of religion is therefore 'the cruel oppressor, the merciless enemy of the poor and wretched'.[48] This disagreement is not simply one of different moral responses to the same facts. It is one about the nature of things. For Burke, poverty and sorrow are inescapable, and the need for the consolations of religion therefore ineradicable. For Marx, it is in the nature of things that men should rise up, tear off and tear up the religious mask of oppression and abolish the condition that requires illusion. For such an undertaking Burke would predict nothing but defeat and shame.

For the Marxist, religion is essentially political, an instrument with which the ruling class maintains its rule. For Burke, too, religion is political and politics is religious. The state is a religious institution. The chief psychological function of religion is to give the believer a sense of his own dignity, comfort in distress, a guide to action and hope for the future. These are also among the important functions of the state.

> . . . He who gave our nature to be perfected by our virtue, willed also the necessary means of its perfection – He willed therefore the state.

... They who are convinced of this his will ... cannot think it reprehensible, that this our corporate fealty and homage ... should be performed ... with modest splendour, with unassuming state, with mild majesty and sober pomp. For those purposes they think some part of the wealth of the country is as usefully employed as it can be, in fomenting the luxury of individuals. It is the public ornament. It is the public consolation. It nourishes the public hope. The poorest man finds his own importance and dignity in it. ...[49]

Thus the state fulfils the same functions as religion: consolation, hope, a sense of importance. To the radical, this is deplorable. To the conservative, it is not only admirable. It is true.

A common objection to the view that religion performs a conservative political function is that it often performs a radical political function. Burke was fully aware of this. The political radicalism of the Dissenters alerted him to it. But he also acknowledged that the established church might subvert the state.

... [B]y rooting out any sect, you are never secure against the effects of fanaticism; it may arise on the side of the most favoured opinions; and many are the instances wherein the established religion of a state has grown ferocious, and turned upon its keeper, and has often torn to pieces the civil establishment that had cherished it, and which it was designed to support; France – England – Holland.[50]

Although Burke acknowledges this fact, he cannot explain it. This is not a mere oversight. For he has observed a fact which does not fit his general theory of society and he can only leave it as an important anomaly.

Property is the other great foundation of society. 'The characteristic essence of property, formed out of the combined principles of its acquisition and conservation, is to be *unequal*.' Men are by nature equal, and equal they remain in the most primitive societies. Where men are equal, the institution of property is necessarily weak. Property and inequality are created by society. But society itself is natural. Men therefore naturally move from equality to inequality. Inequality marks progress. It 'grows out of the nature of things by time, custom, succession, accumulation, permutation, and improvement of property'.[51]

Burke expresses sympathy for the poor, sometimes in violent language ('. . . and if it should come to the last extremity, and to a contest of blood, God forbid! God forbid! – my part is taken; I would take my fate with the poor, and low, and feeble').[52] But he sets his face firmly against any interference with the existing structure of property. (A passage in the *Reflections* suggests that he favoured high taxes, but not, it is clear, in order to redistribute wealth.)[53]

He gives several reasons for the inviolability of property. Firstly, he seems to have regarded it as a natural right. Government was instituted for the protection of property. And 'too much and too little are treason against property'.[54]

Secondly, he held a free economy to be natural. Government interference, especially with relations between employers and employees, was against nature. Labour was a commodity 'like every other' and its price varied with demand. This is in the nature of things.[55]

The third and fourth grounds Burke gives for opposing the redistribution of property are empirical consequences of the second, metaphysical, principle. The third ground is that the rich are few and the poor many, so that taking from the rich to give to the poor does much harm to the rich and little good to the poor.[56] The fourth is that, if the government 'arbitrarily' forces wages up, either business will be ruined or the price of the product will rise. In either case, the worker is the loser.[57]

Fifthly, equality is the enemy of liberty. Political democracy and economic equality are not compatible with ordered liberty.[58]

Burke's firm rejection of any redistribution of wealth, or any intervention by the government to alleviate the condition of the poor, is very harsh and also raises internal problems for his theory, some of which we have already encountered. It raises theological problems. 'God has given the earth to the children of men, and he has undoubtedly, in giving it to them, given them what is abundantly sufficient for all their exigencies; not a scanty, but a most liberal provision for them all.' Yet it has pleased the Divine Providence to withold necessities from the poor.[59]

It raises problems of political theory. The state is our father, loving and lovable. But if he feeds his starving children, he violates the nature of things.[60]

It raises problems of moral theory. Compassion should be shown to the poor, 'the more the better', but 'let there be no lamentation of their condition' nor pity. Natural feeling and natural law are the basis of morality. Yet, although many men have a natural partiality for equality, natural law forbids it.[61]

It raises empirical problems. We saw in Chapter 2 that Burke held both that the poor were happy and miserable. He also held that the rich were often unhappy. Not only do they suffer private sorrows like the poor, but being rich is very boring. The rich are 'our often very unhappy brethren' who require our charity.[62]

The Burke who seeks to elicit our sympathy for the rich while forbidding pity for the starving belies the picture of the Christian moralist and humanitarian which some scholars have painted. Supporting these unprepossessing economic doctrines is a serious methodological fault. Burke, at his best, opposes the real, practical desires and interests of men to abstract radical dogmas. But, in his treatment of inequality, he sets against the real needs of the poor the cruel abstractions of his natural-law dogmas.

That this is precisely what he does is best illustrated by a passage from the *Reflections*, from which I have already quoted. Many wretched men, he wrote, are doomed to work from dawn to dark in the innumerable servile, degrading, unseemly, unmanly, and often most unwholesome and pestiferous occupations of the social economy. He continued:

If it were not generally pernicious to disturb the natural course of things, and to impede, in any degree, the great wheel of circulation which is turned by the strangely directed labour of these unhappy people, I should be infinitely more inclined forcibly to rescue them from their miserable industry, than violently to disturb the tranquil repose of monastic quietude.[63]

Only respect for 'the natural course of things' prevented Burke from advocating *force* to rescue the working class from its dehumanized labour.

Burke's argument that inequality benefits the poor, because, if there were equality, there would be much less wealth to share, still lives. Inequality and degrading labour seem to be universal features of economically developing societies, though there are considerable variations in the amount and kinds of inequality and labour in different societies. This general argument for inequality, stated with sufficient caution, retains some plausibility.

At the societal level, Burke argues that inequality of wealth, power and status is stabilizing, productive and creative. At the individual level, he maintains that the interests of employer and employee are the same: what is good for the one is good for the other. It is the interest of the employer that his work be well done, and that cannot be unless the employee is healthy and happy. On the other hand, if the employer does not make a good profit, he cannot provide properly for the employee. The profit of the employer is thus 'the first and fundamental interest' of the employee. And if the employer is excessively greedy? 'Why so much the better – the more he desires to increase his gains, the more interested is he in the good condition of those, upon whose labour his gains must principally depend.' The greater the employer's profit, the more he can afford to give to the employee.[64]

Burke is here once again putting abstractions before realities. He shows himself that the 'natural' laws governing the relationship between employer and employee may work entirely to the disadvantage of the latter.

And, first, I premise that labour is . . . a commodity. . . . When any commodity is carried to market, it is not the necessity of the vendor, but the necessity of the purchaser that raises the price. The extreme want of the seller has rather (by the nature of things with which we shall in vain contend) the direct contrary operation. If the goods at market are beyond the demand, they fall in their value; if below it, they rise. The impossibility of the subsistence of a man, who carries his labour to a market, is totally beside the question in his way of viewing it. The only question is, what is it worth to the buyer?

In other words, beggars can't be choosers. The poorer the labourer, the lower his wages will be. He may even starve. But, if the employer can get away with starvation wages, he will and must: it is the nature of things.[65] Burke's contention that it is the necessity of the employer and not that of the employee which determines wages contradicts his claim that the contract of employment is in the interest of both parties equally.

If the market is in the interest of the labourer, it should not be hard to obtain his submission to it. But Burke was very worried about the submissiveness of the poor. Often they are unable to see that the inequality of classes is in their interest. Religion is the solution to this problem of false consciousness. If the poor are inadequately rewarded in this world, they must be taught that a better fate awaits them in the next.[66] Burke leaves himself very vulnerable to his own anti-metaphysical argument. Prattling about eternal justice will not be accepted in payment for a biscuit. 'To provide for us in our necessities', Burke claimed, 'is not in the power of government'. This claim was false when made. Even in 1785, the British Government spent £2 million on poor relief.[67]

In making his case that the poor benefit from inequality, Burke sometimes relies on the laws of nature, sometimes on the good nature of the rich. The rich, he says, are trustees for those who labour. Whether they mean it or not, they execute their trust, 'some with more, some with less fidelity and judgment'. On the whole, the duty is performed 'and every thing returns, deducting some very trifling commission and discount, to the place from whence it arose'. The rich are, therefore, the friends, guardians, patrons and protectors of the poor.[68]

Burke refutes this rather extravagant claim himself. He refers several times to 'opulent oppression' and to 'the wealth and pride of individuals' which at every moment 'makes the man of humble rank and fortune sensible of his inferiority, and degrades and vilifies his condition'. Some of the friends and guardians of the poor execute their trust by feeding their dogs and horses 'with the victuals which ought to nourish the children of the people'. It is the poor who feel most of the 'practical oppression' in this world.[69]

The rich live off the surplus value created by the poor. They 'are the pensioners of the poor, and are maintained by their superfluity'. This superfluity, 'the surplus product of the soil', is spent in part on learning and culture, but much is also spent on 'all the innumerable fopperies and follies in which opulence sports away the burthen of its superfluity'. The rich, Burke tells us, are idle, frivolous, vicious and irresponsible. If justice means that men are rewarded according to merit, Burke's own account of rich and poor shows that the system of inequality he defends represents an unjust redistribution of property from poor to rich.[70]

There is a deep contradiction here between the principle of metaphysical harmony and the Hobbesian view of human nature. God created a Universe of order. If inequality is natural, it must have its own principles of order. Burke finds these in the deference of the poor and the trusteeship of the rich. But Hobbesian man does not play this game. The powerful exploit the weak, says Burke. Man is made to shrink from pain, and poverty, and disease. It is natural that the poor should resent having to labour for the luxury of the rich. Revolution may arise from 'penury and irritation, from scorned loyalty, and rejected allegiance'. When it does, it has its roots deep in human nature and in the unalterable constitution of things.[71]

Burke is ambivalent towards the rich, the poor and also the rising middle class. We saw, in Chapter 3, his rather tortuous treatment of 'avarice'. He is equally ill at ease with its socio-logical cousin, ambition. Ambition is a vice, a sickness, but is the vice of great minds, the sickness of 'every extensive genius'.[72]

Burke recognized, admired and feared the force of the bourgeois revolution. He acknowledged its political power, its enterprise and its tendency to subvert the old order.[73] He valued material progress, for he held it to be the basis of the progress of civilization. But he saw that progress destroys as it creates, and he was afraid that the destruction might get out of hand.

The sociology of religion and the sociology of property meet in Burke's sociology of intellectuals. Ideas have power.

They are also contagious. They spread like wildfire. They are unstable. They arise, grow, become strong and refined, degenerate, dissolve, and make way for new ideas.[74]

Men need a religion as guide, comfort and hope. If they are forced from one religion to another, they will, in time, settle down to their new faith.[75] Religions, like other systems of ideas, are born, flourish, change and die. This theme of the sociological mutability of even the most fundamental beliefs exists in tension with the metaphysical (and epistemological) doctrine which states that certain truths are immutable. For Burke's critique of radical politics rests, to an important extent, on the denunciation of intellectuals who were undermining popular belief in putative eternal truths, while his sociology of belief emphasizes the natural birth, life and decay of all belief-systems.

Thus Burke the metaphysician and Burke the sociologist give rather different accounts of the relations between ideas and society. The former suggests that fundamental metaphysical truths develop into social institutions through a long and painful historical process. The latter suggests that certain social conditions are associated with certain ideas. The two approaches are not necessarily incompatible, but they constitute different perspectives which may lead to different conclusions.

Sociologically, Burke held, theory itself, that is abstract thought, especially abstract political thought, was 'one sure symptom of an ill-conducted state'.[76] Theory was not a natural activity, it did not arise from some property of the human mind, it was a response to a deviation of society from the normal and the natural.

It did not follow that, because radical critiques of the *status quo* were 'symptoms' of an *ill-conducted* state, there should be even a presumption in favour of their validity. Political radicalism arose from two sources. One was the oppressed. In this case, it was respectable, but not necessarily valid. 'Great distress has never hitherto taught, and whilst the world lasts it will never teach, wise lessons to any part of mankind. . . . Desperate situations produce desperate councils and desperate measures.' With this doctrine, Burke seeks to fuse popular sympathy with political élitism. The oppressed know how they suffer, but not why, nor what is the best remedy.[77]

The second source of radical ideas is the well-off. Such ideas may be 'the diseases of minds pampered with security and power; who, having nothing to desire, look in liberty for more than liberty can give, and wander without principle through the vast void of speculation'.[78]

Thus, not only is being oppressed not a necessary condition of having radical ideas, but being the opposite of oppressed – pampered security – is conducive to radicalism. Bertrand Russell once said that the influence of boredom on human affairs had been greatly underestimated. It was not by Burke. He was much impressed by the restless quality of human nature, by the way in which satiety breeds dissatisfaction, and by the *excitement* some men derive from radical ideas.

> The life of adventurers, gamesters, gipsies, beggars, and robbers is not unpleasant. It requires restraint to keep men from falling into that habit. The shifting tides of fear and hope, the flight and pursuit, the peril and escape, the alternate famine and feasts of the savage and the thief, after a time, render all course of slow, steady, progressive, unvaried occupation, and the prospect only of a limited mediocrity at the end of long labour, to the last degree tame, languid, and insipid.[79]

Perhaps Burke's conservative romanticism made him sensitive to radical romanticism. But it is important to note that, in accordance with his denunciation of moral perfectionism, he is here *defending* the insipid and the mediocre in politics.

One social group is especially prone to political adventurism: the intellectuals. The love of paradox is a common characteristic of intellectuals, who are often attracted to novelty and bored by the familiar. It is precisely the familiar that Burke wishes to defend.[80]

The tendency to paradox is a psychological quality of intellectuals. But it is not only the psyche, but the social location of intellectuals which, in Burke's view, gives them their distinctive political character. Intellectuals are spinners of theories about the world, but their experience of the world is narrow. At this point Burke conjoins an epistemological, a moral and a sociological argument. Epistemologically, political wisdom requires long and varied practical experience: the most refined speculation is no substitute for this. Moral questions are not abstract but concrete and complex: they require a knowledge of the multifarious circumstances of social life. Sociologically, the intellectual is cut off from the requisite variety of experience. The intellectual in politics is a clever fool – and a dangerous one.[81]

To be dangerous, he must be something worse than paradoxical and unpractical. The poison is at the very heart of the intellectual process. It is the essence of the intellectual to generalize, to search out the roots of the problem, to look for general principles. In politics this is dangerous.

Remove a grievance, and, when men act from feeling, you go a great way towards quieting a commotion. But the good or bad conduct of a government, the protection men have enjoyed, or the oppression they have suffered under it, are of no sort of moment, when a faction, proceeding upon speculative grounds, is thoroughly heated against its form. When a man is, from system, furious against monarchy or episcopacy, the good conduct of the monarch or the bishop has no other effect, than further to irritate the adversary.

Because intellectuals delight in the search for fundamental principles, they tend to find solutions too big for the problem. Because they judge society by such principles, they are liable to find it fundamentally defective. Radicalism is inherent in theory.[82]

Burke believed that intellectuals in his time had other dangerous characteristics. One was their commitment to science. The scientific mind favoured experiment. In politics, however, experiment was dangerous. In his *Letter to a Noble Lord*, Burke wrote of the leftish Duke of Bedford:

His grace's landed possessions are irresistibly inviting to an *agrarian* experiment. They are a downright insult upon the rights of man. They are more extensive than the territory of many of the Grecian republics; and they are without comparison more fertile than most of them. . . . There is scope for seven philosophers to proceed in their analytical experiments, upon Harrington's seven different forms of republics, in the acres of this one duke. Hitherto they have been wholly unproductive to speculation; fitted for nothing but to fatten bullocks, and to produce grain for beer, still more to stupify the dull English understanding. Abbe Siéyès has whole nests of pigeon-holes full of constitutions ready made, ticketed, sorted, and numbered. . . . What a pity it is, that the progress of experimental philosophy should be checked by his grace's monopoly![83]

Burke was not opposed to political experiment *per se*. He was opposed to experiment for experiment's sake. A cautious, experimental approach to the correction of real political evils he would approve.

But it was not only the experimental spirit of science that was dangerous when applied to politics, but also its tendency to treat people as things.

The geometricians, and the chemists, bring, the one from the dry bones of their diagrams, and the other from the soot of their furnaces, dispositions that make them worse than indifferent about those feelings and habitudes, which are the support of the moral world. . . . These philosophers consider men in their experiments no more than they do mice in an air-pump, or in a recipient of mephitic gas. Whatever his grace may think of himself, they look upon him, and every thing that belongs to him, with no more regard than they do upon the whiskers of that little long-tailed animal, that has been long the game of the grave, demure, insidious, spring-nailed, velvet-pawed, green-eyed philosophers, whether going upon two legs, or upon four.[84]

Theory is also related to arrogance. Theoriests aspire to profound truths so that, if they are not restrained by fear of God or men, they are apt to overrate their own importance. The abstraction of theory adds to this arrogance a lack of humanity. 'Nothing can be conceived more hard than the heart of a thorough-bred metaphysician. . . . It is like that of the principle of evil himself, incorporeal, pure, unmixed, dephlegmated, defecated evil.[85]

The arrogance of the intellectual was, to a large extent, a result of his being a new arrival on the social scene. So too was his ambition.

Ambition is come upon them suddenly; they are intoxicated with it, and it has rendered them fearless of the danger, which may from thence arise to others or to themselves. . . . [W]hen the possibility of dominion, lead, and propagation presented itself, and that the ambition, which before had so often made them hypocrites, might rather gain than lose by a daring avowal of their sentiments, then the nature of this infernal spirit, which has 'evil for its good', appeared in its full perfection.[86]

Here again we see Burke's fear of social mobility, of fluid elements in the social structure. But creativity and fluidity tend to go together. The intellectuals and the men of money are the new, mobile, progressive forces in society. The money men are dangerous because money is power. So are the intellectuals because ideas too may be powerful. Of the two, the intellectuals are the more dangerous, for self-interest is tractable, speculation is not.[87] The ambition of the intellectuals becomes a threat when the possibility of their power presents itself, when their ideas become fashionable. For Burke, the influence of radical intellectuals cannot be a rational response to changed circumstances. It must come straight from hell.

Burke was obsessed by the belief that , of all social forces, ideas were the hardest to keep within safe bounds. Abstraction and imagination were social dangers. For these qualities of political theory made it like a distorted mirror-image of religion. Burke never denied that religion might be cruelly fanatical. So too might political theory. 'It must always have been discoverable by persons of reflection, but it is now obvious to the world, that a theory concerning government may become as much a cause of fanaticism as a *dogma* in religion.' Over and over again, Burke wrote of revolutionary ideology as a religion. He referred to 'the new fanatical religion . . . of the rights of man', with its priests and its high mysteries. Speaking of the Reformation, he declared that it was at first thought necessary 'to oppose to popery another popery, to get the better of it'. Now, he suggested, atheism was opposing to Christian superstition another superstition, to get the better of it.[88]

Was it the scepticism or the fanaticism of intellectuals that Burke saw as the chief threat to order? The answer is that the first undermined the old order and the second destroyed it.

Scepticism could inhibit action in support of existing society, but it could not by itself motivate action. Men must have a faith to move them. That is why scepticism led to its apparent opposite, fanaticism.[89]

The final question to consider in this chapter is Burke's view of history. History is society in motion. How did Burke's society move?

Burke's universe was one of order, governed by immutable laws. This order and these laws, far from ruling out change, were the basis of progress. The 'great law of change' was 'the most powerful law of nature', one which we must all obey.[90]

Burke viewed history as the unfolding of God's will, which was to develop the perfection inherent potentially in Man. Society was the chief instrument of this will, so that society was both maker and product of history. Progress, however, was not inevitable, unilinear or universal. History was the story of regress as well as progress, the regress being sometimes temporary, at other times apparently permanent.[91]

If progress was neither inevitable nor universal, it had broadly characterized the history of Europe, and especially the history of England. We have already seen that Burke did not idealize the past. History consisted for the greater part of the miseries brought upon the world by pride, ambition, avarice, revenge, lust, sedition, hypocrisy, ungoverned zeal, and other disorderly appetites. None the less, throughout history Christianity had done much to dispel barbarism and to promote learning, art, civility and commerce. It was therefore the chief source of progress.[92]

In what did progress consist? Not, on the whole, in greater wisdom, for Burke held that the great moral and political truths had been long understood. In material life, certainly, and Burke was not one to despise this. In science, arts and literature, 'which have illuminated and adorned the modern world'. In refined manners, to which he attached great importance, for they expressed a sensitive morality and were themselves expressed in fine art. And in political institutions.[93]

For Burke, political progress had two meanings. The first was that of adjustment, adjustment of each part of the social system to all the others, adjustment of social institutions to

changing circumstances. The second was the gradual realization of right and justice. Here he spoke the language of natural
rights. These passages suggest that, contrary to what is usually
thought, Burke's view of the crucial difference between his
political theory and that of the French revolutionaries was not
that they believed in natural rights and he believed in prescriptive rights, but rather that they believed in the immediate,
wholesale implementation of abstract rights, regardless of the
consequences, whereas, in his view, rights could only be
implemented gradually, through cautious mutual adjustment
of different parts of the social whole. Thus, progress as
adjustment and progress as the establishment of right were
mutually dependent.[94]

Burke did not believe the British constitution to be perfect.
He did, however, believe that it was sound in essentials, requiring only occasional piecemeal reform. But its virtues were not
necessarily permanent. Indeed, towards the gloomy end of his
life, he feared that it might be in its death throes.[95]

The French Revolution, for Burke, was regressive, not progressive. It subverted that order of things 'under which our
part of the world has so long flourished, and indeed been in a
progressive state of improvement, the limits of which, if it had
not been thus rudely stopped, it would not have been easy for
the imagination to fix'.[96]

But Burke did concede that disorder might lead to progress.
Conflict might be not only conducive, but even necessary to
improvement, as the cases of Magna Carta and the 1688
Revolution showed. Indeed, in speaking of the American
Revolution, he suggested that attempts to block progress, and
he had economic progress chiefly in mind, would lead to
revolution. Significantly, he considered such attempts as
defiance of Providence. There were therefore cases in which
revolutionary forces were progressive.[97]

## NOTES

1. R. A. Nisbet, 'The French Revolution and the Rise of
Sociology in France', *American Journal of Sociology*, 49, 1943–4,

pp. 156–64; 'Conservatism and Sociology', *American Journal of Sociology*, 58, 1952–3, pp. 167–75.

2.  R. A. Nisbet, *The Sociological Tradition* (New York: Basic Books, 1966), p. 18.

3.  *The Works and Correspondence of Edmund Burke* (London: Rivington, 1852), vol. III, p. 271; vol. IV, p. 389; vol. V, p. 264.

4.  Edmund Burke, *Reflections on the Revolution in France* (Harmondsworth: Penguin Books, 1968), p. 175.

5.  *Works and Correspondence*, vol. V, pp. 254, 342; vol. VI, p. 345.

6.  Supra, p. 31.

7.  *Works and Correspondence*, vol. VI, p. 188.

8.  *Works and Correspondence*, vol. V, pp. 254 *et seq.*, 148.

9.  John C. Weston, Jr., 'Edmund Burke's View of History', *The Review of Politics*, 23, 1961, p. 212; C. P. Courtney, *Montesquieu and Burke* (Oxford: Blackwell, 1963), p. 152.

10.  *Works and Correspondence*, vol. IV, p. 389; vol. V, pp. 324, 286.

11.  Ibid., vol. III, pp. 372, 351; *Reflections*, pp. 170, 352.

12.  *Reflections*, pp. 152–3.

13.  *Works and Correspondence*, vol. IV, p. 487.

14.  *Reflections*, p. 186; *Works and Correspondence*, vol. III, p. 244.

15.  *Works and Correspondence*, vol. IV, p. 487.

16.  *Works and Correspondence*, vol. III, p. 183; vol. IV, p. 487; vol. VI, p. 15.

17.  *Reflections*, pp. 194–5.

18.  *Works and Correspondence*, vol. IV, p. 466; Francis Canavan, *The Political Reason of Edmund Burke* (Durham, North Carolina: Duke University Press, 1960), p. 116.

19.  *Reflections*, pp. 196–9; Canavan, pp. 86–8.

20.  *Works and Correspondence*, vol. V, p. 482.

21.  H. V. F. Somerset, ed., *A Notebook of Edmund Burke* (Cambridge: Cambridge University Press, 1957), p. 74.

22.  *Works and Correspondence*, vol. IV, pp. 389 *et seq.*; Courtney, p. 159.

23.  *Works and Correspondence*, vol. V, p. 307.

24.  *Works and Correspondence*, vol. V, p. 310; *Reflections*, pp. 193–4, 265–6.

25.  *Works and Correspondence*, vol. VI, pp. 207, 213; Canavan, p. 67.

26.  *Works and Correspondence*, vol. VI, p. 460.

27.  Ibid., vol. II, p. 517; *Reflections*, p. 194.

28.  *Works and Correspondence*, vol. IV, pp. 462–3 (emphasis Burke's); Alfred Cobban, *Edmund Burke and the Revolt against the Eigtheenth Century* (London: Allen & Unwin, 1960), p. 90.

29. *Reflections*, pp. 315, 120, 135, 194; *Works and Correspondence*, vol. III, p. 432.

30. *Works and Correspondence*, vol. III, p. 325; vol. IV, pp. 584–5, 363; vol. VI, p. 241; *Reflections*, pp. 201, 281.

31. Cobban, p. 50.

32. Cobban, ibid.; *Works and Correspondence*, vol. V, p. 310.

33. *Reflections*, pp. 300, 122; Canavan, pp. 149, 160.

34. *Reflections*, p. 187.

35. *Works and Correspondence,* vol. V, p. 57; *Reflections*, pp. 187–188.

36. *Reflections*, p. 370; see also Burleigh Taylor Wilkins, *The Problem of Burke's Political Philosophy* (Oxford: Clarendon Press, 1967), p. 107.

37. *Reflections*, p. 186; *Works and Correspondence*, vol. V, p. 489.

38. *Works and Correspondence*, vol. V, p. 149; Vol. III, p. 291; vol. VI, p. 265.

39. *Reflections*, p. 351; *Works and Correspondence*, vol. VI, pp. 286, 373; vol. III, pp. 125, 137, 387; vol. V, p. 233; Wilkins, p. 198.

40. *Works and Correspondence*, vol. IV, p. 387; vol. I, p. 593; *Reflections*, pp. 141, 150, 129, 132, 138.

41. *Works and Correspondence*, vol. V, pp. 46, 47; *The Correspondence of Edmund Burke* (Cambridge and Chicago University Presses, 1958–1970), vol. VII, p. 389.

42. *Reflections*, pp. 174, 372.

43. *Works and Correspondence*, vol. VI, p. 57; vol. V, p. 486; Wilkins, p. 77.

44. *Reflections*, pp. 194–5, 196; *Works and Correspondence*, vol. IV, p. 483.

45. *Reflections*, p. 189.

46. *Reflections*, p. 372.

47. David McLellan, *Karl Marx: Early Texts* (Oxford: Blackwell, 1971), p. 116.

48. McLellan, ibid.; *Reflections*, p. 372.

49. *Works and Correspondence*, vol. VI, p. 57; vol. V, p. 297; *Reflections*, pp. 196–7.

50. *The Speeches of the Right Honourable Edmund Burke* (London: Longman, Hurst, Rees, 1816), vol. IV, p. 57; *Reflections*, p. 94; *Works and Correspondence,* vol. VI, pp. 238, 38, 285.

51. *Reflections*, p. 140 (emphasis Burke's), pp. 138, 372, 124, 271, 195 *et seq.*; *Works and Correspondence*, vol. VI, pp. 181, 62, 207; vol. V, p. 193; Thomas W. Copeland, *Our Eminent Friend Edmund Burke* (New Haven: Yale University Press, 1949), p. 166.

52. *The Works of the Right Honourable Edmund Burke* (London: Rivington, 1812–15), vol. 10, p. 139.
53. *Reflections*, pp. 371–2.
54. Wilkins, p. 198; *Reflections*, p. 203.
55. *Works and Correspondence*, vol. V, pp. 191, 194.
56. *Works and Correspondence*, vol. V, pp. 189–90, 195; vol. I, p. 559; *Reflections*, p. 140.
57. *Works and Correspondence*, vol. V, p. 195.
58. Ibid., vol. IV, p. 424.
59. Ibid., vol. I, pp. 578, 551; vol. V, p. 194; vol. III, pp. 340, 513; vol. V, p. 203.
60. Ibid., vol. V, pp. 396, 189, 203.
61. Ibid., vol. V, pp. 190, 397; vol. I, p. 578; vol. IV, p. 578; *Reflections*, p. 372.
62. *Reflections*, pp. 124, 201.
63. Ibid., p. 271.
64. *Works and Correspondence*, vol. V, pp. 193–4.
65. Ibid.,
66. *Reflections*, p. 372; *Works and Correspondence*, vol. V, p. 190.
67. *Works and Correspondence*, vol. V, p. 189; R. M. Hutchins, 'The Theory of Oligarchy: Edmund Burke', *The Thomist*, V, 1943, p. 71.
68. *Works and Correspondence*, vol. V, pp. 190, 209.
69. *Reflections*, pp. 376, 197, 203; *Works and Correspondence*, vol. IV, p. 533.
70. *Works and Correspondence*, vol. IV, p. 189; *Reflections*, pp. 271–3.
71. *Works and Correspondence*, vol. III, pp. 314, 351; vol. V, p. 237; *Correspondence*, vol. IX, p. 162.
72. *Works and Correspondence*, vol. VI, pp. 296–7.
73. *Reflections*, pp. 211, 308, 311.
74. *Works and Correspondence*, vol. V, p. 149; vol. IV, p. 556.
75. Ibid., vol. VI, p. 57.
76. Ibid., vol. III, p. 322.
77. *Correspondence*, vol. IX, p. 162; *Works and Correspondence*, vol. IV, pp. 363–4.
78. R. M. Hutchins, 'The Theory of the State: Edmund Burke', *Review of Politics*, V, 1943, p. 152.
79. *Works and Correspondence*, vol. IV, p. 364.
80. Canavan, p. 71.
81. *Reflections*, pp. 132–3, 124, 148, 345; *Works and Correspondence*, vol. IV, pp. 474, 359–60; Canavan, p. 50.
82. *Works and Correspondence*, vol. IV, pp. 476–7.
83. Ibid., vol. V, pp. 242–3 (emphasis Burke's).

84.  Ibid., vol. V, p. 242.
85.  Ibid., p. 241.
86.  Ibid., pp. 242, 332.
87.  Ibid., p. 241.
88.  *Works and Correspondence*, vol. IV, p. 476 (emphasis Burke's);
vol. V, pp. 241, 58, 141, 144; vol. VI, p. 59; vol. III, p. 424.
89.  Somerset, p. 69; Wilkins, p. 109.
90.  Canavan, p. 169.
91.  Weston, p. 220; Canavan, p. 130; *Works and Correspondence*,
vol. VI, pp. 179, 216, 220, 226.
92.  *Reflections*, p. 247; Somerset, p. 90; *Works and Correspondence*,
vol. III, pp. 352, 377–8; vol. VI, pp. 180, 266, 220, 225.
93.  *Works and Correspondence*, vol. VI, pp. 180, 287.
94.  *Works*, pp. 218–20.
95.  *Works and Correspondence*, vol. IV, p. 489; vol. VI, p. 368.
96.  *Correspondence*, vol. VII, p. 387.
97.  *Works and Correspondence*, vol. III, p. 260.

# 5

# The Principles of Politics

The most important concept which links Burke's theory of government to his theory of revolution is that of 'tyranny'. Tyranny is the most evil form of government. The best is that which is least tyrannical. The hall-mark of non-tyranny is law. The hallmark of tyranny is lawlessness.

'Law' is both a metaphysical and a political concept. Law is the fabric of the Universe. It governs governments, governors and governed. No human exercise of power is legitimate unless it accords with the divine law.[1]

'Law' is closely related conceptually to 'reason', 'order', 'justice' and 'freedom'. 'law-and-order' has today become a cliché invoked to support conventional calls for the control of crime. For Burke, law and order were the foundations upon which the mansion of civilization was constructed. Governments provide social order through law, which is the necessary precondition of justice, and therefore of freedom. Government is at the same time subject to reason and reason's executive power. This is rational politics. Its reward is rational freedom.[2]

Opposed to reason is 'will'. Burke declared himself the enemy of 'all the operations of opinion, fancy, inclination, and will, in the affairs of government'. Opposed to order is revolution; to law, anarchy; to (rational) government, tyranny. Thus, the relation between revolution and tyranny is, for Burke, both causal and conceptual. Revolution is the assertion of will, not reason; it is dis-order, an-archy. Anarchy is not so much no-government as no-law. Government without law is tyranny. Will is both the subverter of order and unchecked tyrant. Metaphysical will is manifested in politics as excessive liberty. The metaphysical character of will explains the super-ficially paradoxical political fact that extreme claims to liberty lead to tyranny: both are lawless.[3]

This may seem the straightforward application of Burke's metaphysical conservatism, based on the premise that nature entails order. But straightforward conservatism it is not. It is decidedly double-edged. For if reason is paramount to govern-ment, the way is open to appeal from government and positive law to a higher reason, even to overthrow government in the name of a higher reason. Since some governments may be tyrannies (contrary to reason), some revolutions may be jus-tified (rational).

The possibility that, within Burke's system of thought, the natural law may sanction some revolutions raises the question, much debated in recent years, as to precisely what view Burke took of the natural rights of man. I shall show why this question is a difficult one, and I shall propose an answer to it; but, before I do so, I shall show why it is important.

Various conceptions and doctrines of 'natural rights' or 'human rights' have played an important part in the liberal tradition, from Locke to the present. It is often said that a 'great debate' took place at the end of the eighteenth century between Edmund Burke and Thomas Paine about the validity of the concept of the 'rights of man' and that this dispute was at the heart of their disagreement about the justifiability of the French Revolution.

Yet scholars do not agree as to what Burke's views about natural rights actually were. Some hold that the conventional view – namely, that he rejected the concept – is quite mistaken. Since Burke is widely taken to be one of the most important critics of this most important political concept, it is obvious why it is essential to identify precisely what view he did take of it.

The textual evidence is, at first sight, conflicting: there are passages for and passages against the idea of natural rights. Some have suggested a 'contextual' explanation for textual inconsistency: Burke resorted to the concept of natural rights when his sympathies were evoked (e.g., by the plight of the Irish Catholics) and criticized it when it was employed by those of whom he disapproved (e.g., the French revolutionaries).

The evidence that Burke subscribed to the idea of natural human rights is of two kinds: first, liberal use of natural-rights language, and, second, the coherence of the concept with his theory of natural law and government.

Natural-rights rhetoric is common in Burke and is used with respect to various problems at different times, e.g., 'the real essential rights of mankind' (1774 – in defence of the American colonists); 'the common rights of men' (1777 – same subject); 'the rights of human nature' (1782 – the oppression of Irish Catholics); 'the rights of humanity and the laws of nature' (same); 'the true and genuine rights of men' (1791 – in praise of revolution in Poland).[4]

Those quotations have several interesting features. First, in all of them Burke uses the concept of rights to defend subjects and oppose governments and is, to this extent, in the classical liberal tradition. Second, the date of the last quotation shows that the onset of the French Revolution had not caused him to abandon the language of human rights. Third, the first of the two 1782 quotations relates 'rights' to 'human nature' so that the violation of the one is synonymous with the violation of the other, both constituting tyranny. Fourth, the second 1782 quotation associates human rights with the law of nature, thereby confirming that the latter may have a popular and dissident cutting-edge. Finally, the use of the prefixes 'real', 'true' and 'genuine' before the 1774 and 1791 rights terms signals that a special meaning is intended. There is a clue here that the debate between Burke and his radical enemies was not about whether to embrace or reject the concept of the 'rights of man' but over its 'true' meaning. Note that Burke qualified his favourable use of the 'rights of man' with the prefix 'real' as early as 1774: this qualification was not produced by the French Revolution.

Are these quotations examples of mere rhetoric or of the deployment of a genuine theoretical concept? There is good reason to believe that they are the latter. 'The rights of men', Burke wrote in 1783 in connection with the oppression of the Indian people, 'that is to say, the natural rights of mankind, are indeed sacred things; and if any public measure is proved mischievously to affect them, the objection ought to be fatal.'[5] When Burke said 'sacred', he meant *sacred*: this is not a term he ever used lightly. The rights of men are part of the divine order. In addition, if a natural-rights objection is 'fatal' to a public measure, then it must derive from the natural law, for nothing else yields standards to which positive law is subordinate. Thus, the concept of the natural rights of man is integrated into Burke's theoretical system.

Burke suggests that natural rights are not only *above* government and law, they are *before* them: men had natural rights before they formed society. 'To take away from men their lives, their liberty, or their property, those things, *for the protection of which society was introduced*, is great hardship and intolerable tyranny' (1772 – opposing a petition to relax the doctrinal commitments of Anglican clergymen). This seems very close to the position of Locke. In 1761, Burke had stated this view even more strongly: 'Every body is satisfied, that a conservation and secure enjoyment of our natural rights is the great and ultimate purpose of civil society; and that therefore all forms whatsoever of government are only good as they are subservient to that purpose *to which they are entirely subordinate*' (on the persecution of Irish Catholics).[6]

What, then, are we to make of Burke's apparently clear repudiation of this doctrine?

What were the rights of man previous to his entering into a state of society? Whether they were paramount to, or inferior to social rights, he neither knew nor cared. Man he had found in society, and that man he looked at – he knew nothing of any other man – nor could he argue on any of his rights (1792 – speech against Unitarians).[7]

But it is this passage which is rhetorical and anomalous, for it is impatient, careless, and inconsistent with most of his other statements on the subject. Burke often showed that he cared, and thought he knew, about the relative paramountcy of natural and social rights.

In two important texts of 1790 – the *Reflections* and his

speech on the repeal of the Test and Corporation Acts – Burke declared unequivocally that social rights *abrogated* natural rights.

Abstract principles of natural right had been long since given up for the advantages of having, what was much better, society, which substituted wisdom and justice, in the room of original right. *It annihilated all those natural rights*, and drew to its mass all the component parts of which those rights were made up. . . . [H]ow can any man claim, under the conventions of civil society, rights which do not so much as suppose its existence? Rights which are absolutely repugnant to it? One of the first motives to civil society, and which becomes one of its fundamental rules, is, that no man should be judge in his own cause. By this each person has at once *divested himself of the first fundamental right of uncovenanted man*, that is, to judge for himself, and to assert his own cause. *He abdicates all right to be his own governor.* . . . Men cannot enjoy the rights of an uncivil and of a civil state together.[8]

It seems hard to reconcile the view that 'the great and ultimate purpose of civil society' is the 'conservation and secure enjoyment of our natural rights' with the view that society annihilates these rights and that the *point* of going into society is to get rid of them. But we do not have here a simple contradiction. Immediately after Burke tells us that society annihilated natural rights, he says that it 'drew to its mass all the component parts of which those rights were made up'. What are the 'component parts' of natural rights? How can they be drawn to the mass of society if the rights themselves have been annihilated?

We may risk some speculative interpretation here. Suppose that Burke, despite what he said, did not mean 'annihilated' but rather 'transformed'. If natural rights are *transformed* by society, then we can say without self-contradiction that natural rights are incorporated into society, yet given up *qua* natural (pre-social) rights, while remaining pertinent to the evaluation of governments. The merit of this interpretive move is that it enables us to make coherent sense of all Burke's statements on natural and social rights. It obviously raises the crucial question: what is the nature of the transformation?

Burke answers this question with his distinction between the real rights of men and false claims of right. Civil society is made for the advantage of men and 'all the advantages for which it is made become his right'. Men have therefore the right to live under the rule of law and to justice. They have, too, more specific rights: to the fruits of their industry, to inherit property, to care for their children, to education and to practise religion.[9] These real rights are social rights. They are *transformed* precisely in being made social, that is, in being integrated into the system of more or less stable and harmonious human relationships that constitutes society. Rights thereby become rules. The real rights of men, therefore, collectively amount to the fundamental right to live in freedom under law.

Real rights are always social, but not always identical with legal rights. Men can never have rights incompatible with society as such; but they may have rights not permitted by a particular society. Thus, the real rights of men may be used to criticize actual governments.

The *pretended* rights of man, by contrast, cannot be integrated into a functioning society. They thus tend to destroy it. False claims of right are intrinsically revolutionary, anarchic and tyrannical. Their practical consequences are truly terrible.

Massacre, torture, hanging! These are your rights of men! These are the fruits of metaphysic declarations wantonly made, and shamefully retracted! . . . The leaders of [the French Revolution] tell [the people] of their rights, as men, to take fortresses, to murder guards, to seize on kings . . . and yet these leaders presume to order out the troops, which have acted in these very disorders to coerce those who shall judge on the principles, and follow the examples, which have been guaranteed by their own approbation.

This we may call Burke's 'Kronstadt thesis'. Leaders provide followers with a 'rights' ideology suitable for destroying the old society but incompatible with the reconstruction of the new because subversive of all society. Leaders therefore call in troops to suppress the assertion of the very rights which are supposed to be *raison d'être* of the new order. Burke insists that the leaders, in behaving so, are not betraying their principles but rather realizing their necessary implications. He captures his distinction between the false and the true rights of man very neatly when he refers to the French National Assembly 'occupied as it was with the declaration and violation of the rights of man'. The two activities are necessarily related: declaring false rights and violating real ones.[10]

It is now clear that what really constitutes the falsity of false rights is that they are abstract. It is '*abstract* principles of natural right' which are given up for the advantages of society.

Abstract principles . . . he disliked, and never could bear . . . But of all abstract principles, abstract principles of natural right . . . were the most idle, because the most useless and the most dangerous to resort to.

The abstract character of the radicals' natural-rights doctrine violated not only the moral axiom that man is social but also the epistemological thesis that morality must be based upon experience rather than logic.

You have theories enough concerning the rights of men; – it may not be amiss to add a small degree of attention to their nature and disposition. It is with man in the concrete; – it is with common human life, and human actions, you are to be concerned.[11]

The evidence so far suggests that Burke held a severely modified natural-rights theory. The question arises as to whether this collapses completely into Utilitarianism. His critique of radical natural-rights theory hints occasionally at Utilitarianism. Abstract principles of natural right, he says, are *useless*; they undermine social bonds which form the *happiness* of mankind. Some scholars have thought that Burke was a sort of Utilitarian. Were they right?

Burke does sometimes give empirical happiness priority over abstract rights.

All government . . . is founded on compromise and barter. We balance inconveniences; we give and take; we remit some rights, that we may enjoy others; and we choose rather to be happy citizens, than subtle disputants.

He opposed parliamentary reform on the ground that it was supported merely by speculative theories of government against which he relied on 'the happy experience of this country of a growing liberty and a growing prosperity for five hundred years.'[12]

Similarly, he distinguished between grievances felt in experience and those derived from theories. Those of the Irish Catholics, Americans and Indians were of the first kind; those of the radical intellectuals of the second.[13]

Burke also describes the ends of government in Utilitarian terms. 'I was persuaded that government was a practical thing, made for the happiness of mankind, and not to furnish out a spectacle of uniformity, to gratify the schemes of visionary politicians.'[14]

At times Burke pushes further into Utilitarian country: '. . .the happiness or misery of mankind, estimated by their feelings and sentiments, and not by any theories of their rights, is, and ought to be, the standard for the conduct of legislators towards the people.'[15]

If Burke is here veering away from natural-rights theory towards Utilitarianism in order to repudiate the radical political implications of the former, he is on a dangerous tack. For, although Utilitarianism is not necessarily democratic (people may be happy under undemocratic governments), it is populistic in so far as it insists that the happiness of all the people should count, and count equally, in determining the government's policies.

Burke pulls up very fast when he sees this destination in view, but he can do so only at the cost of great shock to the system. Against abstract natural rights Burke sets an apparently concrete, humane, democratic Utilitarianism. 'Government is a contrivance of human wisdom to provide for human *wants*. Men have a right that these wants should be provided for by this wisdom.' Yet it is a *law of nature* that it is not within the power of government to provide for us in our necessities. Thus Burke tears us away from abstract rights to provide for our wants, only to deny us our necessities in the name of an abstract law of nature.[16]

If Burke's commitment to Utilitarianism is, for this reason, suspect, a sort of Utilitarianism does act as a brake on his commitment to natural rights. It does so by applying the two moral principles of circumstance and consequence. The rightness of a claim of right depends upon the circumstances in which the right is to be applied. Circumstances shape consequences.

A man desires a sword; why should he be refused? A sword is a means of defence, and defence is the natural right of man, – nay, the first of all his rights, and which comprehends them all. But if I know that the sword desired is to be employed to cut my own throat, common sense, and my own self-defence, dictates to me, to keep out of his hands this natural right of the sword.[17]

Everyone knows that Burke lamented the passing of the age of chivalry and the arrival of the age of calculation. But how far did his commitment to counting the cost of political actions commit him to *calculating* the cost?

In contrast to his reputation as a champion of the chivalric spirit, Burke's attitude to cost-benefit Utilitarianism was generally favourable. It is true that there is one very hostile passage in the *Reflections*.

No theatric audience in Athens would bear what has been borne, in the midst of the real tragedy of this triumphal day; a principal actor weighing, as it were in scales hung in a shop of horrors, – so much actual crime against so much contingent advantage, – and after putting in and out weights, declaring that the balance was on the side of the advantages. They would not bear to see the crimes of new democracy posted as in a ledger against the crimes of old despotism, and the bookkeepers of politics finding democracy still in debt, but by no means unable or unwilling to pay the balance. In the theatre, the first intuitive glance, without any elaborate process of reasoning, would shew, that this method of political computation would justify every extent of crime.[19]

None the less, Burke often does talk the language of political computation. 'For you know that the decisions of prudence (contrary to the system of the insane reasoners) differ from those of judicature: and that almost all the former are determined on the more or the less, the earlier or the later, and on a balance of advantage and inconvenience, of good and evil.'[19]

These two passages may seem reconcilable if we focus upon the contrast in the first between *actual* crime and *contingent* advantage. In a revolution, Burke may be saying, the crimes are real, the advantages hypothetical, and thus the revolutionary promises are not worth the cost. But this account does not explain his excoriation of political computation as such. And *both* seem inconsistent with the following warning from the *Reflections*: ' . . . the real effects of moral causes are not always immediate; but that which in the first instance is prejudicial may be excellent in its remoter operation; and its excellence may arise even from the ill effects it produces in the beginning.'[20]

Burke's attitude to cost-benefit Utilitarianism is, therefore, not wholly clear nor clearly consistent. But his position was something like this: political judgement *does* consist of weighing the advantages and disadvantages of applying a given principle; but real costs and benefits weigh more heavily than speculative ones, though remoter consequences must be considered; when in doubt, natural moral feeling ('the first intuitive glance') is a better guide than logic.

Although the juxtaposition of quotations can produce some striking apparent inconsistencies in Burke's thought, it has a fairly high degree of overall coherence. He believed that the real rights of men brought them happiness, and that human happiness was ordained by the law of nature. 'In reality there are two, and only two, foundations of law; and they are both of them conditions without which nothing can give it any force; I mean equity and utility.' Natural law and natural rights give the principles governing man's political life. Utility shows us how these principles are to be applied in actual circumstances. Either without the other leads, not merely to error, but very likely to tyranny. And tyranny violates at the same time the law of nature and the conditions of human happiness.[21]

But we do Burke both less and more than justice if we conclude on the bland note of 'overall coherence'. Burke could be very acute; he could be very inconsistent; and he could be very nasty. On the one hand, he shrewdly remarks that the pursuit of happiness for others may be a dangerous enterprise: 'Let me add, that the great inlet, by which a colour for oppression has entered into the world, is by one man's pretending to determine concerning the happiness of another, and by claiming a right to use what means he thinks proper in order to bring him to a sense of it.' On the other hand, he could, in 1797, advocate that the British Government let loose on the people of France 'famine, fever, plagues, and death' and 'with a pious violence' force down blessings upon them.[22]

If equity and utility are the two, and only two, foundations of law, what is the status of the conventional view that Burke was a champion of *tradition*? In fact, 'tradition' is not a concept of Burke's political theory. But he was a traditionalist. How did Burke relate traditionalism to his particular mixture of natural law and Utilitarianism?

Burke's chief traditionalistic concept is 'prescription'. His classic statement of the doctrine of prescription was made in 1782 during a debate in the House of Commons on electoral reform. The British constitution, he said, 'is a prescriptive constitution; it is a constitution, whose sole authority is, that it has existed time out of mind.' If the *sole* authority of the British constitution, which it was the principal object of Burke's political theory to justify and to defend, was prescription and time, what theoretical work is there for equity and utility to do?[23]

Notwithstanding the last quotation, prescription is not the ultimate ground of political institutions. It is itself grounded in the law of nature. Its protection was among the causes for which civil society itself was instituted. It is, however, 'the most solid of all titles, not only to property, but, which is to secure that property, to Government'. Being the *most* solid of all titles, it supersedes every other title. It appears, therefore, that prescription has priority over utility or natural right.[24]

Having given the principle of prescription the heaviest firing power possible, Burke is fully armed to make his most famous use of it: as a weapon to destroy the radical doctrine of the rights of man. But precisely at this critical juncture he hesitates and loses confidence in his theoretical armoury.

Against these their rights of men let no government look for security in the length of its continuance, or in the justice and lenity of its administration. The objections of these speculatists, if its forms do not quadrate with their theories, are as valid against such an old and beneficent government as against the most violent tyranny, or the greenest usurpation.

In pitting prescription against radical speculation, Burke does not dare to rely on prescription alone. Although prescription is the *sole* authority of the British constitution; although it supersedes every other title; he needs other grounds for attacking the pretended rights of man. These other grounds are 'justice', 'lenity' and 'beneficent government', concepts redolent of both natural law and Utilitarianism.[25]

Although Burke did occasionally speak as if age, in institutions or persons, constituted virtue in itself, the virtue of prescriptive right is grounded in a more complex theory. Prescription, according to Burke, is solidly founded because its merits 'are confirmed by the solid test of long experience, and an increasing public strength and national prosperity'. Prescription protects what is *real* and *beneficent*; the pretended rights of man offer at best speculation, at worst tyranny.[26]

This argument obviously rests upon one massive assumption of fact: the beneficence of the eighteenth-century British constitution. On this ground, he is clearly highly vulnerable to attack. 'The old building stands well enough.' This position requires a certain moral complacency and a well-developed capacity to ignore awkward facts. But, if Burke is weak on the facts here, he is at the same time, characteristically, theoretically interesting. For what he wishes to protect by his doctrine of the prescriptive constitution are the *liberties* of the English people, 'the rights of Englishmen'. He is not defending age against rights, but age-old rights. Prescription is the form taken by the real rights of men.[27]

It is plain, therefore, that Burke's doctrine of prescription is but a part of his general preference for political institutions (including rights) that have evolved through historical experience over those derived logically from abstract principles. What is less clear is whether he is claiming that prescriptive rights are ultimately justified because they are prescriptive or because prescription is the method by which some absolute, ahistorical standard of right is achieved. On the one hand, he says that Englishmen (with his approval) claim their rights on grounds of prescription 'without any reference whatever to any other more general or prior right'. On the other hand, there is this: 'Let me say, for the honour of human nature and for the glory of England, that we have better institutions for the preservation of the rights of man than any other country in the world.' Thus, when all is said, a certain cloudiness remains over Burke's view of the rights of man, and, as a result, his political theory never conclusively lays to rest the critical, or even the radical potentialities of the concept.[28]

Prescription, for Burke, proves utility. Old institutions have shown themselves to be useful. This is so because wisdom accumulates through experience. The individual is foolish, but the species is wise. The individual should, therefore, be cautious and rely on traditional practice, 'established recognized morals' and 'the general, ancient, known policy of the laws of England'. This brings us to the interesting question of Burke's attitude to ancestor-worship.[29]

The path is a curious one, taking unexpected turns. Burke begins, almost like Descartes, with the aim of eliminating all error from his thought. 'I endeavoured to put myself in that frame of mind which was . . . the most reasonable; and which was certainly the most probable means of securing me from all error.' Then he assumes his own fallibility. 'I set out with a perfect distrust of my own abilities. . . .' Suddenly, we are brought face to face with ancestorism: 'I set out with a perfect distrust of my own abilities; a total renunciation of every speculation of my own; and with a profound reverence for the wisdom of our ancestors, who have left us the inheritance of so happy a constitution, etc., etc. . . .'[30]

Ancestorism is particularly strongly represented in the *Reflections*. 'Always acting as if in the presence of canonized forefathers, the spirit of freedom, leading in itself to misrule and excess, is tempered with an awful gravity.' 'We know that we have made no discoveries; and we think that no discoveries are to be made, in morality; nor many in the great principles of government, nor in the ideas of liberty, which were under-stood long before we were born. . . .' And in the *Appeal from the New to the Old Whigs*: 'The example of our own ancestors is abundantly sufficient to maintain the spirit of freedom in its full vigour, and to qualify it in all its exertions.'[31]

These passages, well-known and striking though they are, must be interpreted with great care. They are rhetorical exaggeration and are not to be taken literally. The textual evidence to support this view is overwhelming. Burke did not believe that all, or most, of his ancestors were wise and saintly. His *English History* expresses almost exactly the oppo-site view. Many of his ancestors were brutes and the older the ancestry, the more brutish it was likely to be.[32]

Burke's unfriendly view of his ancient forefathers was not only determined by a respect for historical fact. It served an important ideological purpose. In the seventeenth and eight-eenth centuries, radicals sometimes based their critique of contemporary society on the claim that the true English tradi-tion was pre-Norman, democratic and egalitarian. As a tradi-tionalist anti-democrat and anti-egalitarian, Burke needed to cut this argument down. Superficially, his ancestorism seemed to lend it support. But he repudiated this reading on two grounds. First, the ancient British were barbarians. Second, respect for English tradition does not mean the earlier, the better. Tradition, on the contrary, represents the historical accumulation of wisdom, so, on the whole, the later, the better. The English constitution is 'a deliberate election of ages and of generations'; it is 'made by the peculiar circumstances, occasions, tempers, dispositions, and moral, civil, and social habitudes of the people, which disclose themselves only in a long space of time'; 'the species is wise, *and when time is given to it*, as a species it almost always acts right'. Burke's ancestorism is never Anglo-Saxonism, but an expression of anti-Paineism. It is well expressed, with characteristically incisive malice, in the following barb: 'We have discovered, it seems, that all which the boasted wisdom of our ancestors has laboured to bring to perfection for six or seven centuries, is nearly, or altogether, matched in six or seven days, at the leisure hours and sober intervals of citizen Thomas Paine.'[33]

The doctrine of prescription, therefore, and the accompanying reverence for 'canonized forefathers' do not constitute in Burke's thought, a basis for a reactionary appeal to some ideal past, but, on the contrary, entail a belief in progress. Ancestor-worship is a necessary, but not a sufficient condition of good government, for it must be tempered by attention to present circumstances. Change is the most powerful law of nature, and thus the work of our ancestors is constantly to be modified. Prescription does not rule out reform. It does, however, require cautious reform. For even justified reform may violate some prescriptive interest. This violation is an evil to be minimized. Gradualness therefore reconciles prescription to change.[34]

Burke was, then, a 'progressive'. Progress, for him, consisted in the increasing realization of rational liberty. Yet there is undoubtedly a tension between the progressive and the backward-looking elements in his thought. He held that the revolutionary settlement of 1689 was the high peak of human political achievement and the eighteenth-century English constitution as near perfect as human institutions could be. Yet there is also a nostalgia for (his view of) the late Middle Ages, as every reader of the *Reflections* knows. The age of chivalry is gone. Which age was that? Occasionally, Burke seems to place it between the twelfth and the fourteenth centuries.[35]

He is open to two criticisms here. First, if history is progress, why stop at 1689? Burke says: I concede the need for reform, but not in fundamentals. But why should there not be further progress in fundamentals? Burke may reply: because changing fundamentals upsets the whole apple-cart. There is a good answer to this. Burke confuses fundamental reform with revolution. Fundamental change is compatible with gradualness. In the eighteenth century, one could have been a gradualist and still desired fundamental reform of the electoral system. Burke's case for cautious reform did not entail his belief that the English constitution was fundamentally near-perfect.

Burke might have opposed fundamental reform on the alternative ground that the English constitution did not need it, because it was so good. But good by what standards? By those of natural law? Appeal to this criterion, however, opens up just the sort of theoretical speculation about ideal standards of government that he was so concerned to suppress. By the standards of the English tradition? This answer brings us round in a circle. Why should not this tradition evolve into fundamentally new forms, etc., etc.?

Burke's conservatism is thus subvertible both by his progressivism and by his commitment to natural law. But, once again, his argument is interesting, even though unsuccessful. Let us place the label 'quasi-perfectionism' on the belief that in the fairly recent past progress reached its highest point, so that present-day society is nearly perfect, requiring only minor reforms and adaptations to changing circumstances. Burke was a quasi-perfectionist and quasi-perfectionism is the dominant ideology of the Western world today, even though it is somewhat less confidently held now than it was twenty years ago. The chief elements of the modern quasi-perfect society are civil liberty, parliamentary democracy and the welfare state. This ideology, though quite different in content from Burke's, has much of the same conservative spirit; a sense of great achievements hard-won and jealously to be guarded, and a consequent fear of political radicalism.

This shows the relevance of Burke's theory to modern liberalism. If this doctrine is quasi-perfectionist, is it subvertible by progressivism or by some absolute-standard normative theory? Are liberals committed to the view that we must progress beyond liberalism? Is modern liberal theory, shot through with anxiety though it is (as was Burke's) too complacent about the moral status of liberal achievements?

Modern liberalism is unlike, and superior to, Burke's political thought in being more hospitable to, or in recognizing the necessity of, rapid change and in tolerating or valuing experiment and innovation. But it is faced with a similar dilemma to that which faced Burke, and which he failed to resolve: how to conserve cherished achievements while adapting to a rapidly changing world which may require the abandonment/transcendence of some part of those achievements. In other words, quasi-perfectionism may be unviable. Burke's world was soon to pass away. The future of liberalism is unknown. The study of Burke is relevant because quasi-perfectionist views similar in form to his are still held by persons of power and influence, because they are very plausible, and because they failed in his time.

The second criticism that may be made of Burke's traditionalism is that there is a contradiction between his belief in progress and his nostalgia for the 'chivalrous' past. Burke's response might be this. Civilization is primarily the achievement of Christianity struggling through many centuries against barbarism. The battle for civilization is always hard, always liable to setbacks, but it had been largely won, at least in the sphere of culture and manners, by the late Middle Ages. In the sphere of politics, the final victory took longer, but it came, in England, in 1689. In the late eighteenth century, however, new forces were appearing in both the cultural and political worlds which threatened this great historical achievement. So, while the eighteenth century was, on the whole, the most civilized of centuries, it was timely to reaffirm the virtues of the Middle Ages. Thus the doctrine of progress and nostalgia for the past might be reconciled.

Burke's medievalism and his progressivism are, therefore, not formally incompatible. Yet many of his readers, from his days to ours, have found it intolerably, even absurdly, reactionary. It is worth remembering, therefore, that, in his appreciation of medieval culture, Burke was ahead of, not behind his times. Political nostalgia is always sentimental. Burke's was no exception. His defence of 'chivalry' was, in its time, reactionary. The defence of Marie Antoinette is no longer a popular cause. But distrust of sophisters, economists and calculators is still with us. Burke's medievalism was a weapon to attack *bourgeois* values (which, in their French revolutionary form, he did not believe to be progressive). There is, then, some continuity even between reactionary Burke and modern critics of bourgeois culture.

Prescription is grounded in the natural law. It is also an important basis for social order, which is in turn a prerequisite of civilization.[36] This explains its central place in Burke's political theory. Yet even he was aware that the doctrine raised difficulties. In the middle of one of his strongest defences of prescription, he wrote this.

I see the national assembly openly reprobate the doctrine of prescription, which one of the greatest of their own lawyers tells us, with great truth, is a part of the law of nature. He tells us, that *the positive ascertainment of its limits*, and its security from invasion, were among the causes for which civil society itself had been instituted.[37]

So, prescription does have limits. What are they?

Prescription is the child of natural law and, if it inherits the sanctity, it is also subject to the authority of its parent. Prescription cannot stand against natural law. This may seem obvious, given the pre-eminent position of natural law in Burke's theoretical structure. But it is not easy for him to allow this, for prescription represents experience and natural law is a matter of speculation. But prescriptive right may be abstract, too, and the real experience may be of evil. There is such a thing as 'hereditary tyranny'.[38] In such cases, Burke's solution seems unequivocal. 'Precedents merely as such cannot make Law – because then the very frequency of crimes would become an argument of innocence.' 'There is a time, when the hoary head of inveterate abuse will neither draw reverence, nor obtain protection.'[39]

But, if hoary institutions may be judged by the standards of natural law, the whole doctrine of prescriptive right seems in mortal peril. In order to shore up the defence of prescription against subversion by radicals using natural-law arguments, Burke lays down some rather stringent conditions for their proper application: (1) the object affected by the abuse must be important; (2) the abuse itself must be great; (3) it must be habitual, not accidental; (4) it must be utterly incurable in the body as it now stands constituted.[40]

Burke also protects prescriptive institutions from attack by natural-law arguments with his doctrine of 'old violence'. 'It is possible that many estates about you', he writes to a Captain Mercer in 1790, 'were obtained by arms; . . . but it is old violence; and that which might be wrong in the beginning, is consecrated by time and becomes lawful.'[41]

But Burke is now faced with several difficulties. First, from the moral point of view, how can mere time convert crime into right? Is this not, to use his own words, 'to make the

success of villainy the standard of innocence'?[42] Burke's reply
is based partly on order and partly on utility. If the criminal
origin of old titles could be used to challenge them, social
order would never be secure and more good would be lost
than justice gained. Real utility is better than abstract justice.
However, for the doctrine of old violence to legitimate an
institution through prescription, the original crime must have
been transmuted into justice and beneficence. Long-standing
tyranny is still tyranny.[43]

The second difficulty facing Burke's doctrine of old violence is that it casts doubt on the very concept of political crime.
If any such crime can be converted into a legitimate political
institution through the passage of time (provided time
ameliorates the villainy), it is, when committed, only, so to
speak, provisionally a crime. If present institutions had criminal origins, why should not the crimes of the French Revolution mellow into venerable forms? Was Burke vulnerable to
the criticism made by a pamphleteer of his day:

. . . that a government recently made,
Is always a nuisance, that never can plead
Prescription, in favour of plunder and trade:
And he says, 'tis a maxim in politics true,
Old robbers ought never to tolerate new?[44]

Burke knew that some would think it right, or at least practical, to accord respectability to the French Revolution because
it was there and seemed set to stay.[45] Against this view he
argued that the Revolution had not settled, and that it was
therefore practical to overthrow it. The Revolution offended
natural law on every fundamental point – it violated religion,
property, monarchy, aristocracy, prescription – so that it
could never become legitimate. Every benefit of the Revolution was speculative; every crime actual. The doctrine of old
violence did not apply.

Was he right? A Utilitarian might find the doctrine of old
violence plausible. It might indeed cause more harm than good
to question the origins of long-enjoyed rights. He might also
find this no argument for tolerating present evils, for it might

do more good than harm to fight them. Thus, Burke's position may be defended as consistently Utilitarian provided certain very strong factual assumptions are accepted.

But Burke looked at the Fench Revolution at close range: balancing high, real, immediate costs against speculative gains, and finding the balance negative. If we, from our place in history, look at the French Revolution, we may apply Burke's doctrine of old violence. We may see French history much as Burke saw English, as the story of liberty struggling through much violence and vice to precarious victory. Thus, from the short-term Utilitarian standpoint, Burke's condemnation of the French Revolution had some plausibility. From the long-term progressivist standpoint, it now seems weak. Both standpoints are Burkean.

A third difficulty in Burke's doctrine of crime and prescription lies in his treatment of conquest. Burke defended the prescriptive rights of Indians and Irish Catholics against tyrannical invasion by their English rulers. But he never acknowledged their prescriptive right not to be ruled by the English at all. The rights of conquest appear to override prescription – for English imperialism, though not for French revolutionaries.[46] Burke might be tempted to argue that English imperialism, unlike the French Revolution, represented the spreading of the natural law and beneficent government, if it were not for the fact that he did not believe that to be the case with respect to India and Ireland.

Prescription, therefore, is not wholly consistent with natural law. There may be 'hereditary tyranny'. An ancient government may be persistently unjust. It may, similarly, offend the principle of utility. 'Old establishments are tried by their effects', says Burke, thereby admitting that the results may be negative.

Prescription does not rule out reform or adaptation to changing circumstances. But circumstances may be too radical for a traditionalist theory to handle. Burke not only admits this; on occasion he insists on it.

Whoever goes about to reason on any part of the policy of this country with regard to America, upon the mere abstract principles of government, or even upon those of our own ancient constitution, will often be misled. Those who resort for arguments to the most respectable authorities, ancient or modern, or rest upon the clearest maxims, drawn from the experience of other states and empires, will be liable to the greatest errors imaginable. The object is wholly new in the world. It is singular; it is grown up to this magnitude and importance within the memory of man; nothing in history is parallel to it. All the reasonings about it, that are likely to be at all solid, must be drawn from its actual circumstances.[47]

Novel circumstances challenge not only traditional wisdom but also 'well-tried' policies and even ancient institutions. They can destroy the marriage of traditionalism and pragmatism which is at the heart of Burke's political theory.

At times prescription falls to utility. The following comes from a report of a parliamentary speech made by Burke in 1790.

Mr. Burke . . . said he was happy to find that gentlemen had taken up the question on the principles of reason, as well as on the authority of precedent. In a question which concerned the safety and welfare of the people, every consideration, except what had a tendency to promote these great objects, became superseded – *Salus populi suprema lex, prima lex, media lex.*[48]

This is almost the language of the French revolutionaries. Traditionalism is close to collapse.

Prescription is not only a principle with which to defend ruling classes against subversives. It is available, Burke makes clear, to the people to defend their rights against their rulers and, if necessary, as a weapon of attack. New violence by rulers against old rights of the people provides motivation, and may provide justification, for rebellion.[49] But a rebellion motivated by the desire to protect old rights may lead to a revolution which destroys old rulers and old rights together. How this comes to be is analysed in Burke's sociology of revolution, as we shall shortly see. But, first, we must talk about democracy.

## NOTES

1. *The Works and Correspondence of Edmund Burke* (London: Rivington, 1852), vol. I, p. 560; vol. III, p. 479; Edmund Burke, *Reflections on the Revolution in France* (Harmondsworth: Penguin Books, 1968), pp. 192, 195.

2. *Reflections*, p. 104; *Works and Correspondence*, vol. I, p. 558.

3. *Works and Correspondence*, vol. V, p. 225; vol. IV, pp. 471–2, 428.

4. *Works and Correspondence*, vol. III, p. 312; vol. IV, p. 480; *The Correspondence of Edmund Burke* (Cambridge and Chicago University Presses, 1958–1970), vol. II, p. 529; vol. IV, pp. 411, 416.

5. *Works and Correspondence*, vol. III, p. 451.

6. *The Works of the Right Honourable Edmund Burke* (London: Rivington, 1812–15), vol. 10, p. 16; *Works and Correspondence*, vol. VI, p. 23; emphasis mine in both quotations.

7. *The Speeches of the Right Honourable Edmund Burke* (London: Longman, Hurst, Rees, &c., 1816), vol. IV, p. 51.

8. *Speeches*, vol. III, p. 476; *Reflections*, p. 150; emphasis mine in both quotations.

9. *Reflections*, p. 149.

10. Ibid., pp. 345, 354.

11. *Speeches*, vol. III, pp. 475–6; *Works and Correspondence*, vol. I, p. 562.

12. *Works and Correspondence*, vol. III, pp. 284, 222.

13. Ibid., vol. II, p. 177.

14. Ibid., vol. III, p. 321.

15. *Works*, vol. 10, p. 46; *Works and Correspondence*, vol. IV, p. 485.

16. *Reflections*, p. 151 (Burke's emphasis); *Works and Correspondence*, vol. V, pp. 189, 203. See also *Reflections*, p. 370.

17. *Reflections*, p. 90; *Works*, vol. 10, p. 58; *Works and Correspondence*, vol. III, p. 264.

18. *Reflections*, p. 176.

19. *Works and Correspondence*, vol. IV, p. 514; vol. III, pp. 68, 284.

20. *Reflections*, p. 152.

21. *Works and Correspondence*, vol. VI, pp. 23, 17, 15; *Works*, vol. 10, p. 102; Carl B. Cone, *Burke and the Nature of Politics: The Age of the French Revolution* (Lexington: University of Kentucky Press, 1964), p. 225; *Reflections*, p. 265.

22. *Works and Correspondence*, vol. VI, p. 23; vol. V, p. 359.

23. *Works*, vol. 10, p. 96.

24. *Reflections*, p. 260; *Works and Correspondence*, vol. VI, p. 67; vol. I, p. 577; *Works*, vol. 10, p. 96.

25. *Reflections*, pp. 148, 149.

26. *Reflections*, p. 148; *Works*, vol. 10, p. 96.

27. *Works and Correspondence*, vol. III, p. 68; vol. VI, p. 64; *Reflections*, pp. 118, 119, 109, 111.

28. *Reflections*, p. 119. Peter J. Stanlis, *Edmund Burke and the Natural Law* (Ann Arbor: University of Michigan Press, 1965), p. 131.

29. *Works and Correspondence*, vol. IV, p. 440.

30. Ibid., vol. III, p. 269.

31. *Reflections*, pp. 121, 182; *Works and Correspondence*, vol. IV, p. 487.

32. John C. Weston, Jr., 'Edmund Burke's View of History', *The Review of Politics*, 23, 1961, p. 220; *Works and Correspondence*, vol. VI, pp. 188, 371.

33. *Works*, vol. 10, p. 97 (emphasis mine); *Works and Correspondence*, vol. IV, p. 388; vol. V, p. 457.

34. Francis Canavan, *The Political Reason of Edmund Burke* (Durham, North Carolina: Duke University Press, 1960), p. 170.

35. Weston, pp. 205–6; *Reflections*, p. 181.

36. *Reflections*, pp. 111, 192.

37. Ibid., p. 260 (emphasis mine).

38. *Works and Correspondence*, vol. VI, p. 290.

39. Canavan, pp. 122–3.

40. Burleigh Taylor Wilkins, *The Problem of Burke's Political Philosophy* (Oxford: Clarendon Press, 1967), p. 191.

41. *Works and Correspondence*, vol. I, p. 577; vol. VI, pp. 67, 64, 65, 66.

42. Ibid., vol. IV, p. 472.

43. Ibid., vol. IV, p. 577; vol. VI, p. 366.

44. Cone, pp. 499–500.

45. *Works and Correspondence*, vol. I, pp. 597, 607; vol. V, p. 271; *Correspondence*, vol. VI, p. 140.

46. *Speeches*, vol. IV, p. 6; *Works and Correspondence*, vol. IV, p. 566.

47. *Works and Correspondence*, vol. III, p. 85.

48. *Speeches*, vol. III, p. 513 (emphasis Burke's).

49. Wilkins, p. 62.

# 6

# Government for the People

Prescription sanctifies two institutions in particular: government and property.

Prescription is the most solid of all titles, not only to property, but, which is to secure that property, to Government. They harmonise with each other, and give mutual aid to one another.

But this understates the importance of property in Burke's political theory, for property does far more than 'give aid' to government: it is the foundation of church, state and society.[1]

Burke held that it was natural for property to govern and right for government to protect property. This suggests that his political theory was an ideology of the property-owning class. This is true, but only part of the truth. For he had to reconcile prescriptive government, government by property, with good government, government by talent. And he had to reconcile government by property with government for the people.

We find here a political manifestation of a problem we have already seen arising out of Burke's traditionalistic version of natural law. Is traditional wisdom necessarily the best? Is traditional government necessarily the best? Is the traditional ruling class necessarily that most fit to govern? What is to be the role of political talent outside the traditional ruling class? If, as Burke affirmed, good government required 'much thought, deep reflection, a sagacious, powerful, and combining mind', why did he not favour government by meritocrats rather than by hereditary aristocrats? What political form most favoured government by the wisest and most virtuous?

The natural law produces for Burke the dilemma of government by prescription or talent. It also produces the problem of democracy. For natural law clearly prescribes that government be for all the people. So, why not democracy?

Burke (certain *obiter dicta* notwithstanding) detested democracy. His *Reflections on the Revolution in France* was a polemic against democracy. It is, therefore, all the more striking that we can detect in his thought a democratic pull from natural law.

Now as a law directed against the mass of the nation has not the nature of a reasonable institution, so neither has it the authority: for in all forms of government the people is the true legislator; and whether the immediate and instrumental cause of the law be a single person, or many, the remote and efficient cause is the consent of the people, either actual or implied; and such consent is absolutely essential to its validity.[2]

The consent of the people may be 'implied'. By whom and how? The people is the true legislator 'in all forms of government'. Is the doctrine of the people's consent therefore consistent with all forms of government?

Burke answers these questions.

The people, indeed, are presumed to consent to whatever the legislator ordains for their benefit; and they are to acquiesce in it, though they do not clearly see into the propriety of the means, by which they are conducted to that desirable end. This they owe as an act of homage and just deference to a reason, which the necessity of government has made superior to their own.[3]

Government by the people truly means rule by a small minority of the virtuous and the wise.[4]

This appears to indicate a rather high-minded meritocracy, not an hereditary aristocracy. And this is what Burke appears to advocate.

You do not imagine that I wish to confine power, authority, and distinction to blood, and names, and titles. No, Sir. There is no qualification for government, but virtue and wisdom, actual or presumptive. Wherever they are actually found, they have, in whatever state, condition, profession or trade, the passport of Heaven to human place and honour.[5]

However, Burke makes two strong reservations about meritocracy. The first is that actual virtue and wisdom must be clearly demonstrated by experience.

. . . I do not hesitate to say, that the road to eminence and power, from obscure condition, ought not to be made too easy, nor a thing too much of course. If rare merit be the rarest of all rare things, it ought to pass through some sort of probation. The temple of honour ought to be seated on an eminence. If it be open through virtue, let it be remembered too, that virtue is never tried but by some difficulty, and some struggle.[6]

We may note here, once again, Burke's uneasiness about social mobility. He maintains that there is no qualification for government but merit, but appears to sense that a truly meritocratic society would subvert stability based upon reverential traditionalism. The 'probation' doctrine of rule by merit is his attempt to recognize, as natural law requires, that the best should govern, while retaining the idea of prescriptive government by a traditional ruling class.

None the less, Burke had said that, wherever merit is found, in whatever state, condition, profession or trade, it had 'the passport of Heaven to human place and honour'. But, in the same work, Burke wrote this.

The occupation of an hair-dresser, or of a working tallow-chandler, cannot be a matter of honour to any person – to say nothing of a number of other more servile employments. Such descriptions of men ought not to suffer oppression from the state; but the state suffers oppression, if such as they, either individually or collectively, are permitted to rule.[7]

Why should not the passport of Heaven to human place and honour be available to wise and virtuous hair-dressers and tallow-chandlers, to say nothing of a number of more servile employments?

Burke appears to have this question covered. The passport-to-Heaven passage is explicitly stated to be a corrective to the generalization about hair-dressers, etc. Thus (it appears) he is indeed extending the passport to deserving members of such descriptions of men.

This response must itself be qualified, however. In discussing the role of lawyers in politics, he makes the following general comment on qualifications for government.

. . . [W]hen men are too much confined to professional and faculty habits, and, as it were, inveterate in the recurrent employment of that narrow circle, they are rather disabled than qualified for whatever depends on the knowledge of mankind, on experience in mixed affairs, on a comprehensive connected view of the various complicated external and internal interests which go to the formation of that multifarious thing called a state.[8]

So, although virtue and wisdom may be found in any condition, there is a wide range, from the most servile through hair-dressers to lawyers, which is unconducive to the production of that wisdom necessary to government. If the passport of Heaven is an exception to the dismissal of hair-dressers, the critique of lawyers suggests that Burke is not expecting many such passports to be issued.

The people is the true legislator. But they are presumed to have consented to the superior reason of their actual legislators. The only qualifications for becoming such a legislator are virtue and wisdom, actual or presumptive. Presumption not only transfers sovereignty from the people to their legislators, but helps to determine who is eligible to be a legislator. This is the second reservation about meritocracy.

A true natural aristocracy . . . is formed out of a class of legitimate presumptions, which, taken as generalities, must be admitted for actual truths. To be bred in a place of estimation; to see nothing low and sordid from one's infancy; . . . to be habituated to the censorial inspection of the public eye; to look early to public opinion; to stand upon such elevated ground as to be enabled to take a large view of the wide-spread and infinitely diversified combinations of men and affairs in a large society; to have leisure to read, to reflect, to converse; . . . to be habituated in armies to command and to obey; . . . to be led to a guarded and regulated conduct, from a sense that you are considered as an instructor of your fellow-citizens in their highest concerns, and that you act as a reconciler between God and man – to be employed as an administrator of law and justice, and to be thereby amongst the first benefactors of mankind – to be a professor of high science, or of liberal and ingenuous art – to be amongst rich traders, who from their success are presumed to have sharp and vigorous understandings, and to possess the virtues of diligence, order, constancy, and regularity, and to have cultivated an habitual regard to commutative justice – these are the circumstances of men, that form what I should call a *natural* aristocracy. . . . Men, qualified in the manner I have just described, form in nature, as she operates in the common modification of society, the leading, guiding, and governing part.[9]

This is the natural ruling class. It is constructed theoretcially from three components: (1) certain character traits considered necessary to good government (e.g., broad vision, capacity to command); (2) certain social conditions considered conducive to the production of these traits (e.g., high social status, leisure); and (3) certain occupations presumed to create these conditions. The occupations Burke has chiefly in mind are landowner, army officer, clergyman, judge, professor and merchant.

This appears to be an aristocracy of talent, even if Burke allows presumption to narrow the social field in which talent may be found, for each occupation is justified by him on the ground that it breeds virtue and/or wisdom. But this overstates his commitment to meritocracy. For, just when talent seems to be taking up a strong position in his theory of government, it is firmly placed behind property. 'Nothing is a due and adequate representation of a state', says meritocratic Burke, 'that does not represent its ability, as well as its property.' But, continues property Burke without a pause, 'as ability is a vigorous and active principle, and as property is sluggish, inert, and timid, it never can be safe from the invasions of ability, unless it be, out of all proportion, predominant in the representation.'[10] Burke not only considers ability vigorous and property sluggish, but also that ability is apt to invade property. This propensity of ability justifies giving predominance to property. Here is indeed a strong expression of his fear of innovating talent, a fear so strong that he is pushed back from advocating government by the wise and virtuous to defending that of the sluggish, inert and timid.

Burke often speaks of 'property' in an undifferentiated way, but at times he indicates that aristocratic property has priority over commercial. This is strongly hinted at in the 'natural aristocracy' passage, where more prominence is given to those 'bred in a place of estimation' than to the rich traders, who come well down the list. But he is more explicit than this. In his third *Letter on a Regicide Peace*, he writes: 'The present war is, above all others . . . a war against landed property. That description of property is in its nature the firm basis of every stable government.' Elsewhere, he suggests that the exclusive rule of an hereditary nobility may be 'no bad mode of government'.[11]

Burke ascribes a number of important moral and political qualities to the aristocracy: stability, attachment to tradition, moral responsibility. These are conservative, natural-law qualities we would expect him to require of his ruling élite. But he also saw the aristocracy as the bastion of freedom.

And if in our own history, there is any one circumstance to which, under God, are to be attributed the steady resistance, the fortunate issue, and sober settlement, of all our struggles for liberty, it is, that while the landed interest, instead of forming a separate body, as in other countries, has, at all times, been in close connexion and union with the other great interests of the country, it has been spontaneously allowed to lead, and direct, and moderate all the rest.[12]

The strain between Burke's theory of the aristocratic élite and empirical reality is great. The evidence for this is abundant in his own writings. 'Fat stupidity' and 'gross ignorance', he says, is to be found at courts, at the head of armies and in senates as much as at the loom and in the field. The first Earl of Bedford was a 'jackal in waiting', 'a prompt and greedy instrument of a levelling tyrant, who opressed all descriptions of his people'. The present Duke of Bedford has no public merit of his own to justify his wealth and social position except 'the awful hoar of innumerable ages' and 'the sacred rules of prescription'. In his last years, he was to describe his 'natural aristocracy' as greedy, self-indulgent, cowardly and decadent. During the war with revolutionary France, he declared: 'I do not accuse the people of England. As to the great majority of the nation, they have done whatever in their several ranks, and conditions, and descriptions, was required of them by their relative situations in society.' Explicitly, he accuses the Government. But he is clearly indicting by implication the ruling class. [13]

There is, then, a degree of uncertainty in Burke's attitude to aristocracy. As a result, it is not hard to juxtapose passages apparently pointing in opposite directions. Writing in November 1790, he exclaimed: 'Indeed, indeed, the entire destruction (for it is no less) of all the Gentlemen of a great Country, the utter ruin of their property, and the servitude of their persons, can never be otherwise than most affecting to my mind; and I never can approve any principles or any practices which lead to such a conclusion.' Nine years earlier, he had said this in Parliament.

I am accused, I am told abroad, of being a man of aristocratic principles. If by aristocracy they mean the peers, I have no vulgar admiration, nor any vulgar antipathy, towards them; I hold their order in cold and decent respect. I hold them to be of an absolute necessity in the Constitution; but I think they are only good when kept within their proper bounds. . . . If by the aristocracy, which indeed comes nearer to the point, they mean an adherence to the rich and powerful against the poor and weak, this would indeed be a very extraordinary part. . . . When, indeed, the smallest rights of the poorest people in the kingdom are in question I would set my face against any act of pride and power countenanced by the highest, that are in it; and if it should come to the last extremity, and to a contest of blood, God forbid! God forbid! – my part is taken; I would take my fate with the poor, and low, and feeble. [14]

These passages are not truly inconsistent. Both denounce tyranny: the first by the poor over the rich, the second by the rich over the poor. Nevertheless, Burke concedes too often that property is apt to be oppressive to sustain his identifica-tion of wise and virtuous government with government largely by property.

Burke's doctrine of natural aristocracy requires, therefore, a ruling class composed of three elements: the hereditary landed aristocracy, other men of property, men without property of exceptional virtue and wisdom. Although this ruling class has a duty to preserve the bases of the existing social order, includ-ing the existing institution of property, and thus may be said to have a duty to rule in its own interest, it also has a duty, prescribed by natural law, to govern in the interest of all the people. This raises the question of the relation between rulers and ruled.

The doctrines of implied consent and natural aristocracy seem to have left little room for any democratic content in Burke's political theory. None the less, it is subject to demo-cratic pressure. This pressure is, on occasions, quite strong. These occasions are not, however, spread evenly throughout his work. They tend to be either (a) in early or middle life, or (b) in connection with Ireland. In his *Thoughts on the Cause of the Present Discontents* (1770), he wrote this.

The virtue, spirit, and essence of a House of Commons consists in its being the express image of the feelings of the nation. It was not instituted to be a control *upon* the people. . . . It was designed as a control *for* the people.[15]

The function of the House of Commons is to control the executive and legislative branches of government, but mem-bers of the Commons 'can never be a control on other parts of government, unless they are controlled themselves by their constituents'. The House of Commons should be dependent on the people. As late as 1780, in his *Speech on the Plan for Economical Reform*, he exhorted his fellow members: 'Let us give a faithful pledge to the people, that we honour, indeed, the crown; but that we *belong* to them; that we are their auxiliaries, and not their task-masters.' The House of Com-mons, he says in the *Thoughts*, acts 'from an immediate state of procuration and delegation' and not 'as from original power'.[16]

The representation of the people by the Commons, says Burke, must be actual, not implied or presumed.

It is material to us to be represented really and *bona fide*, and not in forms, in types, and shadows, and fictions of law. The right of election was not established merely as a *matter of form*, to satisfy some method and rule of technical reasoning. . . . It is a right, the effect of which is to give to the people that man, and *that man only*, whom, by their voices actually, not constructively given, they declare that they know, esteem, love, and trust. This right is a matter within their own power of judging and feeling; not an *ens rationis* and creature of law; nor can those devices, by which any thing else is substituted in the place of such an actual choice, answer in the least degree the end of representation.

'Let the commons in parliament assembled be one and the same thing with the commons at large. The distinctions that are made to separate us are unnatural and wicked contrivances. Let us identify, let us incorporate ourselves with the people.'[17]

In his late (1791) *Appeal from the New to the Old Whigs*, Burke, in the midst of a passage rejecting democracy, concedes that the people should control those in authority. No legislator, at any period of the world, he maintains, has willingly placed the seat of active power in the hands of the multitude, for there it admits of no control. However, even here he says: 'The people are the natural control on authority; but to exercise and control together is contradictory and impossible.[18] The argument is against literal government by the people, not against government controlled by the people.'

Earlier, in the 1770 *Thoughts*, he seemed to go further.

Indeed, in the situation in which we stand, with an immense revenue, an enormous debt, mighty establishments, government itself a great banker and a great merchant, I see no other way for the preservation of a decent attention to public interest in the representatives, but the interposition of the body of the people itself, whenever it shall appear, by some flagrant and notorious act, by some capital innovation, that these representatives are going to overleap the fences of the law, and to introduce an arbitrary power. This interposition is a most unpleasant remedy. But, if it be a legal remedy, it is intended on some occasion to be used; to be used then only, when it is evident that nothing else can hold the constitution to its true principles.[19]

The interposition of the people is allowed only under certain conditions. What these conditions are is not clear. At first, popular action seems to be justified to preserve 'a decent attention to public interest in the representatives', a weak requirement since it is not hard to argue plausibly that representatives are neglecting this duty. But, after the 'interposition' phrase itself, the conditions become more stringent. The representatives must be about to 'overleap the fences of the law' and to 'introduce an arbitrary power'. Here Burke suggests that popular revolt is justified only to preserve the constitution against innovating tyrants. But, he insists, 'it is intended on some occasion to be used'. Indeed, he indicates that it is needed 'in the situation in which we stand' – in 1770.

In this passage conservative Burke and radical Burke are both present. Conservative Burke reminds his audience that popular action is 'a most unpleasant remedy', to be used only when it is necessary to save the constitution. Radical Burke reminds them that such necessity arises from time to time. When it does, it is not the people's representatives who must act against an arbitrary executive, but the people who must act against their representatives.

Further support for the view that there is a populistic, direct-action strand in Burke's thought can be found in the *Speech on Economical Reform*.

... [W]e ought to attend ... to those who approach us like men, and who, in the guise of petitioners, speak to us in the tone of a concealed authority. ... But the petitioners are violent. Be it so. Those, who are least anxious about your conduct, are not those that love you most. Moderate affection, and satiated enjoyment, are cold and respectful; but an ardent and injured passion is tempered up with wrath, and grief, and shame, and conscious worth, and the maddening sense of violated right. A jealous love lights his torch from the firebrands of the furies. They who call upon you to belong wholly to the people, are those who wish you to return to your proper home; to the sphere of your duty, to the post of your honour, to the mansion-house of all genuine, serene, and solid satisfaction.[20]

The people should control their representatives. But who are 'the people'? If Burke was an anti-democrat, must we read 'the people' to mean a small élite? Two facts say no. The first is that the language of these passages does not support such an interpretation. Burke refers to 'the people', 'the body of the people itself' and 'the commons at large'. The second is that he produces theoretical arguments in favour of democracy. When he does this, he is usually discusing Ireland.

A country in which only some are free, said Burke in connection with Ireland, is 'the very description of despotism'. Liberty is the portion of the mass of the citizens. To be subject to the state without being a citizen is 'civil servitude'.[21]

Two interpretations of this doctrine are possible. The first is that the 'liberty' which is the portion of the mass of the people refers to such real rights of man as the right to acquire property and implies no right to political participation. Such an interpretation is supported by a passage like this.

No one can imagine then, an exclusion of a great body of men, not from favours, privileges and trust, but from the common advantages of society, can ever be a thing intended for their good, or can ever be ratified by any implied consent of theirs.[22]

In Burke's theory, 'the common advantages of society' do not include the right to democratic government. Nor do they include 'trust', which connotes political power. The passage may therefore be read as implicitly permitting the exclusion of 'a great body of men' from political rights.

But a second interpretation is possible. Burke says exclusion from *citizenship* is servitude. 'Citizenship' connotes the vote for us. It is hard to be sure whether or not it did for Burke. He certainly wrote at times as if it did.

The object pursued by the Catholics is . . . in some degree or measure to be again admitted to the franchises of the constitution. . . . I have always considered the British constitution, not to be a thing in itself so vicious, as that none but men of deranged understanding, and turbulent tempers, could desire a share in it: on the contrary, I should think very indifferently of the understanding and temper of any body of men, who did not wish to partake of this great and acknowledged benefit.[23]

The Catholic objective which Burke supports is to be admitted to 'the franchises of the constitution'. This suggests, once again, the vote. But does the phrase 'in some degree or measure' mean that Burke wished to concede a quite limited right to vote to Irish Catholics? Rational men would wish to partake of the British constitution. Does this mean that all rational men would want the vote? Does it follow that universal suffrage is rational? Or, since the actual British constitution granted only an extremely limited franchise, did Burke desire for Ireland only what existed in England? The passage is opaque. But it rings democratically.

The problem in Ireland, as Burke saw it, was not that a minority ruled the majority, for he defended that in England, but that a selfish minority oppressed the majority.[24] Ireland was a tyranny, while England was ruled by a natural aristocracy. This is Burke's theoretical distinction. But if the fact be conceded that England's actual aristocrats were oppressive, then his rather democratic Irish arguments would apply to England.

In writing about Ireland, Burke tended strongly to undercut his general élitist position. The year is 1792. The French Revolution is into its third year. Burke has written his *Reflections* and his *Appeal from the New to the Old Whigs*, his two principal anti-democratic tracts. In this year he none the less writes of the Irish Catholics:

If they should be told, and should believe the story, that if they dare attempt to make their condition better, they will infallibly make it worse – that if they aim at obtaining liberty, they will have their slavery doubled – that their endeavour to put themselves upon any thing which approaches towards an equitable footing with their fellow-subjects will be considered as an indication of a seditious and rebellious disposition – such a view of things ought perfectly to restore the gentlemen, who so anxiously dissuade their countrymen from wishing a participation with the privileged part of the people, to the good opinion of their fellows. But . . . I think arguments of this kind will never be used by the friends of a government which I greatly respect. . . .[25]

But arguments of this kind were being used by Burke at that

very time against English and French radicals. Political, economic and social inequality serve the general interest: this contention is a main pillar of his political theory. Rule by the few is in the interest of the many: in England and in France. In Ireland it is a tale told by knaves and believed by fools.

Burke also advances on behalf of the Irish Catholics another standard argument for democracy: that participation in a political system strengthens the loyalty of the participant to the system.

> The admission of the most respectable and decent ranks of the Roman Catholics to a share of constitutional rights, must certainly strengthen, instead of diminishing, the security of the state as it now stands. A greater number of persons will be interested in conservation. . . . If the experience of mankind is to be credited, a seasonable extension of rights is the best expedient for the conservation of them.[26]

This is a conservative statement. Only 'the most respectable and decent ranks' of the Catholics are to be admitted to constitutional rights, and then only to a 'share' of them. The objective is conservation, not reform, nor even justice. Burke proposes a 'seasonable' extension of rights, thus permitting himself to disallow another claim of right as unseasonable. Despite all this, the passage contains a democratic logic. If the extension of participation strengthens the state, why not universal suffrage? Why not, at the very least, a more hospitable attitude to the extension of the suffrage?

There are texts which support still more firmly the view that Burke was advocating for Ireland not only more constitutional liberty but greater political democracy.

> They who are excluded from votes (under proper qualifications inherent in the constitution that gives them) are excluded, not from the state, but from the British constitution. They cannot by any possibility, whilst they hear its praises continually rung in their ears, and are present at the declaration which is so generally and so bravely made by those who possess the privilege – that the best blood in their veins ought to be shed, to preserve their share in it; they, the

disfranchised part, cannot, I say, think themselves in a happy state, to be utterly excluded from all its direct and all its consequential advantages.[27]

The passage is not wholly clear: what does the parenthesis in the first sentence mean? But the general point is. Those excluded from the vote are excluded from the constitution and are unhappy. Burke is clearer still in a letter of 1782.

The taking away of a vote is the taking away the shield which the subject has, not only against the oppressions of power, but of that worst of all oppressions, the persecutions of private society, and private manners. No candidate for parliamentary influence is obliged to the least attention towards them, in cities or counties; on the contrary, if they should become obnoxious to any bigotted, or any malignant people among whom they live, it will become the interest of those who court popular favour, to use the numberless means, which always reside in magistracy and influence, to oppress them.[28]

Burke is here denouncing the 'taking away' of the vote, i.e., the abrogation of a prescriptive right. But if, as he suggests, the prescriptive right to vote provides a shield for liberty, why should not those who have never had the vote, to whom he concedes the right to rational liberty, be granted the same protection?

Burke did not favour universal suffrage for Ireland. He favoured a property qualification, but wished it to be low. In a letter to his son, dated 29 February, 1792, he wrote:

The hundred pound qualification is not a thing to be even whispered, because it would tend to make the world believe . . . that the committee are like Lord Kenmare and his friends, who look only to the accommodation of a few gentlemen, and leave the common people who are the heart and strength of the cause of the Catholics, and are the great objects in all popular representation, completely in the lurch. What has been proposed is full high enough. And it ought to be stuck to.[29]

What had been proposed was a lower property qualification. But if a hundred pound qualification would leave the common people in the lurch, why would not the lower qualification have done so, though to a smaller degree? Once again, Burke's theory carries him beyond his policy.

Burke was aware that his advocacy of the vote for Irish Catholics might be used to support the cause of electoral reform in England. He expressly built defences against such moves. There was, he maintained, a basic distinction between the claims of the Irish Catholics and those of the English reformers. The former wished the right of election 'should be ratified, confirmed, and extended to a new class of citizens'. The latter wanted 'a new right of election, and that the whole constitution of representation should be new cast'.[30]

This distinction is doubly dubious. Firstly, the English reformers could, on Burke's argument, call for the extension of the old right of election to a new class of citizens, an extension he opposed. Secondly, it is sophistical to claim that the extension of the suffrage from an oppressive class of one religion to include a substantial section of the oppressed adherents of another is nothing more than a ratification and extension of an old right of election. Burke's proposal for Ireland was at least as radical as some of those he opposed in England. He did not rely solely on the prescriptive right of Catholics to vote, for he advocated extension of the suffrage to 'a new class of citizens'. His attempt to distinguish between the Irish and English cases for electoral reform therefore failed.

However, he has a second argument to distinguish Ireland and England. This rests on the concept of *virtual representation*. 'Virtual representation is that in which there is a communion of interests, and a sympathy in feelings and desires between those who act in the name of any description of people, and the people in whose name they act, though the trustees are not actually chosen by them.' Virtual representation, he says, is in many cases better than actual. 'The people may err in their choice; but common interest and common sentiment are rarely mistaken.'[31]

This preference for virtual representation is harmonious with the doctrine of natural aristocracy but not harmonious with his affirmation of 1770 that it is 'material to us to be represented really and *bona fide*, and not in forms, in types, and shadows, and fictions of law'.

However, the Catholics of Ireland did not even have virtual representation. They had the contrary: actual oppression. By and large, Burke thought, the English were adequately represented. Legally, the sense of the people of England was to be collected from the House of Commons. If there was any doubt whether the House of Commons represented perfectly the whole Commons of Great Britain – and Burke thought there was none – there was no question but that the Lords and Commons together represented the sense of the whole people to the Crown and to the world. The legal presumption that Parliament represented the will of the people was not irrebuttable, but 'before the legally presumed sense of the people should be superseded by a supposition of one more real . . . , some strong proofs ought to exist of a contrary disposition in the people at large, and some decisive indications' of their wishes.[32]

The distinction between the Irish and English cases for electoral reform rests upon the validity of Burke's application of the virtual-representation doctrine to England. Factually, one may doubt whether Parliament represented the interests of the commons at large as perfectly as Burke claimed. Theoretically, Burke is forced to rely on the fictional device of presumption, which he had himself expressly condemned and which violates the whole ostensible bias of his philosophy to prefer the empirically real to the abstractly theoretical.[33]

Democracy meant, for Burke, rule by the *will* of the majority. Rule by *will*, as distinct from *reason*, was against the natural law. Rule by many wills was the worst of political evils since numbers gave added force to will. Government should be rational, that is, just and wise. This required virtue and wisdom, not the counting of wills. The necessary virtue and wisdom were rare. Those who possessed them were the natural aristocracy.[34]

Burke identified the natural aristocracy with the hereditary aristocracy and the rich merchants, which makes his theory an upper-class ideology. But here I am concerned with its philosophical, not its sociological, status. Burke advocated government by reason and claimed that this entailed government by these classes. Reason, he argued, arose from experience. Rationality will, therefore, be found among those with the most extensive experience of men, and, still more importantly, those who are the chief repositories of the experience of the ages. The whole nation is to some extent such a repository (see the discussion of 'epistemological populism' in Chapter 2). But the hereditary aristocracy scores highest on both counts. It is both, by its social position and training, best equipped for government, and the chief curator of inherited culture.

Thus, the 'reason' which Burke gives priority over 'will' is traditional reason, which also has priority over the innovating reason of individuals or groups. To ensure that 'reason' remains conservative, he puts the idea of the 'social contract' to his own distinctive use.

Before society, there is no sovereignty. Society is created by voluntary agreement. This agreement is the constitution. Once made, it is 'a permanent standing covenant', binding on every individual in society, independent of any choice by him. The nature of this constitution is 'collected from the form into which the particular society has been cast'.[35] Since the present form of society is the evidence for what the constitution is, and the consititution is assumed to be based on an initial voluntary contract, Burke has it both ways in two ways: his aristocratic society has a democratic consensual origin/justification and his compulsory society has a voluntary origin/justification.

This prescriptive constitution, sanctioned both by voluntary agreement and natural law as 'a partnership . . . between those who are living, those who are dead, and those who are to be born' cannot be altered at will or by force, even if the will or the force be that of the majority. There was nothing 'natural' about majority rule for Burke. The only natural constitution was the traditional one. Against that, majority rule had no claim, not only because it represented subjective will against objective reason, but because it was a violation of the social contract. Majority rule is therefore against the original and implied present consent of the people. Democracy is undemocratic.[36]

The philosophical distinction between will and reason is reflected by the political distinction between will and interest. 'The will of the many, and their interest, must very often differ; and great will be the difference when they make an evil choice.' When the will and the interest of the people diverge, rulers have a duty to pursue their interest despite their wishes. 'I did not obey your instructions', Burke told his Bristol constituents in 1780; 'No. I conformed to the instructions of truth and nature, and maintained your interest, against your opinions, with a constancy that became me.'[37]

This right and duty of the Member of Parliament to follow his independent judgement against the wishes or instructions of his constituents is one of Burke's most famous doctrines. It is often cited today, typically with approval, when similar problems of the relation between M.P. and his constituents arise. Two points should, however, be remembered. First, it is based on a natural-law epistemology, entailing a belief in absolute truth in politics, and on an anti-democratic political theory, both of which would be less widely approved today. Second, it contradicts his 1770 view that the people should control the House of Commons.

Burke supports the doctrine with two arguments. The first is the doctor-patient analogy.

The people are the masters. They have only to express their wants at large and in gross. We are the expert artists: we are the skilful workmen, to shape their desires into perfect form, and to fit the utensil to the use. They are the sufferers, they tell the symptoms of the complaint; but we know the exact seat of the disease, and how to apply the remedy according to the rules of art.[38]

The second anti-democratic argument is one from justice.

No man carries further than I do the policy of making government pleasing to the people. But the widest range of this politic complaisance is confined within the limits of justice. . . . I never will act the tyrant for their amusement. If they will mix malice in their sports, I shall never consent to throw them any living, sentient creature whatsoever, no not so much as a kitling, to torment.[39]

It is often thought that political élitism must be based upon mistrust of 'the people'. How far is this in fact true of Burke? Let us consider some texts.

I reverentially look up to the opinion of the people, and with an awe, that is almost superstitious.

This is extreme, and clearly needs at least one qualification.

[The desires of the people], when they do not militate with the stable and eternal rules of justice and reason . . . ought to be as a law to a House of Commons.

He sometimes expresses himself more moderately.

I am not one of those who think that the people are never in the wrong. They have been so, frequently and outrageously, both in other countries and in this. But I do say, that in all disputes between them and their rulers, the presumption is at least upon a par in favour of the people. Experience may perhaps justify me in going farther. When popular discontents have been very prevalent, it may well be affirmed and supported, that there has been generally something found amiss in the constitution, or in the conduct of government. The people have no interest in disorder. When they do wrong, it is their error, and not their crime.[40]

By contrast, Burke also expressed a less favourable view of the people. 'The impetuous desire of an unthinking public will endure no course, but what conducts to splendid and perilous extremes.'[41] There is no reconciling the people deserving of reverential awe with the impetuous and perilous public. The best that can be said for Burke at this point is that a quite similar ambivalence characterizes many other political theories.

Although Burke's attitude to 'the people' may sometimes seem democratic, his definition of 'the people' is not. Those who, 'in any political view', are to be called 'the people' consist only of those 'of adult age, not declining in life, of tolerable leisure for such discussions, and of some means of information, more or less, and who are above menial dependence'. He reckoned there to be about 400,000 such people in

1796. Similarly, he said that the French nation, according to its fundamental constitution, consisted of the monarch, the church, the military, the corporate bodies of justice and of burghership.[42] Burke therefore excludes the majority of real people from his definition of the political 'people' or the constitutional nation. This from the man who suggested that exclusion from the constitution was civil servitude.

We must conclude that, despite his flirtations with democratic notions, Burke was an anti-democrat. The sovereignty of the people was, he believed, 'the most false, wicked, and mischievous doctrine that ever could be preached to them'. It was so because it entailed the rule of will, and this in turn entailed the subversion of rational government. Democracy meant anarchy.[43]

Democracy also meant tyranny. This is a central thesis of Burke's political theory. 'I hate tyranny, at least I think so; but I hate it most of all where most are concerned in it. The tyranny of a multitude is but a multiplied tyranny.' There is nothing in democracy that provides a guarantee, or even a barrier, against tyranny. On the contrary, democracy is more likely to be tyrannical than other forms of government and also likely to be more tyrannical. For when the people have power, there is no check on them; they will pursue their opponents without the restraint that all minority, even single, rulers must observe.[44]

Burke opposed democracy because he thought it threatened liberty: this view has had many supporters from his day to ours, even among nominal democrats. But, if in this he was part of a respected tradition, can the same be said for his opposition to all proposals for reforming the eighteenth-century electoral system?

Burke did not consistently oppose reform. He was more favourable towards it early in his career than he was later. He changed his view because he believed the circumstances in which reform was being debated were changing. Reform, at the end of his career, had, he believed, revolutionary implications. It was proposed in a radical climate formerly absent, and this led him to dig in his heels.

One reason he gave for opposing reform was that the

reformers attached too much importance to constitutional forms. It may be argued that Burke attached too little importance to them, in England if not in Ireland. Even if this is so, his criticism of his opponents' constitutional optimism was not without some force.[45]

Robert Hutchins, a trenchant modern liberal critic of Burke, has maintained that prescription is 'the most disingenuous of all Burke's arguments for opposing the extension of the suffrage and the reform of the House of Commons' because both had been frequently altered in the immediately preceding centuries. But, on this issue, Burke preferred Utilitarian to prescriptive arguments. The existing system of representation, he said, had been found 'perfectly adequate to all the purposes for which a representation of the people can be desired or devised'. The system worked and most of the people were satisfied with it. He denied that the places which were heavily represented were more free, more just, more prosperous or happier than those which had less representation. The criterion of reform, he insisted, should not be theoretical improvement, but practical.[46]

Reform, Burke thought, was not merely unnecessary, it was fraught with great peril. The Constitution was at stake. Moderate reformers might not be able to keep their extreme supporters in check. Parliamentary reform was a slippery slope to revolution.[47] At this stage, Burke's conservative pragmatism changes to panic.

What form of government, then, did Burke advocate? One answer is: none. We have seen that he criticized those who attached excessive importance to political forms. 'It was not for any particular system of government that he contended, but for some government. Let it be a pure monarchy, a democracy, or an aristocracy, or all mixed, he cared not, provided a government did exist.'[48]

But this does not ring true. Burke never contended for pure monarchy, democracy or aristocracy. He contended for a mixed constitution, as he understood it to exist in England. 'We are resolved to keep an established church, an established monarchy, an established aristocracy, and an established democracy, each in the degree it exists, and in no greater.'

Sometimes he considered the Constitution to consist of three parts only: monarchy, aristocracy, democracy. 'Democracy' meant the House of Commons.[49]

Burke defended this mixed constitution not merely on grounds of prescription. It accorded with several of his basic principles. It defied, for instance, that principle of simple abstract perfectionism which he believed led in practice to tyranny. 'The whole scheme of our mixed constitution is to prevent any one of its principles from being carried as far, as taken by itself, and theoretically, it would go. . . . To avoid the perfections of extreme, all its several parts are so constituted, as not alone to answer their own several ends, but also each to limit and control the others. . . .'[50]

The mixed constitution is appropriate for a plural society. Interests in such a society are 'various, multiform, and intricate'. All these interests must be considered, compared, and reconciled if possible. The constitutional machinery for doing this must be one of balanced powers. Such a constitution makes for moderation. It renders 'all the headlong exertions of arbitrary power, in the few or in the many, for ever impractical'. It prevents 'the sore evil of harsh, crude, unqualified reformations'. It is a constitution of conservation and liberty.[51]

We have examined the democratic and the aristocratic strains in Burke's thought, and his doctrine of the balanced constitution. But what justification, apart from tradition, did he give for monarchy?

The monarchy, Burke held, was not only 'great and ancient' but 'the key-stone that binds together the noble and well-constructed arch' of the constitution. It was 'the presiding and connecting principle of the whole'.[52]

Burke supported an active, but not an absolute monarchy. The monarchy was one power to be balanced with the others in the mixed constitution. It was subject to natural law, metaphysically and morally, and subject, politically, to the checks of corporate bodies representing the different interests of the realm. Royal power might not destroy popular rights nor might popular rights swallow royal power.[53] Because the monarchy is the key-stone of the constitution, and because the constitution is a constitution of liberty, the monarchy, so long as it acts within the constitution, is a bulwark of liberty.[54]

Burke defended monarchy, not kings. There were inadequate kings; there were wicked kings. But this did not destroy the principle of monarchy. No political institution would work if those who peopled it were corrupt. Monarchy was a necessary check on abuses by the other powers, as they were necessary checks on the abuses of monarchy.[55]

I have so far ignored one much-discussed part of Burke's political theory: his doctrine of party. I wish only to show how party fits into the structure of his thought. The political party he favours is a combination of men acting upon a common principle. This well-known definition reflects several of his basic ideas. Politics should be based on principle, but principle in action. It concerns power, but power restrained by principle. And as politics is a practical discipline, so is it a collective one: it requires combinations of men.[56]

Parties, too, are instruments for freedom. They check royal absolutism. They also, Burke thought, check radical subversion of the Constitution. Party was necessary to the constitutional balance. Party was therefore necessary to liberty.[57]

## NOTES

1.  *The Works of the Right Honourable Edmund Burke* (London: Rivington, 1812–15), vol. 10, p. 96; *The Speeches of the Right Honourable Edmund Burke* (London: Longman, Hurst, Rees, &c., 1816), vol. IV, p. 166; *The Works and Correspondence of Edmund Burke* (London: Rivington, 1852), vol. I, p. 577; vol. V, pp. 309, 388; *The Correspondence of Edmund Burke* (Cambridge and Chicago University Presses, 1958–70), vol. VII, p. 389.

2.  *Works and Correspondence*, vol. VI, p. 15.

3.  Ibid., p. 16.

4.  *Works and Correspondence*, vol. IV, pp. 467, 471; Edmund Burke, *Reflections on the Revolution in France* (Harmondsworth: Penguin Books, 1968), p. 192.

5.  *Reflections*, p. 139.

6.  *Reflections*, pp. 139–40.

7.  Ibid., p. 138.

8. Ibid., p. 133.
9. *Works and Correspondence*, vol. IV, p. 466 (emphasis Burke's).
10. *Reflections*, p. 140.
11. *Works and Correspondence*, vol. V, p. 414; vol. IV, p. 513.
12. *Works and Correspondence*, vol. IV, p. 414; *Correspondence*, vol. IV, p. 450; vol. VII, p. 62; Francis Canavan, *The Political Reason of Edmund Burke* (Durham, North Carolina: Duke University Press, 1960), p. 98.
13. *Reflections*, p. 201; *Works and Correspondence*, vol. V, pp. 233, 229, 231, 241, 237, 424, 487.
14. *Correspondence*, vol. VI, p. 179; *Works*, vol. 10, p. 138.
15. *Works and Correspondence*, vol. III, pp. 146–7 (emphasis Burke's).
16. Ibid., vol. III, pp. 153, 174, 147; vol. IV, p. 404; emphasis Burke's.
17. Ibid., vol. III, pp. 154, 403–4 (emphasis Burke's).
18. Ibid., vol. IV, p. 459.
19. Ibid., vol. III, p. 164.
20. Ibid., p. 403.
21. *Works and Correspondence*, vol. VI, p. 54; vol. IV, p. 512.
22. Ibid., vol. VI, p. 16.
23. Ibid., vol. IV, p. 534.
24. Ibid., vol. VI, p. 54.
25. Ibid., vol. IV, p. 534.
26. Ibid., vol. II, p. 176.
27. Ibid., vol. IV, p. 515.
28. *Correspondence*, vol. IV, p. 409.
29. *Works and Correspondence*, vol. IV, p. 538; *Correspondence*, vol. VII, p. 83.
30. *Works and Correspondence*, vol. II, pp. 176, 177.
31. Ibid., vol. IV, p. 540.
32. Ibid., vol. V, p. 374.
33. R. M. Hutchins, 'The Theory of Oligarchy: Edmund Burke', *The Thomist*, V, 1943, pp. 64–5.
34. *Works and Correspondence*, vol. IV, pp. 458, 459, 463, 363; *Reflections*, p. 191.
35. *Works and Correspondence*, vol. IV, pp. 460, 463; vol. V, p. 125; *Reflections*, p. 105.
36. *Reflections*, pp. 194–5, 105; *Works and Correspondence*, vol. IV, pp. 458, 463, 465.
37. *Reflections*, pp. 141, 191; *Works and Correspondence*, vol. III, pp. 418, 354; vol. V, p. 316; vol. IV, p. 416.

38. *Works and Correspondence*, vol. III, p. 401; vol. IV, p. 533.

39. Ibid., vol. III, p. 443.

40. *Works and Correspondence,* vol. III, pp. 146, 347, 114; *Works,* vol. 10, p. 76.

41. *Works and Correspondence*, vol. I, p. 564.

42. *Works and Correspondence*, vol. V, pp. 284, 36.

43. R. M. Hutchins, 'The Theory of the State: Edmund Burke', *Review of Politics*, V, 1943, p. 149; *Works and Correspondence*, vol. IV, pp. 431–2.

44. *Works and Correspondence*, vol. I, p. 578; *Reflections*, pp. 228, 190, 111, 176.

45. *Correspondence*, vol. II, p. 150.

46. Hutchins, 'The Theory of Oligarchy', p. 73; Canavan, pp. 162–5.

47. *Works and Correspondence*, vol. II, p. 176; vol. III, p. 70; *Correspondence*, vol. IX, p. 336.

48. *Speeches*, vol. IV, p. 166; *Reflections*, p. 228.

49. *Reflections*, p. 188; *Works and Correspondence*, vol. IV, p. 415.

50. *Works and Correspondence*, vol. VI, p. 486.

51. *Works and Correspondence*, vol. IV, p. 486; *Reflections*, p. 122.

51. *Works and Correspondence*, vol. IV, p. 418.

52. *Works and Correspondence*, vol. IV, p. 418.

53. *Works and Correspondence*, vol. IV, pp. 425, 450, 446; *Reflections*, p. 111.

54. *Reflections*, p. 109; *Works and Correspondence*, vol. IV, p. 423.

55. *Works and Correspondence*, vol. IV, p. 380.

56. Ibid., vol. III, p. 170.

57. Frank O'Gorman, *Edmund Burke: His Political Philosophy* (London: Allen & Unwin, 1973), especially pp. 28, 29, 32, 35, 40.

# 7

# The State and Freedom

Burke's theory of the state was liberal in two senses. First, he wished to steer a middle course between royal absolutism and popular democracy. Second, he had a keen awareness of human weakness, therefore of the likelihood that power would be abused, therefore of the dangers of government grown too strong. He opposed the British state's treatment of the Americans; he opposed the French Revolution because, among other reasons, he thought it had developed a tyrannical state.

By contrast, there are strongly illiberal elements in his view of the state. The state, he says, is sacred, and we should regard it with pious awe. God willed it to perfect our virtue.[1] This state seems, from the liberal point of view, over-legitimated, too good to be safe. If God willed the state, why should it need to be checked?

Closely associated with the idea of the state as sacred is Burke's paternalistic imagery.

To avoid therefore the evils of inconstancy and versatility, . . . we have consecrated the state, that no man should approach to look into its defects or corruptions but with due caution; . . . that he should approach to the faults of the state as to the wounds of a father, with pious awe and trembling solicitude. By this wise prejudice we are taught to look with horror on those children of their country who are prompt rashly to hack that aged parent in pieces, and put him into the kettle of magicians, in hopes that by their poisonous weeds, and wild incantations, they may regenerate the paternal constitution, and renovate their father's life.[2]

Presenting the state as an aged parent invokes simultaneously the qualities of wisdom and benevolence. It also enables Burke to transform revolutionaries into parricides.

But the metaphor is not successful. If we think of the parent as 'senile' rather than 'aged', the paternalistic image is more favourable to revolutionaries. It is not right, obviously, to hack even senile parents in pieces, but it is also not right that they should rule millions of rational beings.

Burke's conception of the state as sacred and paternalistic suggests authoritarian implications for its role in society. But the suggestion is misleading. The state, he says, ought to confine itself to public peace and public prosperity. 'In its preventive police it ought to be sparing of its efforts, and to employ means, rather few, unfrequent, and strong . . .' The adjectives are crucial. The interventions of the state should be few, unfrequent, but *strong*. Burke's state is limited, but tough.[3]

What are the rules for intervention? 'The coercive authority of the state is limited to what is necessary for its existence. . . . It considers as crimes (that is, the object of punishment) trespasses against those rules, for which society was instituted.'[4] The second sentence qualifies the first to a significant degree. The coercive authority of the state is limited to what is necessary for its existence, but not for its mere existence. It punishes trespasses against those rules for which society was instituted. It does not just protect itself; it protects those institutions which are its *raison d'être*.

What are these institutions?

. . . [T]he state ought to confine itself to what regards the state, or the creatures of the state, namely, the exterior establishment of its religion; its magistracy; its revenue; its military force by sea and land; the corporations that owe their existence to its fiat. . . .[5]

The intention of this passage is to confine the state's duties to a limited sphere, though the reference to corporations begs the question as to what corporations the state ought to set up and protect. But here is another version of the institutions for the sake of which society was formed.

If civil society be made for the advantage of man, all the advantages for which it is made become his right. . . . Men have a right . . . to the fruits of their industry; and to the means of making their industry fruitful. They have a right to the acquisitions of their parents; to the nourishment and improvement of their offspring; to instruction in life, and to consolation in death. Whatever each man can separately do, without trespassing upon others, he has a right to do for himself; and he has a right to a fair portion of all which society, with all its combinations of skill and force, can do in his favour.[6]

Here we are looking at the problem from the bottom up: the rights of man rather than the rights of the state. Among the rights of man are the right to the fruits of his industry and the right to the *means* of making his industry fruitful. He also has a right to instruction and to the nourishment and improvement of his offspring. Finally, he has a right to a fair portion of 'all which society . . . can do in his favour'.

If we did not know better, we might suspect Burke of harbouring socialist inclinations. But we do know better. We saw, in Chapter 4, that he opposed state intervention in the economy to help the poor. 'Let government protect and encourage industry, secure property, repress violence, and discountenance fraud, it is all they have to do. In other respects, the less they meddle in these affairs the better . . . .'[7]

Burke's *laissez-faire* state limits the real rights of men. A man may have a right to a 'fair portion of all which society . . . can do in his favour', but, beyond protection from force and fraud, and religious consolation for misery, the right has little content. There is a contradiction here. The state should protect those rights, for the conservation of which it was formed. When Burke speaks of rights, they include the right to certain forms of economic justice. When he speaks of the state, he forbids it to meet this obligation.

The limited state is incompatible with both the paternalist state (for the loving parent is forbidden to aid his starving children) and with the real rights of men. It is also apparently incompatible with the principle of utility. 'The object of the state is (as far as may be) the happiness of the whole.'[8] This seems to justify considerable state aid to the miserable, unless great weight is given to the parenthetical 'as far as may be'.

Burke can only escape the statist implications of paternalism, economic rights and utility, by the doctrine that it is in the nature of things that these principles are best realized by the limited state. This doctrine has a heavy load to bear, for he concedes actual misery and injustice while setting up happiness and justice as principles.

Burke argued against state aid to the poor. But this was not an argument against state socialism, for this was not on the agenda at the time he wrote. His argument is directed against state, i.e. monarchical, interference with commerce. It was a bourgeois argument against absolute monarchy and therefore a liberal argument.

Property was, for Burke, a natural right. But, consistently with his general attitude to natural rights, he did not believe it to be absolute. In the *Reflections*, when he is most alert to defend property, he allots to the state 'the full, sovereign superintendence . . . over all property, to prevent every species of abuse'.[9] He does not say what he means by 'every species of abuse', so that, once again, a principle of intervention is established, whose practical implications are unclear.

Thus, with regard to the economy, Burke provides principles for an interventionist state, while advocating *laissez-faire* in practice, justifying this by an appeal to natural economic laws. His view of political freedom is also rooted in his metaphysics.

'I love order so far as I am able to understand it, for the universe is order.' In society, therefore, 'good order is the foundation of all good things'. This good order requires the people 'without being servile' to be 'tractable and obedient'.[10]

Disobedience must therefore be punished. Even where the people are 'provoked to their excesses', the law ought to look to nothing but the offence and punish it. Weak, even if beneficent, government is the greatest of evils, for it encourages disorder and thereby often renders necessary 'the most rigorous and illegal proceedings'. 'Through an extreme lenity it is on some occasions tyrannical.'[11]

In the face of disobedience, government must be severe, for order is the first virtue of society. Or is it? When Burke conducted his campaign against the French Revolution, his objective was not primarily to restore order to France, but to subvert such fragile order as there was in order to restore the prior ruling class. The values of the old regime had priority over the establishment of order in the short term.

The people, without being servile, must be obedient. The no-servility proviso is not innocuous. In 1773, organizing opposition to the government's Indian policy, Burke recommended a systematic campaign in the press, and even suggested 'a procession of proprietors to Westminster Hall as a method of overawing parliament'. 'I like a clamour, whenever there is an abuse. The fire-bell at midnight disturbs your sleep, but it keeps you from being burned in your bed.'[12]

If not a contradiction, there is a tension between the primacy of order and the fire-bell at midnight. This tension is apparent in his Irish writings. In 1796 he writes to the Rev. Thomas Hussey: 'The doctrine of passive obedience, as a doctrine, it is unquestionably right to teach.' In 1792 he had advocated 'a persevering, litigious, dissatisfied obedience'. Obedience still, but restless, not, perhaps, entirely 'tractable'. Then, every now and again, the fire-bell rings out, as in the letter to Lord Fitzwilliam, 10 February 1795: 'All the miseries of Ireland have originated, in what has produced all the miseries of India, a servile patience under oppression, by the greatest of all misnomers called prudence.'[13]

Read literally, Burke may seem consistent. All the people should always obey the law. All the people always have the right to present their grievances in a lawful manner to their rulers. Rulers have the duty to listen to grievances and to apply appropriate remedies. They also have the duty to punish all violations of the law.

But such an account is far too bland a rendering of Burke's tense struggle to master the problems of order and oppression, liberty and resistance. We have, on the one hand, the familiar rhetoric of deference. On the other, we have the fire-bell at midnight. And, in a letter to the Rev. Hussey, 18 January 1796, Burke says: 'Dreadful it is; but it is now plain enough, that Catholic *Defenderism* is the only restraint upon Protestant *Ascendancy*.'[14] Defenderism was armed resistance.

Burke understood the passions of the oppressed. Referring

to the Irish past, he wrote of 'the hideous and abominable things which were done in the turbulent fury of an injured, robbed, and persecuted people'.[15] At this point, the two sides of Burke's rhetoric confront each other. Hideous, abominable, turbulent fury is the language of his attack on the French Revolution. Injured, robbed and persecuted is the language of his sympathy for the Irish Catholics and the Indians, which he denied to the people of France. The passage shows, not only that Burke had a left as well as a right hand, but that he knew that he did. The Burke of order and deference is challenged by the Burke of the oppressed. The structure of his thought is tense rather than firm.

What of liberty? Burke was, in his way, a libertarian. In November 1789 he wrote to Charles-Jean-François Depont: 'You hope, Sir, that I think the French deserving of liberty? I certainly do. I certainly think that all men who desire it, deserve it. It is not the reward of our merit or the acquisition of our industry. It is our inheritance. It is the birthright of our species.'[16]

This appears to secure the right to liberty rather firmly. But Burke continues:

'We cannot forfeit our right to [liberty], but by what forfeits our title to the privileges of our kind; I mean the abuse or oblivion of our rational faculties, and a ferocious indocility, which makes us prompt to wrong and violence, destroys our social nature, and transforms us into something little better than the description of wild beasts. To men so degraded, a state of strong constraint is a sort of necessary substitute for freedom; since, bad as it is, it may deliver them in some measure from the worst of all slavery, that is the despotism of their own blind and brutal passions.

Thus, when Burke says all who desire liberty deserve it, he does not mean what he appears to mean. To have the right to liberty, you must be rational and somewhat docile. Liberty is for Burkean man. Hobbesian man requires 'a state of strong constraint'.

By the time of his *Letter to a Member of the National Assembly* (1791), Burke had changed his mind about the right of the French to liberty.

I doubt much, very much, indeed, whether France is at all ripe for liberty on any standard. Men are qualified for civil liberty in exact proportion to their disposition to put moral chains upon their own appetites; in proportion as their love to justice is above their rapacity. . . . Society cannot exist unless a controlling power upon will and appetite be placed somewhere, and the less of it there is within, the more there must be without. It is ordained in the eternal constitution of things that men of intemperate minds cannot be free. Their passions forge their fetters.[17]

Thus, though liberty is the birthright of our species, it is only attainable in a rational society. However, this qualification to the basic libertarian principle is itself qualified. The possibility of liberty is related to the nature of particular societies. Burke writes this of America.

In this character of the Americans, a love of freedom is the predominating feature which marks and distinguishes the whole: and as an ardent is always a jealous affection, your colonies become suspicious, restive, and untractable, whenever they see the least attempt to wrest from them by force, or shuffle from them by chicane, what they think the only advantage worth living for. This fierce spirit of liberty is stronger in the English colonies probably than in any other people of the earth. . . .[18]

Burke invites our sympathy, not simply for the American love of freedom, but for its ardent, even fierce spirit, and the untractable conduct in which it results when liberty is threatened.

No doubt Burke thought the American conception of liberty more rational than the French. But he allows the Americans a right to ferocity which he denies to the French. With respect to the Americans, he says to the British Government: 'Reflect how you are to govern a people, who think they ought to be free, and think they are not. Your scheme yields . . . nothing but discontent, disorder, disobedience. . . .'[19] He never asked Louis XVI to reflect how he was to govern a people, who thought they ought to be free, and thought they were not. And when the king's schemes yielded discontent, disorder and disobedience, he condemned the popular disorder, not the policies that had provoked it.

The problem of liberty, for Burke, lay in the fact that it entailed power, power to do good or evil. 'Considerate people, before they declare themselves, will observe the use which is made of power.' The spirit of freedom led, in itself, to misrule and excess. For, without wisdom and virtue, what is liberty? 'It is the greatest of all possible evils; for it is folly, vice, and madness, without tuition or restraint.'[20]

Liberty, therefore, to be welcomed, must be combined with government, public force, an effective and well-distributed revenue, with morality and religion, peace and order, with civil and social manners, the solidity of property, and inequality. 'All these (in their ways) are good things too; and, without them, liberty is not a benefit whilst it lasts, and is not likely to continue long.'[21] Burke also insists that liberty be combined with the rule of law.[22]

Burke sought to balance 'a government of real energy for all foreign and all domestic purposes, with the most perfect security to the liberty and safety of individuals'. This is the 'spirit of rational liberty' to which he subscribes on the opening pages of the *Reflections*. Such a balance is maintained through institutions and feelings rooted in national tradition.[23] These are the sociological and psychological conditions of rational freedom.

Liberty must always be balanced with order: in affirming this, Burke is consistent. But his description of how the balance is to be maintained differs in the different contexts of the French and American revolutions. Burke constantly calls the French to order. Here, by contrast, is 'American' Burke.

Liberty, too, must be limited in order to be possessed. The degree of restraint it is impossible in any case to settle precisely. But it ought to be the constant aim of every wise public council to find out by cautious experiments, and rational cool endeavours, with how little, not how much, of this restraint the community can subsist; for liberty is a good to be improved, and not an evil to be lessened. It is not only a private blessing of the first order, but the vital spring and energy of the state itself, which has just so much life and vigour as there is liberty in it.[24]

But the view that Burke proposed a balance between order and liberty is too neat. Consider the question of freedom of speech. Burke held that every citizen should be permitted decently to express his sentiments upon public affairs, without hazard to his safety, even though they went against a predominant opinion.[25] Yet, in *Thoughts and Details on Scarcity* (1795), he wrote this: 'The great use of government is as a restraint; and there is no restraint which it ought to put upon others, and upon itself too, rather than that which is imposed on the fury of speculating under circumstances of irritation.' Lest there be some doubt as to what he means by 'restraint', Burke states that the government owes to the people the duty of 'timely coercion'. It is true that speculation is only to be coerced 'under circumstances of irritation'. It is also true that it is the 'fury' of speculating which is to be restrained. None the less, it is clear that Burke's distrust of the speculative mind could lead him to advocate the forceful suppression of dissent in troubled times.[26]

*Thoughts and Details on Scarcity* is a treatise on economics. It is worth considering why Burke took up the question of freedom of thought in such a work. The reason was that he was concerned, more concerned than ever before in 1795, about the *political* consequences of the spread of radical ideas among the poor. His concern derives from his sociological view of the relations between ideas and politics.

It is the interest, and it is the duty, and because it is the interest and the duty, it is the right of government to attend much to opinions; because, as opinions soon combine with passions, even when they do not produce them, they have much influence on actions. Factions are formed upon opinions; which factions become in effect bodies corporate in the state; – nay factions generate opinions in order to become a centre of union, and to furnish watchwords to parties; and this may make it expedient for government to forbid things in themselves innocent and neutral.[27]

Since opinions, even those innocent in themselves, may become the basis of factions, which themselves become 'in effect bodies corporate in the state', to deny, on libertarian grounds, the government the right to control opinions is to deny it the right to control factions subversive of the state. In practice, Burke at this time supported savage penalties for those agitating on behalf of reform.[28]

There are three special aspects of liberty to which Burke addressed himself. The first is the question of work. Burke acknowledged, as we saw in Chapter 4, that many men were doomed to work from dawn to dark in innumerable degrading occupations. He deplored this, but resigned himself to it on the ground that it was necessary. This 'solution' to the problem of servile and degrading work is unsatisfactory, not only because it justifies a concrete evil by an abstract principle in violation of Burke's own moral methodology, but because it raises the question of the relation of work to liberty without pursuing the implications of having done so. If he had followed this trail, it would have led him to the problem of reconciling the freedom to employ others with the right of those others to be free from servile employment. The doctrine of the necessity of market relations conceals rather than solves this problem, while the 'dawn to dark' passage briefly reveals its existence.

A second aspect of liberty with which Burke concerned himself was slavery. Burke opposed slavery, thereby placing liberty before prescriptive property rights. But, consistently with his own principles, he did not propose to solve the problem by the direct application of the abstract right to liberty to produce a policy of immediate abolition. He proposed gradual reform,[29] arguing that this would lead to less suffering than would immediate abolition, since the slaves were unprepared for such a sudden and radical change in their situation. On slavery, liberty was his principle, caution his method.

On a third aspect of liberty, religious toleration, Burke was also 'progressive'. It is tempting to explain his religious toleration by reference to the fact that his immediate family was composed of both Protestants and Catholics. This explanation, valid so far as it goes, does not go far enough. It explains his advocacy of toleration towards Catholics, but not his extension of it to 'Jews, Mahometans and even Pagans', indeed to all religions.[30]

It also conceals a fundamental theoretical point behind a

merely biographical one. For in Burke's political thought, which rests always upon a theological foundation, the essential divide is not between Protestantism and Catholicism, not even between Christianity and other religions, but between religion itself and atheism. Toleration he was not prepared to extend to atheists.

At the same time that I would cut up the very root of atheism, I would respect all conscience. . . . The . . . infidels are outlaws of the Constitution; not of this country, but of the human race. They are never, never to be supported, never to be tolerated.[31]

Were the reasons for Burke's rejection of atheism religious or political? This question makes a presupposition which Burke would have rejected: that the two can be properly separated. Burke did wish to withhold toleration from religious groups which he believed to be engaged in radical politics and explicitly gave a political reason for his position. But the dual basis of his ferocious hostility to atheism is well revealed in the following passage.

Under the systematic attacks of [the infidels], I see some of the props of good government already beginning to fail; I see propagated principles, which will not leave to religion even a toleration. . . . Let it be but a serious religion, natural or revealed, take what you can get; cherish, blow up the slightest spark. One day it may be a pure and holy flame. By this proceeding you form an alliance, offensive and defensive, against those great ministers of darkness in the world, who are endeavouring to shake all the works of God established in order and beauty.[32]

Atheists seek to shake all the works of God. Among the chief works of God is the state. Atheism is, therefore, intimately related to political radicalism. Neither can be tolerated.

Burke's view on the state and freedom must be understood in relation to his view of the British Constitution. When he speaks of 'rational liberty', he is usually speaking of the British Constitution.

Our constitution is like our island, which uses and restrains its subject sea; in vain the waves roar. In that constitution I know, and

exultingly I feel, both that I am free, and that I am not free dangerously to myself or to others. I know that no power on earth, acting as
I ought to do, can touch my life, my liberty, or my property.[33]

The British Constitution brings on, more than any other
subject, Burke's famous grand style. 'Our political system is
placed in a just correspondence and symmetry with the order
of the world, . . . wherein, by the disposition of a stupendous
wisdom, moulding together the great mysterious incorpora-
tion of the human race . . .' and so forth. This style is difficult to
illustrate by quotation, since one of its leading features is the
great length of passages, with the use of such techniques as
cumulative repetition and crescendo. This aspect of Burke
must be read whole to be understood at all.

It is necessary, none the less, to pick out the chief *ideas* Burke
held about the Constitution. Firstly, it is part of the pattern of
nature and the order of the world. It is as it is by the disposition
of a stupendous wisdom. Secondly, it remains in a condition of
unchangeable constancy, even though it also moves through
perpetual decay, fall, renovation and progression. Thirdly, it is
a constitution of liberty, but this liberty is considered as an
inheritance, and so considering it fortifies the fallible and
feeble contrivances of our reason with the unerring and
powerful instincts of nature. Fourthly, by always acting 'as if
in the presence of canonised forefathers', the spirit of freedom,
which, in itself, leads to misrule and excess, 'is tempered with
an awful gravity'. This 'awful gravity' should be particularly
noted. It is what tempers misrule and excess. It is also that
feature of the British Constitution which Burke seeks to con-
vey by his rhetoric. 'By this means our liberty becomes a noble
freedom. It carries an imposing and majestic aspect.'[34]

The next question we must ask is why Burke believed both
that the British constitution was a constitution of rational
liberty and that the British ruling class ruled tyrannically.

If the Constitution was a solid rock, and liberty one of its
chief principles, liberty itself was less than solid. In 1775, with
reference to America, Burke declared: ' . . . [I]n order to prove
that the Americans have no right to their liberties, we are every
day endeavouring to subvert the maxims which preserve the

whole spirit of our own. To prove that the Americans ought not to be free, we are obliged to depreciate the value of freedom itself. . . .'[35] Of one particular bill brought forward by the British Government, Burke wrote, again in 1775: 'No cruelty, no tyranny ever heard of in history or invented in fable has at all equalled it.'[36]

Burke also believed that the British Government exercized, and had for a long time exercized, directly, or indirectly through the Protestant Ascendancy, a tyranny over the Catholic majority in Ireland.[37] Writing to the Rev. Hussey in December 1796, he insisted that the Irish tyranny was as bad as the French.

Shall you and I find fault with the proceedings of France, and be totally indifferent to the proceedings of Directories at home. You and I hate Jacobinism as we hate the Gates of Hell – Why? Because it is a system of oppression. What can make us in love with oppression because the syllables Jacobin are not put before the *ism*? When the very same things are done under the *ism* preceded by any other name in the Directory of Ireland.[38]

Note that Burke writes of events in Ireland as taking place 'at home'. Irish tyranny may once have been the harshness of foreign conquest, but now it is plain British tyranny.

Similarly, Burke was convinced that the government of India by the East India Company was 'one of the most corrupt and destructive tyrannies that probably ever existed in the world'.[39] Nor was the charge to be laid exclusively against the Company. The 'Indian interest', which was collaborating in the oppression of the Indian people, was 'a great part of the kingdom, of all ranks, classes and descriptions, spiritual and temporal', including the Court.[40]

Yet, although Burke believed British rule in America, Ireland and India to be tyrannical, and although he believed that these policies and regimes led to the introduction of tyrannical elements into the government of Britain, he would not admit that this tyranny was part of the British Constitution.

As British tyranny did not lead Burke to question the Constitution, it also made little impact on his doctrine of paternalistic imperialism.

The parliament of Great Britain sits at the head of her extensive empire in two capacities: one as the local legislature of this island, . . . The other, and I think her nobler capacity, is what I call her imperial character; in which, as from the throne of heaven, she superintends all the several inferior legislatures, and guides and controls them all, without annihilating any. As all these provincial legislatures are only co-ordinate with each other, they ought all to be subordinate to her; else they can neither preserve mutual peace, nor hope for mutual justice, nor effectually afford mutual assistance. It is necessary to coerce the negligent, to restrain the violent, and to aid the weak and deficient, by the overruling plenitude of her power.[41]

Why should Britain enjoy this plenitude of power? Because, says Burke, it has been called by Providence to be the 'tutelary angel of the human race'. 'By adverting to the dignity of this high calling, our ancestors have [in America] turned a savage wilderness into a glorious empire: and have made the most extensive, and the only honourable conquests, not by destroying, but by promoting the wealth, the number, the happiness of the human race.'[42]

The British Empire was justified because it brought peace, justice and aid to the weak, because it promoted the wealth and happiness of the human race. Did it? Did Burke believe it did? The passage last quoted was written in 1775, the year in which he was saying that Britain had brought tyranny to America. One might add that his opinion that the European conquest of America was honourable was probably more widely shared among the conquerors than among the conquered.

Despite mounting evidence to the contrary, Burke clung tenaciously to the idea of the beneficent Empire. After four more years of the American struggle, in 1779, he could still write: 'My principles make it my first, indeed almost my only earnest wish, to see every part of this Empire, and every denomination of men in it happy and contented, and united on one common bottom of equality and justice.' As late as 1795, he denounced Irish independence from England as a disaster.[43] The Empire could enjoy the constitution of rational liberty.

But it actually suffered from tyranny. Burke offered the people of the British Empire his speculative abstractions, while they lived with the tyranny he himself portrayed, at length and with feeling.

He was susceptible to doubt. In a letter about America, he wrote in 1775: 'I have been a strenuous advocate for the superiority of this country – but I confess I grow less zealous when I see the use which is made of it.' In his speech on Fox's East India Bill (1783), he wondered if Britain was fit to govern India at all. 'But there we are: there we are placed by the Sovereign Disposer; and we must do the best we can in our situation.'[44] When the facts contradict the theory, appeal to Providence to save the theory.

If God had willed the British Empire, he had certainly not willed one for revolutionary France, appearances to the contrary notwithstanding.

I can speak it to a certainty, and support it by undoubted proofs, that the ruling principle of those who acted in the revolution as statesmen had the exterior aggrandizement of France as their ultimate end in the most minute part of the internal changes that were made. We . . . cannot easily form a conception of the general eagerness of the active and energetic part of the French nation, itself the most active and energetic of all nations, previous to its revolution, upon that subject.[45]

Had the Sovereign Disposer willed the exterior agrandizement of France? Perhaps He had. but Burke would fight it none the less. Why? Because France was a tyranny. But so was the British Empire. Burke had contradicted himself and placed his God in an embarrassing moral position.

Burke opposed French expansion partly because it was the Revolution expanding and partly because it was France doing so. Burke, the Irishman, was an English nationalist. This nationalism contradicted the implications of universal community contained in the Christian religion, to which he subscribed, thereby causing further difficulties in his system of thought.

Speaking of India, he drew attention to 'the faith, the covenant, the solemn, original, indispensable oath, in which I am bound, by the eternal frame and constitution of things, to the whole human race'.[46] But here is a different Burke.

To commiserate the distresses of all men suffering innocently, perhaps meritoriously, is generous, and very agreeable to the better part of our nature – a disposition that ought by all means to be cherished. But to transfer humanity from its natural basis, our legitimate and homebred connexions; to lose all feeling for those who have grown up by our sides, in our eyes, the benefit of whose cares and labours we have partaken from our birth, and meretriciously to hunt abroad after foreign affections, is such a disarrangement of the whole system of our duties, that I do not know whether benevolence so displaced is not almost the same thing as destroyed, or what effect bigotry could have produced, that is more fatal to society.[47]

It may be said that this passage is consistent with the one quoted just before it. Burke praises compassion for all men suffering innocently. He condemns only loss of compassion for those who have grown up by our sides and the meretricious hunt for foreign affections. He wrote this in the context of Ireland. He was denouncing those Protestants who befriended their foreign co-religionists while oppressing their Catholic fellow-countrymen. This is consistent with compassion for suffering Indians.

This argument ignores the underlying theory. Burke says that the natural basis of humanity is in those with whom we have grown up, with whom we have exchanged the benefits of love and labour, with whom we constitute a real society. The hunting after foreign affections may be benevolence, but it is benevolence so displaced that it may be as fatal to society as bigotry. National solidarity is necessary to society. Foreign benevolence threatens it.

It is true that the internationalism here denounced is domestic tyranny, but it is also religious solidarity. Burke places loyalty to nation before loyalty to religius denomination. His sympathy for Catholics enables him to celebrate the unity of Britain. Religious toleration could make of the country 'one family, one body, one heart and soul, against the family-combination, and all other combinations of our enemies'.[48]

But, if Burke was a nationalist, he was an internationalist too. The civilization he sought to defend was European, not just British. Europe constituted a commonwealth with a common basis of religion, laws, and manners. It embraced diversity of local customs and institutions, but it had the same basis of general law. The nations of Europe had 'the very same Christian religion, agreeing in the fundamental parts, varying a little in the ceremonies and in the subordinate doctrines'. The political and economic systems of Europe had common origins in Roman Law, Germanic custom and feudal institutions. 'From all those sources arose a system of manners and of education which was nearly similar in all this quarter of the globe; and which softened, blended, and harmonised the colours of the whole. . . . From this resemblance in the modes of intercourse, and in the whole form and fashion of life, no citizen of Europe could be altogether an exile in any part of it.'[49]

The European system of manners was based on the spirit of chivalry. But the age of chivalry, Burke lamented in his *Reflections*, was gone. That of sophisters, economists, and calculators had succeeded it. As a result, the glory of *Europe* was extinguished for ever.[50]

Chivalry entailed a generous, proud and dignified submission to rank, 'which kept alive, even in servitude itself, the spirit of an exalted freedom'; the 'unbought grace of life'; manly sentiment and heroic enterprise; sensibility of principle, which 'ennobled whatever it touched' and mitigated ferocity. This spirit, said Burke, made power gentle and obedience liberal, harmonized the different shades of life, and 'incorporated into politics the sentiments which beautify and soften private society'.[51]

All this consituted 'the decent drapery of life', a body of ideas 'furnished from the wardrobe of a moral imagination, which the heart owns, and the understanding ratifies, as necessary to cover the defects of our naked shivering nature, and raise it to dignity in our own estimation'. The old spirit of chivalry is favourably contrasted with the new scientific view of man. 'On this scheme of things, a king is but a man; a queen is but a woman; a woman is but an animal. . . . The murder of a king, or a queen, or a bishop, or a father, are only common homicide. . . .'[52] The materialist conception of man (and woman) annihilates morality, manners and the sense of human dignity. It leads naturally to murder, parricide and regicide.

Chivalry was based upon submission to rank, but it also mitigated power. The chivalrous spirit of fealty freed kings from fear, and thus, Burke said, freed both kings and subjects from the precautions of tyranny. 'Kings will be tyrants from policy when subjects are rebels from principle.'[53]

Europe, on the eve of the French Revolution, was flourishing. Its condition owed much to France. The subversion of French institutions was therefore a threat to all Europe.[54]

The war against the French Revolution was a war in defence of civilization. The cause was that of Christian Europe against 'the empire of anarchy and irreligion'.[55]

Although Burke held that the spirit of chivalry had given to modern Europe its character, and distinguished it to its advantage from the states of Asia, and possibly from those states which had flourished in the most brilliant periods of the ancient world,[56] he did not defend modern Europe as such, but its animating spirit. There were civilized societies and there was barbarism. Barbarism could be found in Europe, as in the French Revolution. Civilization could be found outside it, as in India. Where it was to be found, it was to be cherished.[57]

Burke valued liberty, but the liberty he valued was 'rational' liberty, and his concept of rational liberty can only be understood by reference to his whole system of thought. Rational liberty is that type of liberty enjoyed by those who live in a civilized society.

Since Burke is conventionally, and rightly, considered to be a leading theorist of conservatism, and since he valued highly liberty of a kind, it is worth asking how far he may also be considered a liberal. This raises the difficult problem of specifying the defining elements of liberalism. It is quite beyond my present ambition to do this in a rigorous way. It is sufficient to point to those elements in Burke's thought that would commonly be regarded as liberal, and those that would not.

Burke defended the individual and his (imperfect) representative institutions against the power of the executive. He advocated a limited state, with powers checked by the institutions of civil society. He supported, with qualifications, freedom of speech and freedom of the press; with almost no qualification, the rule of law; and, passionately, property rights. He favoured, very strongly, religious toleration, except where religion was associated with political radicalism; and reform where there was a clear abuse.

All this is quite liberal. But it is qualified by a rather illiberal conservatism. Burke was quite ready to suppress freedom of speech, and even freedom of religion, if he thought the safety of the state or other basic values were threatened. He held this position because he believed (1) that liberty was one among a number of important values; and (2) that ideas could be powerful social forces; therefore, that ideas could threaten these values; therefore, that state control of ideas could be justified.

More clearly illiberal is a strong undercurrent of Burke's thought, which surfaces from time to time: his distrust of social movement, of innovation, especially of intellectual innovation. Burke was a 'progressive' in that he championed the advance of science and the increase of wealth. If Isaac Newton and Adam Smith represent 'the Enlightenment', Burke was for it. If Voltaire does, he was against it. Burke was a man of two worlds: the world of deference and discipline and the world of free thought and free enterprise. The contradiction between these two worlds runs through his thought. The contradiction is brought to the point of crisis by the French Revolution. It is in part because this event forced Burke to confront these two aspects of his own thought that his *Reflections on the Revolution in France* is his masterpiece.

NOTES

1.    Edmund Burke, *Reflections on the Revolution in France* (Harmondsworth: Penguin Books, 1968), p. 194; *The Works of the Right Honourable Edmund Burke* (London: Rivington, 1812–15), vol. 10, p. 108.

2.  *Reflections*, p. 194.
3.  *The Works and Correspondence of Edmund Burke* (London: Rivington, 1852), vol. V, p. 210; vol. III, p. 114; *Reflections*, p. 115; *The Correspondence of Edmund Burke* (Cambridge and Chicago University Presses, 1958–70), vol. VI, p. 10.
4.  *Works and Correspondence*, vol. VI, p. 27.
5.  Ibid., vol. V, p. 210.
6.  *Reflections*, p. 149.
7.  Supra, p. 71; *Works and Correspondence*, vol. V, p. 396; vol. III, p. 391.
8.  *The Speeches of the Right Honourable Edmund Burke* (London: Longman, Hurst, Rees, &c., 1816), vol. IV, p. 58.
9.  *Reflections*, p. 203.
10.  Ibid., p. 372.
11.  *Works and Correspondence*, vol. VI, pp. 60, 196, 241, 307; *Correspondence*, vol. IX, pp. 168, 170.
12.  Carl B. Cone, *Burke and the Nature of Politics: The Age of the American Revolution* (Lexington: University of Kentucky Press, 1957), pp. 243, 215.
13.  *Correspondence*, vol. IX, p. 171; vol. VIII, p. 147; Thomas H. D. Mahoney, *Edmund Burke and Ireland* (Cambridge, Massachusetts: Harvard University Press, 1960), pp. 202, 197.
14.  *Correspondence*, vol. VIII, p. 378 (emphasis Burke's).
15.  *Works and Correspondence*, vol. VI, p. 66.
16.  *Correspondence*, vol. VI, p. 41; *Works and Correspondence*, vol. III, p. 302; *Works*, vol. 10, p. 16.
17.  *Works and Correspondence*, vol. IV, p. 389; *Correspondence*, vol. VI, p. 108.
18.  *Works and Correspondence*, vol. III, p. 253.
19.  Ibid., pp. 220, 257, 253.
20.  *Reflections*, pp. 90–1, 121, 373, *Works and Correspondence*, vol. IV, p. 487.
21.  *Reflections*, pp. 90–1; *Works and Correspondence*, vol. IV, p. 424.
22.  *Correspondence*, vol. VI, pp. 42–6.
23.  *Works and Correspondence*, vol. I, p. 561; *Reflections*, p. 121.
24.  *Works and Correspondence*, vol. III, p. 322; Francis Canavan, *The Political Reason of Edmund Burke* (Durham, North Carolina: Duke University Press, 1960), p. 92.
25.  *Correspondence*, vol. VI, p. 43.
26.  *Works and Correspondence*, vol. V, p. 189.
27.  *Speeches*, vol. IV, p. 57.
28.  Carl B. Cone, *Burke and the Nature of Politics: The Age of the*

*French Revolution* (Lexington: University of Kentucky Press, 1964), pp. 433, 437.

29.  Ibid., pp. 385–8; *Works and Correspondence*, vol. III, p. 262.

30.  *Reflections*, p. 259; *Works and Correspondence*, vol. VI, pp. 23, 25, 56, 58; *Works*, vol. 10, pp. 25, 39; *Correspondence*, vol. III, p. 112; Mahoney, p. 111.

31.  See previous note.

32.  *Works*, vol. 10, pp. 37–9; *Correspondence*, vol. VI, p. 54; Cone, *French Revolution*, pp. 388 *et seq.*

33.  *Works*, vol. 10, p. 104; *Works and Correspondence*, vol. VI, p. 62.

34.  *Reflections*, pp. 120–1.

35.  *Works and Correspondence*, vol. III, p. 259.

36.  *Correspondence*, vol. III, p. 132.

37.  *Works and Correspondence*, vol. IV, pp. 511, 515, 528, 547; vol. VI, p. 65.

38.  *Correspondence*, vol. IX, pp. 170, 169, 165, 163 (emphasis Burke's).

39.  *Works and Correspondence*, vol. III, p. 504; *Correspondence*, vol. VIII, pp. 424, 431–2, 437.

40.  *Correspondence*, vol. VIII, p. 438.

41.  *Works and Correspondence*, vol. III, p. 221.

42.  Ibid., vol. III, pp. 291–2; vol. V, p. 293.

43.  *Correspondence*, vol. IV, p. 121; vol. VIII, p. 246.

44.  *Correspondence*, vol. III, p. 132; *Works and Correspondence*, vol. III, p. 469.

45.  *Works and Correspondence*, vol. V, pp. 333–4.

46.  Ibid., vol. III, p. 489.

47.  Ibid., vol. VI, p. 21.

48.  Ibid., vol. III, pp. 430, 432.

49.  Ibid., vol. V, pp. 305–6.

50.  *Reflections*, p. 170.

51.  Ibid., pp. 170–1.

52.  Ibid., p. 171.

53.  Ibid., p. 172.

54.  Ibid., pp. 173–5.

55.  *Works and Correspondence*, vol. II, p. 4; vol. V, p. 16; *Correspondence*, vol. VI, pp. 457–61; vol. VIII, p. 130.

56.  *Reflections*, p. 170.

57.  *Works and Correspondence*, vol. III, pp. 456–7.

# 8

# The Principles of Progress

We shall begin our analysis of Burke's doctrine of reform and revolution with a consideration of his 'humanitarianism'.

The problem of Burke's humanitarianism is raised by the secondary literature. Dr Frank O'Gorman has written of Burke's 'passionate humanitarian instincts' which, with his 'deep religious feelings', were 'the crucial characteristics of his philosophy'. On the other hand, Dr Conor Cruise O'Brien quotes Harold Laski's view that Burke possessed a generous and compassionate temperament in order to cast doubt on it.[1]

It is obvious that Burke's theory was 'humanitarian' in the sense that it was concerned with the welfare of human beings. Critics who object to the claim that Burke was a humanitarian may object to this or that part of his general moral and political philosophy. But they may acknowledge that parts of the theory appear humanitarian while maintaining that these parts are insincere or merely rhetorical. We must therefore ask whether Burke's humanitarianism was genuine.

A suitable passage for examination is the following one on John Howard, the penal reformer.

I cannot name this gentleman without remarking that his labours and writings have done much to open the eyes and hearts of mankind. He has visited all Europe, – not to survey the sumptuousness of palaces, or the stateliness of temples; . . . but to dive into the depths of dungeons; to plunge into the infection of hospitals; . . . to remember the forgotten, to attend to the neglected, to visit the forsaken, and to compare and collate the distresses of all men in all countries. . . . Already the benefit of his labour is felt more or less in every country; I hope he will anticipate his final reward, by seeing all its effects fully realised in his own.[2]

The passage is unquestionably rhetorical. The phrases 'to remember the forgotten', 'to attend to the neglected', 'to visit the forsaken', rather build up feeling than increase information. But the specificity of references to hospitals and prisons conveys real concern more forcefully than would abstract humanitarian generalities. Burke was also committed to practical reform. His hope that Howard's labours would have beneficial effects in England was no merely pious one, for Howard had already had penal reform statutes passed by Parliament, as Burke well knew.

Thus, in the field of penal reform, Burke's humanitarianism was genuine, concrete, practical and active. In 1767, he favourably reviewed the *Essay on Crime and Punishment* by the reformer Beccaria. In 1789 (note the year) he urged in Parliament a revision of the whole criminal law. In particular, he called for reform of the law relating to imprisonment for debt, prison administration and transportation of convicted criminals. In 1785 he had said that the system of penal transportation violated 'every principle of justice and humanity'.[3]

We saw, in the last chapter, that Burke advocated abolition of the slave trade, though gradually.[4] This gradualism he applied also to penal transportation, advocating, not total abolition, but Australia rather than Africa as the destination, America being no longer available for this purpose, on the ground that Australia was healthier.[5]

Burke's approach to slavery may seem insufficiently humanitarian to the modern reader. Two points will help to place his views in their historical context and thus contribute to an adequate evaluation of them. The first is that they were 'progressive' in relation to the dominant English opinion of his time. The second is that his gradualism required him to tolerate high levels of human misery. For instance, his sketch for legislation to regulate and reform the slave trade provided that every captain of a slave ship who lost not more than one-thirtieth of his slaves by death during the Atlantic crossing should be entitled to a special reward.[6] This proposal does not seem very humanitarian from the standpoint of the slaves.

We saw also, in Chapter 4, that Burke expressed concern for those who worked 'from dawn to dark in the innumerable servile, degrading, unseemly, unmanly, and often most unwholesome and pestiferous occupations, to which by the social economy so many wretches are inevitably doomed'.[7] The remedy he almost countenanced was 'forcibly to rescue them from their miserable industry'. The reason he gave for almost countenancing such a remedy was 'humanity, and perhaps policy'. But this remedy, in the last analysis, he cannot accept. It is, he holds, generally pernicious to impede, in any degree, 'the great wheel of circulation'. A humanitarian might reasonably be expected to consider whether some degree of impediment might be tolerable, in view of the fact that so many wretches were being broken on this great wheel.

In his *Thoughts and Details on Scarcity* Burke was harsher: 'To provide for us in our necessities is not in the power of government.' Neither the state nor the rich can support the poor. On the contrary those who labour 'and are miscalled the poor' must support the rich and the state. The poor must rely on Christian charity and the laws of commerce. Christian charity is a duty, but the manner, mode, time, choice of objects, and proportion, are left to private discretion.[8]

Burke appealed to humanitarian principles when he took up the causes of the Indians and the Irish. He also attacked the French Revolution from an ostensibly humanitarian position. The revolutionaries were 'savages . . . who have declared war upon Europe, whilst they disgrace and persecute human nature, and openly defy the God that made them'.[9]

Burke's humanity was largely reserved for the French upper classes. But he half-acknowledged that the revolutionary ideology contained a humanitarian element. He referred, sarcastically to be sure, to 'the grand philanthropy' of the revolutionaries. He accused the revolutionary tribunals of treading under foot 'their own declared rights of man'.[10] The implication is that the revolutionary rights of man are humane in principle, though they lead to tyranny in practice.

We can see, then, that Burke both was and was not a humanitarian. This being so, what was his attitude to reform?

In a speech of 1790 he is reported to have declared that 'he was no enemy to reformation'. Almost every business in which he had been much concerned, from the first day he had sat in the House of Commons to that time, had been a business of reformation.[11]

Of all this business of reformation, Burke's most important contribution was to the reform of the civil list establishment. Professor Carl Cone has maintained that the very idea of Parliament tampering with the royal establishment introduced a novel principle into the Constitution.

The law was drastic. It eliminated one public and nine household offices which have never been revived. . . . The restrictions it placed upon pensions and secret-service accounts limited the government's ability to influence opinion. . . . Burke's reform . . . established beyond question the authority of parliament to supervise and regulate the civil list. . . . [The] reform was one of the means of reducing crown influence and of increasing the independence of parliament.[12]

Yet, on electoral reform, Burke could be rigidly conservative. Nor was his inflexibilty on this subject simply a response to the French Revolution.[13] Upon what principle did he adopt this position? The answer is the floodgates doctrine. In times of unrest, open the gate of reform a little, and the tide of revolution may soon overwhelm you.[14]

Burke applied the floodgates doctrine to the events which led to the French Revolution. In the following passage from his *Letter to a Member of the National Assembly*, he analyzes the calling of the French Estates–General in 1789.

In the condition in which France was found three years ago, what better system could be proposed, what less, even savouring of wild theory, what fitter to provide for all the exigencies whilst it reformed all the abuses of government, than the convention of the states-general? . . . But I have censured, and do still presume to censure your parliament of Paris for not having suggested to the king, that this proper measure was of all measures the most critical and arduous; one in which the utmost circumspection and the greatest number of precautions were the most absolutely necessary. The very confession that a government wants either amendment in its conformation, or relief to great distress, causes it to lose half its reputation, and as great a proportion of its strength as depends upon that reputation. It was therefore necessary, first to put government out of danger. . . .[15]

Here Burke uses the floodgates doctrine in a form more sophisticated than that which he used to oppose electoral reform in England. To admit that reform is needed is to put government in danger. But, although he favoured great caution, he warmly endorsed the calling of the Estates to reform 'all the abuses of government'.

Burke reserved the floodgates doctrine largely to the question of parliamentary reform in Britain. Why? There are several possible answers. Because he believed there was no widespread grievance about parliamentary representation. Because parliamentary reform touched the heart of the British Constitution to which he was so attached. Because parliamentary reform threatened the interests of the classes of which he was the ideologist.

The cause of maintaining the eighteenth-century electoral system no longer has much support. The floodgates principle appears to have more vitality. Against Burke it might be said that it was precisely inflexibility that brought on revolution in France and reform that prevented it in England. But, if parliamentary reform did prevent revolution in England, it was after the Government had been put out of danger by repression.

Under what conditions did Burke believe reform to be justified? 'There is a time', he once said, 'when the hoary head of inveterate abuse will neither draw reverence, nor obtain protection.'[16] In his *Appeal from the New to the Old Whigs*, Burke wrote in defence of his own consistency as a reformer and, in particular, of the consistency of his *Reflections on the Revolution in France* with his previous record.

To fortify the imputation of a desertion from his principles, his constant attempts to reform abuses have been brought forward. It is true, it has been the business of his strength to reform abuses in government. . . . Before he departs, I will admit for him that he deserves to have all his titles of merit brought forth, as they have been, for grounds of condemnation, if one word, justifying or supporting abuses of any sort, is to be found in that book. . . . On the contrary, it spares no existing abuse. Its very purpose is to make war with abuses. . . .[17]

What is an 'abuse'? When does the 'war with abuses' become

radical subversion? Burke wrote to Sir Hercules Langrishe in 1792:

The crown and the personal safety of the monarch are *fundamentals* in our constitution: yet, I hope that no man regrets, that the rabble of statutes got together during the reign of Henry VIII, by which treasons are multiplied with so prolific an energy, have all been repealed in a body; although they were all, or most of them, made in support of things truly fundamental in our constitution. . . . None of this species of *secondary and subsidiary laws* have been held fundamental. They have yielded to circumstances: particularly where they were thought, even in their consequences, or obliquely, to affect other fundamentals.[18]

This passage suggests that 'secondary and subsidiary' laws may be repealed, even if they were made in support of things truly fundamental to the constitution.

In his *Address to the British in North America* Burke considered the question of constitutional reform.

. . . [T]here is a suspicion that parliament itself is somewhat fallen from its independent spirit. . . . [E]ven if all were true that is contended for, . . . yet as long as the solid and well-disposed forms of this constitution remain, there ever is within parliament itself a power of renovating its principles, and effecting a self-reformation, which no other plan of government has contained. This constitution has therefore admitted innumerable improvements, either for the correction of the original scheme, or removing corruptions, or for bringing its principles better to suit those changes which have successively happened in the circumstances of the nation, or in the manners of the people.[19]

Burke here suggests that the constitution can become corrupt, but that it can reform itself. Indeed, the constitution can be improved, not only to remove corruption, but to correct the original scheme or to bring its principles into accord with changing circumstances.

What doctrine of constitutional reform emerges from these two passages? At first sight, they may appear incompatible. The first suggests that the fundamental/secondary distinction is the same as the untouchable/reformable, while the second seems to allow reform even of fundamentals. A clue to the reconciliation of the two may be found in the phrase 'or for bringing its principles better to suit . . .' The constitution embodies certain, unchangeable principles; these principles are embodied in fundamental institutions, which are sacred; but the policies pursued within the framework of these institutions may be imperfect, and therefore constitute suitable cases for reform. The distinction between these categories is, of course, still not precise. In particular, the electoral system occupies a borderline position between fundamental institution and pragmatic device which might need reform to meet changes in the circumstances of the nation.

We have so far mainly considered what may be reformed, not the conditions under which reform may take place. With respect to secondary laws, Burke applies his doctrines of circumstance and consequence. Secondary laws yield to circumstances, particularly where their consequences affect fundamentals. With respect to the constitution itself, he says it may be improved to adapt its principles to changing circumstances. These are very general criteria, but they show that Burke's approach to reform even of the constitution was pragmatic rather than dogmatically conservative.

In his *Speech on Parliamentary Reform* (1792), Burke claimed that he 'never had resisted reform when he thought it likely to be useful; for instance, the reform moved by the right honourable gentleman opposite seemed to him, if it had been agreed to, productive of good effects, without risk of any harm.'[20] Once again, as late as 1792, on the subject of parliamentary reform, his criteria for change are not very stringent.

One other condition of desirable reform is of especial interest.

But when the reason of old establishments is gone, it is absurd to preserve nothing but the burden of them. This is superstitiously to embalm a carcass not worth an ounce of the gums that are used to preserve it. It is to burn precious oils in the tomb; it is to offer meat and drink to the dead, – not so much an honour to the deceased, as a disgrace to the survivors.[21]

It is not surprising, in view of the reformist principles which we have just been examining, that Burke should advocate the reform, or even abolition, of old establishments that have lost their *raison d'être*. What is remarkable is the imagery of carcasses, which is positively Paineite. For, once admit that old establishments are carcasses, nothing but burdens, then a dangerous opening for radicals is created.

Thus reformer Burke. Conservative Burke also existed, of course. The date is 1769. The subject, parliamentary reform. In reply to an opponent, Burke says this:

Has he well considered what an immense operation any change in our constitution is? How many discussions, parties, and passions, it will necessarily excite? And, when you open it to inquiry in one part, where the inquiry will stop? Experience shows us, that no time can be fit for such changes but a time of general confusion; when good men, finding every thing already broken up, think it right to take advantage of the opportunity of such derangement in favour of an useful alteration. Perhaps a time of the greatest security and tranquillity both at home and abroad may likewise be fit. . . .[22]

How cautious this relatively early discussion of parliamentary reform is. When you open the constitution to inquiry, where will the inquiry stop? This sounds like the floodgates doctrine. But Burke does not rule out changes in the constitution: he confines them to times of general confusion or of great tranquility.

Here is another attempt by Burke to formulate conservative principles of reform.

But it is not human frailty and imperfection and even a considerable degree of them, that becomes a ground for your alteration; for by no alteration will you get rid of those errors, however you may delight yourselves in varying to infinity the fashion of them. But the ground for a legislative alteration of a legal Establishment is this, and this only; that you find the inclinations of the majority of the people, concurring with your own sense of the intolerable nature of the abuse, are in favour of a change.[23]

The important distinction is that between an intolerable abuse and an inevitable imperfection. The condition sounds quite democratic, since 'the inclinations of the majority of the people' must favour the change. But the qualifying phrase, 'concurring with your own sense of . . .', must not be underestimated. Parliament participates independently in deciding what is intolerable.

That the criterion for an intolerable abuse is not merely majority will, but natural justice, is made clearer in a passage from the *Tracts on the Popery Laws*.

In the making of a new law it is undoubtedly the duty of the legislator to see that no injustice be done even to an individual. . . . But in the question concerning the repeal of an old one, the work is of more difficulty; because laws, like houses, lean on one another, and the operation is delicate, and should be necessary; the objection, in such a case, ought not to arise from the natural infirmity of human institutions, but from substantial faults which contradict the nature and end of law itself. . . .[24]

Burke goes on to say that 'a law may in some instances be a just subject of censure, without being at all an object of repeal'. For the criteria for repealing an old law to be met, it is necessary, not that the inclinations of the majority of the people are in favour of the change, but that the law contain substantial faults which contradict the nature and end of law itself.

Too much should not be made of the distinction between the democratic and the natural-law criteria for reform. Burke's doctrine of natural feeling would say that, if the majority of the people regarded an abuse as intolerable, then the nature and end of law were probably not being served. Of more significance is the apparent contradiction between the 'war on all abuses' doctrine and the view that a law may be a just subject of censure without being an object of reform.

It is impossible to effect a perfect reconciliation between the principles of reformer Burke and those of his conservative *alter ego*. Notwithstanding his disclaimer in the *Appeal*, the latter finds his classic expression in the *Reflections*.

I would not exclude alteration neither; but even when I changed, it should be to preserve. I should be led to my remedy by a great grievance.[25]

In his *Speech on Parliamentary Reform* (1792), he put it to the House whether there was any existing grievance great enough to justify the risk 'that must inevitably attend the proposed motion for a parliamentary reform'.[26]

Burke's conservatism could be rigid or flexible. Flexible Burke held that a 'state without the means of some change is without the means of its conservation. Without such means it might even risk the loss of that part of the constitution which it wished the most religiously to preserve.'[27] If it were necessary to preserve the principles and institutions of the constitution, it was clearly justifiable to change its practices. In exceptional circumstances, it might be justifiable, or even necessary, to change the institutions to preserve the principles. The Revolution of 1688 was the strongest case of a justifiable change in constitutional institutions (a change in the line of succession but not, of course, in the institution of monarchy) in order to preserve its fundamental principles.[28]

This is conservative reform, which Burke always allowed in principle. There is another, similar type of conservative reform: reform to restore prescriptive rights which have been violated. About this Burke was ambivalent. On the one hand, the doctrine of 'old violence' suggests that prescription can itself legitimate the abrogation of prescriptive rights. On the other hand, Burke used the doctrine of prescriptive reform to advocate the restoration of old rights, for example in Ireland.[29]

Yet another type of conservative reform which Burke favoured was, paradoxically, the opposite of that rejected by the 'floodgates' doctrine, namely, reform to head off revolution. Here is a classic expression of this principle.

Early reformations are amicable arrangements with a friend in power; late reformations are terms imposed upon a conquered enemy: early reformations are made in cold blood; late reformations are made under a state of inflammation. In that state of things the people behold in government nothing that is respectable. They see the abuse, and they will see nothing else – they fall into the temper of a furious populace provoked at the disorder of a house of ill-fame; they never attempt to correct or regulate; they go to work by the shortest way – they abate the nuisance, they pull down the house.[30]

'Floodgates' says that, in times of unrest, reform may lead to revolution. The 'intolerable abuse' doctrine implies that only in times of unrest is reform justifiable, for if there is no unrest, there can be no intolerable abuse. The 'early reformation' principle says that in times of unrest reform should be carried out to prevent revolution. These doctrines are not formally reconcilable. Burke had no consistent theoretical view about the tactics of conservative reform. He did, however, have a consistent view that reform was justified if the only alternative was revolution.

The conservative character of the 'early reformation' doctrine can also be shown by drawing attention to Burke's distinction between *reformation* (of which he approved) and *change* or *innovation* (of which he did not). 'I knew', he wrote in his *Letter to a Noble Lord*,

> that there is a manifest, marked distinction . . . between change and reformation. The former alters the substance of the objects themselves; and gets rid of all their essential good, as well as all the accidental evil annexed to them. Change is novelty; and whether it is to operate any one of the effects of reformation at all, or whether it may not contradict the very principle upon which reformation is desired, cannot be certainly known beforehand. Reform is, not a change in the substance, or in the primary modification of the object, but a direct application of a remedy to the grievance complained of.[31]

Burke could express his opposition to 'innovation' more strongly. In his *Speech on the Army Estimates*, 9 February 1790, he declared that he would resist 'all violent exertions of the spirit of innovation, so distant from all principles of true and safe reformation: a spirit well calculated to overturn states, but perfectly unfit to amend them'.[32]

Underlying Burke's views about what might be reformed and under what circumstances is the belief that all reform should be cautious. He had a number of reasons for this belief. The first was the awesome nature of the state. In his *Speech on Economical Reform*, he declared that he approached 'the great supreme body of the civil government . . . with that awe and reverence with which a young physician approaches to the cure of the disorders of his parent'.[33]

The second reason was epistemological.

> I would not exclude alteration neither; but even when I changed, it should be to preserve. . . . In what I did, I should follow the example of our ancestors. . . . A politic caution, a guarded circumspection, a moral rather than a complexional timidity were among the ruling principles of our forefathers in their most decided conduct. Not being illuminated with the light of which the gentlemen of France tell us they have got so abundant a share, they acted under a strong impression of the ignorance and fallibility of mankind. He that made them thus fallible rewarded them for having in their conduct attended to their nature.[34]

It is not simply that all men make mistakes, but that we are much more likely to make mistakes in predicting the future than in judging the present. Those who experience a reform are better judges of it than those who plan it. If reform progresses slowly, the effect of each step can be observed. The success or failure of the first step throws light upon the place where the second should be taken. By this method a complete safe reformation may be effected.[35]

This last argument for caution is liberal in so far as caution is advocated in the interest of rational criticism of reforms. Burke has a more conservative argument for gradualism.

> We must all obey the great law of change. . . . All we can do, and that human wisdom can do, is to provide that the change shall proceed by insensible degrees. . . . This mode will, on the one hand, prevent the *unfixing old interests at once:* a thing which is apt to breed a black and sullen discontent in those who are at once dispossessed of all their influence and consideration. This gradual course, on the other side, will prevent men, long under depression, from being intoxicated with a large draught of new power, which they always abuse with a licentious insolence.[36]

Burke was writing about Ireland. The reform in question would have relieved oppressed Catholics from burdens imposed upon them by tyrannical Protestants. Yet Burke would not unfix the interests of the tyrannical Protestants at once, lest they become sullen and discontented. Nor would he relieve the Catholics from the burdens of tyranny at once, lest they abuse their new power with a licentious insolence. Burke did not consider that Catholics slowly unburdened might become sullen and discontented nor that Protestants maintained in most of their old interests might abuse their old power with licentious insolence.

Burke advocated cautious reform, not only to protect illegitimate interests from untimely abrogation, but because he believed that the rash destruction of illegitimate interests would also destroy some that were legitimate.

> To a man who acts under the influence of no passion, who has nothing in view in his projects but the public good, a great difference will immediately strike him, between what policy would dictate on the original introduction of such institutions [as those of pre-revolutionary France], and on a question of their total abolition, where they have cast their roots wide and deep, and where by long habit things more valuable than themselves are so adapted to them, and in a manner interwoven with them, that the one cannot be destroyed without notably impairing the other.[37]

Burke almost proves too much. If the good parts of the constitution are interwoven with the bad, it may be that even gradual reform of the latter will have harmful consequences for the former. Since Burke was committed to the reform of abuses, he had to work his way out of this corner. He is talking about 'cases of extreme emergency', such as existed in England in 1688.

> Even in that extremity . . . the change is to be confined to the peccant part only; to the part which produced the necessary deviation; and even then it is to be effected without a decomposition of the whole civil and political mass, for the purpose of originating a new civil order out of the first elements of society.[38]

The problem is not solved. The spirit of these last two passages is inconsistent. If bad old institutions have truly cast their roots wide and deep; if by long habit good institutions have become adapted to them and interwoven with them, then it is facile to recommend that reform be confined to the peccant part only.

The obvious objection to cautious reform is that it is too slow. Burke says that, on the contrary, its slowness is one of its excellencies. It is not difficult to point out what is wrong with society. It is much harder to put things right. Hasty reform leads to mistakes, which often bring misery to the those whom it was intended to help. Hasty reform also requires multitudes to adapt to new habits and conditions, which may also make them miserable. Thus, slow change is more humane then fast. Impatience wears a human face. In action, it is a tyrant.[39]

Two qualifications must be made to this account of Burke's defence of slow reform. Firstly, the 'early reformation' principle implies that the 'slow reform' doctrine may not be used as an excuse for postponing reform when it is called for. Secondly, reform might sometimes justifiably be swift. Burke is speaking about the relief of Catholics. He is responding to the objection that he supported a reform that was too hasty. No, he says, Parliament was too slow.

They took fourscore years to deliberate on the repeal of an act which ought not to have survived a second session. When at length, after a procrastination of near a century, the business was taken up, it proceeded in the most public manner, by the ordinary stages, and as slowly as a law so evidently right as to be resisted by none would naturally advance. Had it been read three times in one day, we should have shown only a becoming readiness to recognise, by protection, the undoubted dutiful behaviour of those whom we had but too long punished for offences of presumption or conjecture.[40]

Burke was in some ways a political romantic, but his attitude to reform was explicitly anti-romantic.

This virtue of moderation . . . requires a deep courage, and full of reflection, to be temperate when the voice of the multitudes . . . passes judgment against you. The impetuous desire of an unthinking public will endure no course, but what conducts to splendid and perilous extremes.[41]

Untried and uncertain prospects of new advantage recommend themselves to the spirit of adventure 'which more or less prevails in every mind'. This spirit leads men and factions and nations to sacrifice their present goods in favour of wild and irrational expectations.[42] The search for the new, the spirit of adventure, the wild, irrational and impetuous, the splendid and dangerous, all these Burke regards as political diseases. Against these he advocates moderation, pragmatism, patience, even resignation. Dull is safe is good. Exciting is dangerous is bad.

It is important to note, however, the ambivalence in Burke's treatment of this subject. The spirit of adventure prevails in every mind, and is therefore presumably natural. The impetuous public draws us to extremes that are perilous, but also splendid. The radical impulse has in it something human, something admirable. Burke expressed this idea most clearly in his *First Letter on a Regicide Peace*.

I have a good opinion of the general abilities of the Jacobins: not that I suppose them better born than others; but strong passions awaken the faculties; they suffer not a particle of the man to be lost. The spirit of enterprise gives to this description the full use of all their native energies.[43]

We see here, once more, Burke's ambivalence towards talent, energy and enterprise. The Jacobins are his enemies to the death. But he cannot but have a good opinion of their ability. Romantic Burke can give conservative Burke moments of unease.

Burke's approach to reform is, however, generally well integrated with the rest of his political and moral philosophy. For example, he justified social pluralism, the maintenance of conflicting interests in society, on the ground that it interposed 'a salutary check to all precipitate resolution', rendering deliberation 'a matter not of choice, but of necessity', making all change 'a subject of compromise, which naturally begets moderation . . . preventing the sore evil of harsh, crude, unqualified reformations'.[44]

Political moderation is also related to moral imperfectionism.

There is, by the essential fundamental constitution of things, a radical infirmity in all human contrivances. . . . [P]rudence . . . will lead us rather to acquiesce in some qualified plan, that does not come up to the full perfection of the abstract idea, than to push for the more perfect, which cannot be attained without tearing to pieces the whole contexture of the commonwealth. . . .[45]

Men are, in the nature of things, imperfect. Imperfect men make imperfect institutions. But imperfect men also make imperfect reforms. We must not struggle against the nature of things. For, if we do, we may find that, whilst we seek to be in the republic of Plato, we are in no republic at all.[46]

Thus, Burke's critique of political radicalism had deep roots in his moral philosophy, his epistemology, his view of Man, in both his own metaphysics and his critique of metaphysical thought. Radicals were morally and intellectually arrogant. They were also mistaken about the relation of 'thought' to 'life'. They were 'metaphysicians', who dealt in universals and essences and saw no difference between more and less.

These teachers are perfectly systematic. No man who assumes their grounds can tolerate the British constitution in church and state. These teachers profess to scorn all mediocrity; to engage for perfection; to proceed by the simplest and shortest course. They build their politics, not on convenience, but on truth; and they profess to conduct men to certain happiness by the assertion of their undoubted rights.[47]

This is a classic indictment of utopian political thought, not because Burke correctly describes the ideas of his opponents, for he does not, but because he allows to them several qualities upon which they would pride themselves: their concern for human rights; their aspiration for a free and just society; their intellectual rigour. But radicals, Burke says, misunderstand the place of such ideals in political thought. They are abstract universals, not complex realities. Radicals do not know men and society as they really are and, as a result, they are not merely impotent to correct the undoubted evils of the world, but the very rigour of their logic, the very perfectionism of their moral aspiration, leads to disaster. The search for the best sacrifices the mediocre to the worst.

God created Man imperfect. Imperfect Man has accumulated sufficient wisdom through the ages to adapt his institutions to his imperfect nature. Thus, the imperfection (though not the abuses) of these institutions is their virtue.

> The whole scheme of our mixed constitution is to prevent any one of its principles from being carried as far, as taken by itself, and theoretically, it would go. Allow that to be the true policy of the British system, then most of the faults with which that system stands charged will appear to be, not imperfections into which it has inadvertently fallen, but excellencies which it has studiously sought.[48]

Burke also applied this view to the idea of the rights of man.

> The rights of man are in a sort of *middle*, incapable of definition, but not impossible to be discerned. The rights of men in government are their advantages; and these are often in balances between differences of good; in compromises between good and evil, and sometimes between evil and evil.[49]

Utilitarianism is set against utopianism. Convenience is to be preferred to truth. We maximize good by balancing and compromising; we do not seek perfection. We prefer present imperfection to speculative perfection because there is more real good in the former than the latter.

As a philosopher of moderation, Burke is of the first importance in the British political tradition. But the philosophy of moderation is not without its problems. One is that it is apparently self-contradictory. We may call this *the paradox of moderation*. If no virtue should be carried to its extreme, then the virtue of moderation should not be carried to its extreme. When should we then stop being moderate?

Burke realized that this was no mere logical trick, for he wrote that moderation was 'no enemy to zeal and enthusiasm'. Zeal and enthusiasm were proper, if restrained by principle and reason.[50] In this, he attempted to practise what he preached. Neither his prosecution of Warren Hastings nor his polemic against the French Revolution was conducted moderately. But, in both cases, he was pleading the cause of moderate politics. Both were examples of extremism for the sake of moderation.[51] Dr O'Brien has plausibly suggested that it was

the very extremeness of Burke's reaction to the French
Revolution which helped him to understand its unprecedented
importance, which his apparently more realistic and pragmatic contemporaries were slower to realize.[52]

Another problem is raised by Burke's anti-perfectionism.
God created the state so that man's nature might be made
perfect. Burke states emphatically that human nature is per-
fectible.[53] Is this inconsistent with his critique of the perfectionism of radicals? No and yes. No, because the path to
perfection, for Burke, lay through slow evolution. Yes, at a
deeper level, for the Burkean and radical ideas of perfectibility
had common origins and therefore a distant kinship. This is to
say that the ideas of the state, reason, freedom and virtue
abroad in the Enlightenment and the French Revolution were
not as antithetical to those of the Christian tradition as Burke
sometimes made out.

Finally, it should be said that, although the term 'utopianism' is, following Burke, usually applied pejoratively to radicals of the political left, it may properly be applied also to ideas,
theories and persons of the centre and the right. If utopianism
is the unwillingness to accept unwelcome realities, then no
political doctrine holds the copyright on utopianism. Edmund
Burke's defence of the old order was as utopian as Karl Marx's
belief that the classless society was in the offing.

## NOTES

1.  Frank O'Gorman, *Edmund Burke: His Political Philosophy* (London: Allen & Unwin, 1973), p. 54; Conor Cruise O'Brien, Introduction to Edmund Burke, *Reflections on the Revolution in France* (Harmondsworth: Penguin Books, 1968), p. 74.
2.  *The Works and Correspondence of Edmund Burke* (London:
Rivington, 1852), vol. III, p. 422.
3.  Carl B. Cone, *Burke and the Nature of Politics: The Age of the
French Revolution* (Lexington: University of Kentucky Press, 1964),
pp. 178–80.
4.  Supra, p. 141.
5.  Cone, *French Revolution*, pp. 179–80.
6.  *Works and Correspondence*, vol. V, p. 599.

7. *Reflections*, p. 271.

8. *Works and Correspondence*, vol. V, pp. 189, 203–4, 190, 197.

9. *Works and Correspondence*, vol. V, pp. 21, 27; *Reflections*, pp. 160–1.

10. *Works and Correspondence*, vol. V, pp. 357, 55.

11. *The Writings and Speeches of Edmund Burke* (1898–9), vol. III, p. 220.

12. Cone, *French Revolution*, pp. 40, 41, 44, 45–6.

13. Ibid., p. 50.

14. See supra, p. 127.

15. *Works and Correspondence*, vol. IV, p. 385.

16. Ibid., vol. III, p. 353.

17. Ibid., vol. IV, p. 425.

18. Ibid., vol. IV, pp. 524–5 (emphasis Burke's).

19. Ibid., vol. V, p. 545.

20. *The Speeches of the Right Honourable Edmund Burke* (London: Longman, Hurst, Rees, &c., 1816), vol. IV, p. 49.

21. *Works and Correspondence*, vol. III, p. 368.

22. Ibid., p. 70.

23. *The Works of the Right Honourable Edmund Burke* (London: Rivington, 1812–15), vol. 10, pp. 9–10.

24. *Works and Correspondence*, vol. VI, pp. 14–15.

25. *Reflections*, p. 375.

26. *Speeches*, vol. IV, p. 49.

27. *Reflections*, p. 106.

28. *Reflections*, p. 106; *Speeches*, vol. IV, p. 46.

29. Thomas H. D. Mahoney, *Edmund Burke and Ireland* (Cambridge, Massachusetts: Harvard University Press, 1960), p. 208.

30. *Works and Correspondence*, vol. III, p. 353.

31. Ibid., vol. V, p. 223.

32. *Writings and Speeches*, vol. III, p. 220.

33. Francis Canavan, *The Political Reason of Edmund Burke* (Durham, North Carolina: Duke University Press, 1960), p. 172.

34. *Reflections*, pp. 375–6.

35. Ibid., p. 281.

36. *Works and Correspondence*, vol. IV, pp. 554–5 (emphasis Burke's).

37. *Reflections*, p. 266.

38. Ibid., pp. 105–6.

39. Ibid., pp. 280–1.

40. *Works and Correspondence*, vol. III, pp. 438–9.

41. Ibid., vol. I, p. 564.

42. Ibid., vol. IV, p. 404

43. Ibid., vol. V, p. 286.

44. *Reflections*, p. 122.

45. *Works and Correspondence*, vol. I, p. 563.

46. Ibid., vol. II, p. 4.

47. Ibid., vol. IV, pp. 525, 485.

48. Ibid., p. 486.

49. C. P. Courtney, *Montesquieu and Burke* (Oxford: Blackwell, 1963), p. 156 (emphasis Burke's).

50. *The Correspondence of Edmund Burke* (Cambridge and Chicago University Presses, 1958–70), vol. VI, p. 50.

51. Cone, *French Revolution*, p. 125; *Reflections*, p. 61.

52. *Reflections*, p. 72.

53. Ibid., p. 197.

# 9

# The Right of Revolution

Burke is underrated as a theorist of revolution. Modern writers on revolution rarely cite him. The Burke scholar, Dr Frank O'Gorman, has this to say about his treatment of the French Revolution.

There was room for a critic of the revolution in the Europe of the 1790s. Burke was not that critic. He lacked the detachment to fill that role. Burke rejected the new order entirely, from its supposed ideological origins to its allegedly disastrous consequences. The revolutionary thought of Edmund Burke offered neither an analytical interpretation nor a critical rebuttal of the ideals of the French Revolution. In the last analysis, he was mainly concerned to argue the revolution out of existence.[1]

This view is not correct. I have shown that Burke did make a 'critical rebuttal of the ideals of the French Revolution'. I now propose to demonstrate that he did offer an 'analytical interpretation' of the Revolution also.

For Burke, the French Revolution was against the nature of things, a rebellion against God, a rupture with the Universal Order. This was not merely his intemperate way of trying to 'argue the revolution out of existence'. For he had written in an early work, as we saw in Chapter 2, that, in those immense revolutions which bring about great systems of change in the world, we have to acknowledge the hand of God asserting his supreme dominion. The French Revolution bore the stigmata of such an event. Opposition to it might be resistance to the decrees of Providence itself.[2] The Revolution undoubtedly had cosmic significance, but exactly what that significance was Burke was less sure of than he is usually thought to have been.

Burke was not against all revolution. Indeed, it would seem to follow from the foregoing that, the greater the revolution, the more likely that it was God's work. This conclusion is obviously contradicted by Burke's general political conservatism. We must, therefore, examine closely what conception of revolution Burke had, and what he held to justify, and what not to justify, a revolution.

Writing in 1777, in his *Address to the British Colonists in North America*, Burke put forward the following conception of rebellion.

We do not call you rebels and traitors. . . . We do not know how to qualify millions of our countrymen, contending with one heart for an admission to privileges which we have ever thought our own happiness and honour, by odious and unworthy names. On the contrary, we highly revere the principles on which you act, though we lament some of their effects. . . . We view the establishment of the English colonies on principles of liberty, as that which is to render this kingdom venerable to future ages. . . . Those who have and who hold to that foundation of common liberty, whether on this or on your side of the ocean, we consider as the true, and the only true, Englishmen. Those who depart from it, whether there or here . . . are the real rebels to the fair constitution and just supremacy of England.[3]

In the American context, therefore, the rebels are those who betray the English tradition of rational liberty, including, presumably, the King and the British Government. Those who are taking up arms against the state, but are holding to the principles of liberty, are not rebels.

Burke made, partly implicitly, partly explicitly, a distinction between rebellion, revolution and reformation. Rebellion is an attack upon the constitution. Revolution is a change in the constitution. A reformation is the correction of an abuse. A reformation may require a revolution, but a revolution does not necessarily lead to a reformation. The revolution of 1688 was one which led to a reformation. That of 1789 did not. The test to determine whether a revolution had or had not led to a reformation was to observe whether it had increased or diminished liberty.[4]

Burke also implicitly distinguished between a conservative and a radical revolution. The first respects the basic principles and institutions of society, whereas the second destroys them. The fundamental institutions are religion and property. But a revolution in basic institutions must also be a moral revolution. The revolutionaries of France were attempting 'a regeneration of the moral consitution of man'. 'Every thing we hear from them is new, and, to use a phrase of their own, *revolutionary*; every thing supposes a total revolution in all the principles of reason, prudence, and moral feeling.'[5] Burke held that such a revolution could not succeed and would inevitably destroy freedom.

He also held, however, that the world turned upside down had an aesthetic appeal to rival that of the world in proper order. If the state of rational liberty is the object of love and awe, then revolution is the object of awe and terror. But terror has its attractions. Revolution is the Devil's drama.

Plots, massacres, assassinations, seem to some people a trivial price for obtaining a revolution. A cheap, bloodless reformation, a guiltless liberty, appear flat and vapid to their taste. There must be a great change of scene; there must be a grand spectacle to rouse the imagination, grown torpid with the lazy enjoyment of sixty years security, and the still unanimating repose of public prosperity.[6]

Yet some revolutions were justified and some were not. How did Burke distinguish the two?

Firstly, Burke not only believed that certain stringent conditions must be met before revolution was justified, but also held that certain quite stringent conditions must be met before it was justifiable even to discuss under what conditions revolution was justified. In 1793 he wrote of Charles Fox:

It is not easy to state for what good end, at a time like this, when the foundations of all ancient and prescriptive governments, such as ours . . . , are undermined by perilous theories, that Mr. Fox . . . thinks it seasonable to preach up with so much earnestness . . . the doctrine of resistance and revolution at all; or to assert that our last Revolution of 1688 stands on the same or similar principles with that of France. We are not called upon by any circumstances, that I know of, which can justify a revolt, or which demands a revolution, or can make an election of a successor to the crown necessary, whatever latent right may be supposed to exist for effectuating any of these purposes.[7]

One year earlier, he had put it this way:

The foundations, on which obedience to government is founded, are not to be constantly discussed. That we are here, supposes the discussion already made and the dispute settled. We must assume the rights of what represents the public to control the individual . . . until some intolerable grievance shall make us know that it does not answer its end, and will submit neither to reformation nor restraint.[8]

This appears to be an even stronger ban on discussion of the principles of civil obedience and revolution. Talk of revolution is improper not only in perilous times; it always requires special justification: an intolerable grievance. The conditions for justifiably theorizing about revolution seem here to be the same as those for starting one.

The second step Burke takes, as he cautiously emerges from his conservative shell to construct a doctrine of resistance and revolution, is to place the burden of proof on the revolutionaries.

[T]his, I think, may be safely affirmed, that a sore and pressing evil is to be removed, and that a good, great in its amount, and unequivocal in its nature, must be probable almost to certainty, before the inestimable price of our own morals, and the well-being of a number of our fellow-citizens, is paid for revolution. If ever we ought to be economists even to parsimony, it is in the voluntary production of evil. Every revolution contains in it something of evil.[9]

The burden of proof, says Burke, lies heavily on the revolutionaries, whom he characterizes as those who 'tear to pieces the whole frame and contexture of their country' and whose methods he describes as 'unfavourable to all the present happiness of millions of people'.

In politics, Burke continues, men have no right to put the well-being of the present generation wholly out of the question. The care of our own time is our only certain moral trust.

Our duty to the future is not to put its capital at any risk. A revolution, to be justified, must protect the present generation without any risk to future generations.[10]

Burke spells out the implications. The following conditions must be met.

1. There must exist a sore and pressing evil.
2. A great good must be probable almost to a certainty: a condition Burke believed could almost never be met.
3. There must be no other way of 'settling a government fit to obtain its rational ends'.

Burke once again contrasts the concrete with the speculative. Every revolution contains actual evil. The good it promises is at best speculative. The consequences of revolution are uncertain. The benefits of existing government are, except in rare cases of tyranny, real.

When Burke declares that the care of our own time is our only certain moral trust, he does not quite mean what he says. The care of the future is quite as certain a trust. Burke wishes to give no preference to the present over the future. He wishes to preserve the interests of the future by conserving present institutions. The duty to care for the capital of the estate is a duty equally to the present and the future.

But, though the burden of proof is heavy, Burke does not say that it can never be met. Under what conditions would he consider the case for revolution to have been made? In particular, what counts as 'a sore and pressing evil'?

We should expect that one condition that would *not* count would be poverty. The government has no duty to provide for our necessities. Since it does not have this duty, its failure to make such provision cannot be a ground for revolt.

This is not, in fact, quite Burke's position. Let us recall that he deplored the fact that society doomed so many wretches to hard, long labour in degrading and unhealthy occupations, and that he declared himself inclined forcibly to rescue them were it not for the natural course of the great wheel of circulation turned by the strangely directed labour of these unhappy people. Although, as we have already noted, Burke opts not to impede the great wheel, his rhetoric sides with forcible rescue, for the misery is concrete and the wheel abstract.

If this brief passage stood alone, we might consider it a curious anomaly in Burke's thought. But it does not. Writing to the Rev. Thomas Hussey in December 1796, Burke had this to say.

That Jacobinism, which is speculative in its origin, and which arises from wantonness and fullness of bread, may possibly be kept under by firmness and prudence. . . . [B]ut the Jacobinism which arises from penury and irritation, from scorned loyalty, and rejected allegiance, has much deeper roots. They take their nourishment from the bottom of human nature and the unalterable constitution of things, and not from humour and caprice or the opinions of the day about privileges and liberties. These roots will be shot into the depths of Hell, and will at last raise up their proud tops to Heaven itself.[11]

The passage refers to the condition of the Irish Catholics. The 'sore and pressing evil' is not merely poverty, but general tyranny. But 'penury' is assigned an important role in the rise of a form of Jacobinism, and this Jacobinism has its roots in human nature and the unalterable constitution of things. Here, too, Burke seems ambivalent about the right of the oppressed, the penurious, and the rejected to rebel, but inclines towards allowing such a right. 'Jacobinism' may be rooted in the nature of things.

These last two passages are particularly remarkable for having been written during the French Revolution, a time when Burke might be expected not to make any substantial concession to the right of revolution. Earlier, he was, on at least one occasion, still less cautious. He had, he said in the House of Commons in 1781, been accused of not paying sufficient regard to 'men of ample property'. He replied:

When, indeed, the smallest rights of the poorest people in the kingdom are in question, I would set my face against any act of pride and power countenanced by the highest, that are in it; and if it should come to the last extremity, and to a contest of blood, God forbid! God forbid! – my part is taken; I would take my fate with the poor, and low, and feeble.[12]

Notwithstanding the 'God forbid! God forbid!', and the fact
that Burke went on to insist that the poor adhere to 'the rules
of morality and virtuous discipline', the passage has a revolutionary bias. Sceptics may dismiss it as 'mere rhetoric'. But
this is to ignore a fact which refutes a preconceived theory
about Burke's beliefs. The truth is that Burke, the philosopher
of order, inequality, and caution, did, on occasion, suggest that
a revolution by the poor might be justified.

Burke sometimes maintained that revolution was justified if
natural rights had been violated. In 1772, he said: 'When
tyranny is extreme, and abuses of government intolerable,
men resort to the rights of Nature to shake it off.' In 1777, he
justified the Revolution of 1688 as follows: 'The people, at that
time, re-entered into their original rights; and it was not
because a positive law authorised what was then done, but
because the freedom and safety of the subject, the origin and
cause of all laws, required a proceeding paramount and
superior to them.'[13]

Burke conceded the right to overthrow by revolution an
unreformable tyranny. But in November 1796, writing about
Ireland, he imposed a severe qualification upon this right. 'I
believe there are very few cases which will justify a revolt
against the established government of a country, let its constitution be what it will, and even though its abuses should be
great and provoking.'[14]

The concept of tyranny is related to that of the social contract. The foundation of the 1688 Revolution was

a breach of the original contract, implied and expressed in the Constitution of this country, as a scheme of government fundamentally
and inviolably fixed in King, Lords and Commons; – that the fundamental subversion of this ancient Constitution, by one of its parts,
having been attempted, and in effect accomplished, justified the
Revolution; – that it was justified only of that ancient Constitution
formed by the original contract of the British state, as well as for the
future preservation of the same government.[15]

What is this contract, the breach of which justified the Revolution? Burke said that it was expressed and implied in the

British Constitution. This constitution was formed 'by the original contract of the British state'.

What did Burke mean by this last phrase? I believe that the interpretation offered by John C. Weston, Jr., is correct.

One should not be misled by the Lockean language of contract in this passage. When Burke refers to the original contract, he does not mean a contract entered into when a state was formed. Burke means a perpetual contract which binds the successive Kings, Parliaments, and generations of people to obey the constitution in its particular stage of development at any given time.[16]

Burke's language *is* misleading. The constitutional contract was not made at one particular 'ancient' time. It evolved through a long struggle for liberty. But, according to Burke, the constitution of liberty was established before 1688, and the Revolution of that year was a defensive measure against its subversion.

The Constitution was subverted by the King. 'They who led at the Revolution . . . charged [King James] with nothing less than a design, confirmed by a multitude of illegal overt acts, to subvert the Protestant church and state, and their fundamental, unquestionable laws and liberties: they charged him with having broken the original contract between king and people.'[17] The King was the rebel against the Constitution. Compare Burke's similar analysis of the American Revolution, discussed earlier in this chapter.

Very few cases justify revolution, however great the abuses of the constitution. When such a case exists, however, the right of revolution is clear and strong. 'If a king shall abolish or alter courts of law, trial by jury, or religion, or erect a standing army; then the compact is dissolved, and all right and power reverts to the people; and the people, by plots, conspiracies, or any other secret or violent means, may hurl such a king from the throne.'[18]

In 1791, in his *Appeal from the New to the Old Whigs*, Burke was concerned to give the 1688 Revolution a very conservative interpretation. That, he said, was a revolution to end all revolutions in Britain. By re-establishing the constitution of liberty, it sought to remove the causes and need for further revolution. Nothing short of a conspiracy of king, lords and commons for the destruction of the liberties of the nation could justify any similar action in future. Such a conspiracy would be dreadful indeed – but most unlikely.[19]

Thus, although Burke uses his social–contract doctrine to justify revolution, he also uses it to support order and authority. Every person is born into a community as he is born into a family, independently of his will or consent. None the less, just as he contracts an obligation to his parents, so he contracts an obligation to his community. There is the strongest presumption against the right of any individual, or of any number of individuals, to free themselves from this obligation.

When great multitudes act together, under that discipline of nature, I recognise the PEOPLE. . . . In all things the voice of this grand chorus of national harmony ought to have a mighty and decisive influence. But when you disturb this harmony; when you break up this beautiful order, this array of truth and nature, as well as of habit and prejudice; when you separate the common sort of men from their proper chieftains so as to form them into an adverse army, I no longer know that venerable object called the people in such a disbanded race of deserters and vagabonds. For a while they may be terrible indeed; but in such a manner as wild beasts are terrible. The mind owes to them no sort of submission. They are, as they have always been reputed, rebels. They may lawfully be fought with, and brought under, whenever an advantage offers.[20]

Burke has forgotten that, by his own account, it may not be the 'common sort of men', but the king and other chieftains who violate the national harmony and deserve to be called rebels. It is odd that he should forget this, for in the same year in which he wrote the above, he also denounced the 'timidity (operating as perfidy) of the King of France', which, when combined with the conduct of the Emperor of Austria, held out a 'fatal example' to all subjects, 'tending to show what little support, or even countenance, they are to expect from those for whom their principle of fidelity may induce them to risk life and fortune'.[21]

'A positively vicious and abusive government ought to be changed', Burke wrote in November 1789, 'and if necessary, by violence, if it cannot be (as is sometimes the case) reformed.'[22] This was the case in 1688. Writing of the 1688 revolutionaries in the *Reflections*, Burke maintained that a 'grave and overruling necessity obliged them to take the step they took, and took with infinite reluctance, as under that most rigorous of all laws'.[23]

What is the nature of this 'necessity'? Burke made this statement immediately after he had referred to James II's design to subvert the Constitution. The Revolution was necessary in the sense that it was the only means to get rid of tyranny. This interpretation is consistent with Burke's view that the violent overthrow of a vicious and abusive government is necessary if it cannot be reformed. Thus, the 'necessity' is not metaphysical or logical or empirical inevitability – although Burke's talk of 'overruling necessity' sometimes suggests this – but that of an extraordinary moral obligation, overriding and contradicting normal moral obligations, to take the empirically necessary means to ends of overriding moral priority.[24]

But there are passages in which Burke more strongly suggests that a different, less calculating, more cosmic, kind of necessity is at work. In the *Appeal from the New to the Old Whigs*, where he maintains the 'necessity' of the 1668 Revolution several times, he also writes that no man has the right to free himself from his obligations to his community, except the right that 'necessity, which is out of and above all rule, rather imposes than bestows'.[25]

In the *Appeal* Burke also refers to 'necessity . . . for the purpose of self-preservation'.[26] This rings rather different bells. 'Self-preservation' seems quite mundane and uncosmic. And it sounds both more basic and more self-regarding than the restoration of the constitution. But it may be that the distinction between the necessity of preserving oneself and the necessity of preserving the constitution was not made by Burke.

But the most important passage in which Burke advances 'necessity' as a justification for revolution occurs in the *Reflections*. It is part of a famous rhetorical sequence, but the reference to necessity and revolution has been less often noticed than the rest of the sequence. The state, says Burke, ought not to be considered as nothing better than a partnership agreement in a trade of pepper and coffee, calico or tobacco, or some other such low concern, to be taken up for a little temporary interest, and to be dissolved at the fancy of the parties. It is a partnership in all science; in all art; in every virtue; and in all perfection. It is a partnership between the living, the dead, and those who are to be born. 'Each contract of each particular state is but a clause in the great primaeval contract of eternal society, linking the lower with the higher natures, connecting the visible and the invisible world, according to a fixed compact sanctioned by the inviolable oath which holds all physical and all moral natures, each in their appointed place.'[27]

This contract is subject to the will of no one. The 'municipal corporations of that universal kingdom' are not morally at liberty, at their pleasure, and on their speculations of a contingent improvement, 'wholly to separate and tear asunder the bands of their subordinate community', and to dissolve it into 'an unsocial, uncivil, unconnected chaos of elementary principles'.[28]

So far, so familiar. Now comes the important qualification.

It is the first and supreme necessity only, a necessity that is not chosen but chooses, a necessity paramount to deliberation, that admits no discussion, and demands no evidence, which alone can justify a resort to anarchy. This necessity is no exception to the rule; because this necessity itself is a part too of that moral and physical disposition of things to which man must be obedient by consent or force; but if that which is only submission to necessity should be made the object of choice, the law is broken, nature is disobeyed, and the rebellious are outlawed, cast forth, and exiled, from this world of reason, and order, and peace, and virtue, and fruitful penitence, into the antagonist world of madness, discord, vice, confusion, and unavailing sorrow.[29]

What kind of 'necessity' do we have here? Firstly, it is compelling. It is not chosen, but chooses. This resembles that necessity which rather imposes than bestows the right of revolution. Secondly, it is supra-rational. It is paramount to deliberation, admits no discussion, and demands no evidence. Thirdly, it is not an exception to the rule of moderation and reason, for it is equally part of the nature of things.

Is this the same 'necessity' which led the heroes of 1688 to restore the constitution of liberty? Did Burke mean to say that they did not *choose* liberty in preference to tyranny? That they acted without deliberation and demanded no evidence? Or did Burke have more than one conception of 'necessity'?

Interpretation is difficult here. Burke's treatment of the 1688 Revolution does not suggest that he saw it as non-deliberative and unchosen. Yet he justified it by reference to 'necessity'. In the *Reflections* he defined 'necessity' as non-deliberative and unchosen. Yet the *Reflections* is as much a defence of 1688 as it is an attack on 1789. It seems equally implausible that Burke should have forgotten 1688 when he wrote the non-deliberative 'necessity' justification of revolution as that he should have wished to justify 1688 in this way.

Burke seems to have had some such view as the following in mind. Two things justify revolution: (1) tyranny; (2) necessity. Tyranny entails interolerable abuse. An intolerable abuse is an abuse which men are not able to tolerate. Tyranny violates human nature. The 'necessity' which justifies revolution arises from the burdens which tyranny imposes and which its victims cannot bear. They are forced to throw them off. In doing so, men choose freedom, but they are forced by their nature to do so. How they seek freedom may be a matter of deliberation, but that they should seek freedom is not.

In his introduction to the Pelican Classics edition of the *Reflections*, Dr Conor Cruise O'Brien writes that 'Burke understood very well the feelings of conquered people – feelings that were necessarily in his own bones – and he even reluctantly condoned that form of revolutionary action which comes first to a desperate peasantry: agrarian terrorism.'[30] His basis for this claim is a single sentence Burke wrote in a letter to the Rev. Thomas Hussey on 18 January 1796: 'Dreadful it is; but it is now plain enough that Catholic *defenderism* is the only restraint upon Protestant *Ascendancy*.'[31] But Dr O'Brien goes too far in saying that this is a condonation of 'revolutionary action'. It was *defender*-ism Burke reluctantly condoned. Burke sympathized strongly with the plight of the Irish Catholics. But he did not condone, not even reluctantly, Irish radicalism, still less Irish revolution, and his condonation of 'defenderism' was not only reluctant but wrung from him once only. Burke's theory of revolutionary necessity might logically have led him to condone revolutionary action in Ireland. In fact, despite his strong polemics against Protestant tyranny, his Irish policies were consistently those of cautious reform.

Tyranny is a breach of the social contract, which is embodied in the prescriptive constitution. Prescription may therefore justify revolution. Usually a conservative concept, 'prescription' could be put to radical purposes, and in the seventeenth century it was. [32]

Burke favoured revolution only to restore the ancient constitution, but he also favoured progress. If the only good revolutions were backward-looking, how was revolution related to progress?

Burke believed that progress was achieved through struggle, conflict and disorder. His *English History* makes that clear. The good revolution of 1688 was conducive to progress in that it secured the British constitution of ordered liberty. This is quite consistent with its being a 'restoring' rather than an 'innovating' revolution.

Indeed, innovating revolutions hindered or destroyed the prospects of progress. The revolutionaries of France, Burke wrote, 'have projected the subversion of that order of things under which our part of the world has so long flourished, and indeed been in a progressive state of improvement, the limits of which, if it had not been thus rudely stopped, it would not have been easy for the imagination to fix'. [33] Progess was built upon learning and commerce, which in turn depended on order and moral discipline. Religion provided the basis for all of these. The French Revolution was destroying them all. That was why Burke regarded such an innovating revolution as regressive.

If innovating revolutions were regressive, progress could be revolutionary. In his *Speech on Conciliation with America*, Burke referred to a proposal to stop land grants to the growing population of America. There was no way, he said, that the British Government could prevent the expansion of the American colonies. Any attempt to do so would only make enemies of the colonists and bring disaster to Britain. 'Such would, and, in no long time, must be, the effect of attempting to forbid as a crime, and to suppress as an evil, the command and blessing of Providence, "Increase and multiply".'[34] The language is Providentialist. But the idea is not unmarxist. If a state seeks to suppress powerful, inevitable forces of economic expansion, those forces will destroy that state and replace it with one more appropiate to their historic role. If inevitable economic growth might help to explain and justify the American Revolution, why might it not do the same for the French? We shall shortly see how Burke answered that question.

NOTES

   1.  Frank O'Gorman, *Edmund Burke: His Political Philosophy* (London: Allen & Unwin, 1973), p. 141.

   2.  Edmund Burke, *Reflections on the Revolution in France* (Harmondsworth: Penguin Books, 1968), p. 175; *The Works and Correspondence of Edmund Burke* (London: Rivington, 1852), vol. I, p. 607; vol. IV, p. 591; vol. VIII, p. 555.

   3.  *Works and Correspondence*, vol. V, pp. 543–4.

   4.  Ibid., vol. I, p. 561.

   5.  C. P. Courtney, *Montesquieu and Burke* (Oxford: Blackwell, 1963), p. 158; *Works and Correspondence*, vol. V, p. 474.

   6.  *Reflections*, p. 156.

   7.  *Works and Correspondence*, vol. V, p. 125.

   8.  *The Works of the Right Honourable Edmund Burke* (London: Rivington, 1812–15), vol. 10, p. 51.

   9.  *Works and Correspondence*, vol. IV, p. 407.

10.  Ibid.

11.  *The Correspondence of Edmund Burke* (Cambridge and Chicago University Presses, 1958–70), vol. IX, p. 162.

12.  *Works*, vol. 10, p. 139.

13.  *Works*, vol. 10, p. 17; *Works and Correspondence*, vol. V, pp. 535–6.

14.  Francis Canavan, *The Political Reason of Edmund Burke* (Durham, North Carolina: Duke University Press, 1960), p. 139; *Correspondence*, vol. IX, p. 114.

15. John C. Weston, Jr., 'Edmund Burke's View of History', *The Review of Politics*, 23, 1961, pp. 223–4.
16. Ibid., p. 224.
17. *Reflections*, pp. 112–13.
18. Weston, p. 224.
19. *Works and Correspondence*, vol. IV, p. 449.
20. Ibid., pp. 461, 467.
21. Ibid., pp. 584–5.
22. *Correspondence*, vol. VI, p. 48.
23. *Reflections*, p. 113.
24. *Works and Correspondence*, vol. IV, p. 432.
25. Ibid., p. 461.
26. Ibid., p. 446.
27. *Reflections*, pp. 194–5.
28. Ibid., p. 195.
29. Ibid.
30. Ibid., p. 34.
31. *Correspondence*, vol. VIII (emphasis Burke's).
32. L. Stone, *The Causes of the English Revolution* (London: Routledge & Kegan Paul, 1972), p. 104.
33. *Correspondence*, vol. VII, p. 387.
34. *Works and Correspondence*, vol. III, p. 260.

# 10

# The Causes of Revolution

John Plamenatz wrote in *Man and Society* that 'Burke's conception of society, as a well-integrated whole with long-established institutions supported by venerable prejudices, made it impossible for him to give a convincing explanation of anarchy and revolution.'[1]

A common variant of the idea that Burke was unable to explain revolutions is the view that he was only able to explain them, especially the French Revolution, by means of a 'conspiracy theory'. Thus, Francis Canavan wrote that 'Burke saw the French Revolution, not as a popular uprising, but as the result of a conspiracy inspired by a false and dangerous spirit of antisocial criticism.'[2]

I shall try to show that both these views are essentially incorrect.

Burke dealt with the causes of social unrest in his *Observations on 'The Present State of the Nation'*. This work was published in 1769 but refers to the state of the nation in 1765. 'The inclinations of the people', he wrote, 'were little attended to.' A disposition to use force ran through the administration. The nation was uneasy and dissatisfied. 'Sober men saw causes for it, in the constitution of the ministry and the conduct of the ministers. The ministers . . . attributed their unpopularity wholly to the efforts of faction.' However this might be, Burke went on, 'the licentiousness and tumults of the common people, and the contempt of government . . . had at no time risen to a greater or more dangerous height.' The measures taken by the government to suppress the spirit of the people were as violent and licentious as the spirit itself: injudicious, precipitate, and, some of them, illegal. 'Instead of allaying, they tended infinitely to inflame the distemper; and whoever will be at the least pains to examine, will find those measures not only the causes of the tumults which then prevailed, but the real sources of almost all the disorders which have arisen since that time.'[3]

Burke did not deny that the 'efforts of faction' might have contributed to the unpopularity of the government. Nor did he deny the 'licentiousness and tumults of the common people'. But he clearly placed the chief blame on the government. The nation was uneasy and dissatisifed. Sober men saw causes for it in the conduct of the ministers, who attended little to the inclinations of the people and tended to rule by force. The measures taken to suppress the turbulence of the people were equally turbulent and tended infinitely to inflame rather than allay it. The measures of the ministry were the causes of the tumults which then prevailed.

Burke commoly blamed government for disorder. In his *Address to the King* (1777) he declared that the disorders which then prevailed in the empire were due to 'the usual and natural cause of such disorders at all times and in all places, where such have prevailed – the misconduct of government'. They were due to plans laid in error, pursued with obstinacy, and conducted without wisdom.[4]

On several occasions Burke put forward the general principle that oppressive government was 'the usual and natural cause' of mass disorder. On 15 March 1797 he wrote to Earl Fitzwilliam, about Ireland: 'They, who provoke the passions of men beyond the limits of human prudence, are primarily and much the most heavily responsible for all the excesses into which men are led by these passions.' In his *Speech on American Taxation* (1774), he wrote: 'When you drive him hard, the boar will surely turn upon the hunters.' In his *First Letter on a Regicide Peace*, he said: 'Oppression makes wise men mad; but the distemper is still the madness of the wise, which is better than the sobriety of fools.'[5]

This is an aspect of his doctrine of tyranny. Tyranny both justified and provoked (caused) rebellion. Thus it is wrong to say that he believed conspiracy to be the sole, or even the chief cause of revolution.

In his *Letter to the Sheriffs of Bristol* (1777), Burke complained that those who opposed the government's American policy were accused of encouraging rebellion. '*General* rebellions and revolts of a whole people', he declared, 'never were encouraged, now or at any time. They are always *provoked*.'[6]

In his *Address to the King* of the same year, he dealt more fully with the question of faction and rebellion. No faction, he said, could, in any part of the world, be so powerful as to bring about rebellion in America merely by their policy or their talents, when they were few in number, lacking in rank, with no 'natural hereditary dependencies'. America contained millions of people, dispersed over a whole continent, of different, even opposed, religions, manners, governments and local interests. Rebellion meant for these people 'a suspension of all the profits of industry and all the comforts of civil life' added to 'all the evils of an unequal war carried on with circumstances of the greatest asperity and rigour'. It was inconceivable that a small faction could bring such people voluntarily to submit themselves to such a condition 'without some powerful concurring cause'. This concurring cause, Burke suggested, was 'a general sense of some grievance, so radical in its nature, and so spreading in its effects, as to poison all the ordinary satisfactions of life, to discompose the frame of society, and to convert into fear and hatred that habitual reverence ever paid by mankind to an ancient and venerable government'.[7]

Three general principles about faction and rebellion are either stated or implied by this passage.

1. The efforts of a few men of talent without social status could nowhere be a sufficient cause of popular rebellion.
2. No faction could induce a people, geographically dispersed, with disparate and even adverse interests and values, to undergo the evils of revolution and war.
3. A necessary condition for this is a radical and widespread grievance which is decomposing the frame of society.

Burke was speaking of America. But his analysis clearly relied upon general principles of human nature and politics.

Burke's view of the respective roles of faction and oppression in the causation of revolution cannot be fully appreciated without considering his writings on Ireland. Ireland provides a theoretical link between America and France. For Ireland had a government of the same type as America's (oppressive) which was likely, Burke thought, to produce a result like France's (Jacobinism). It is true that Burke did distinguish between the Jacobinism born of speculation and that which arose from penury, but the concession that something so closely associated with the French Revolution as Jacobinism could be produced by oppression shows that Burke was able to explain phenomena like the French Revolution without recourse to conspiracy theory.

Although Burke did not rely on conspiracy theory to explain revolution, he did acknowledge that faction might play some role in the creation of social unrest. Let us now examine more closely what he thought that role was.

Great discontents frequently arise in the best constituted governments from causes which no human wisdom can foresee, and no human power can prevent. . . . Governments of all kinds are administered only by men; and great mistakes, tending to inflame these discontents, may concur. . . . In such circumstances the minds of the people become sore and ulcerated. . . . From their disgust at [public] men, they are soon led to quarrel with their frame of government, which they presume gives nourishment to the vices, real or supposed, of those who administer to it. . . . Then will be felt the full effect of encouraging doctrines which tend to make the citizens despise their constitution.[8]

Burke does not here explain revolution by reference to oppressive government. Great discontents can arise from the best constituted governments, discontents which can lead people to 'quarrel with their frame of government'. But it is only at this point that the full effect of radical doctrines will be felt. So he is not offering a simple conspiracy theory either. Factions, conspiracies, ideologies, fan flames started by other causes. This doctrine appears in the *Appeal from the New to the Old Whigs*, one of Burke's most conservative works, written in 1791 with the French Revolution very much in mind.

Although Burke sometimes explained revolt simply by reference to oppression, at other times he refined this explanation by proposing what we may call the 'blocked-channels-of-reform' explanation. This explanation states that it is not oppression as such that causes men to rebel, but the cumulative effect of three phenomena: (1) radical and widespread grievance; (2) persistent and exhaustive attempts to secure redress; and (3) persistent refusal of the rulers to grant redress. Burke held that these phenomena were present in both America and Ireland. In the beginning of the American controversy, he wrote in his *Letter to the Sheriffs of Bristol* (1777), the American rebels had looked for help from England. They had sought it 'by earnest supplications to government', which government rejected. They found the British resolved to reduce them to unconditional obedience. 'Despairing of us, they trusted in themselves. . . . In proportion as all encouragement here lessened, their distance from this country increased. The encouragement is over; the alienation is complete.'[9]

Burke was on occasion quite specific about the nature of the oppression which caused disorder. The cause of the discontent of the American peoples was taxes.[10] That of the Irish Catholics was not religion but poverty. 'Alas! It is not about popes, but about potatoes, that the minds of this unhappy people are agitated.'[11]

General rebellions are never encouraged, always provoked. But there is a Jacobinism which is speculative in origin, arising from wantonness and fullness of bread. It appears, therefore, that rebelliousness, if not rebellion, can arise in the absence of oppression.[12] The revolutionaries of France were rebels without a cause.

These nefarious monsters destroyed their country for what was good in it: for much good there was in the constitution of that noble monarchy, which, in all kinds, formed and nourished great men, and great patterns of virtue to the world. But though its enemies were not enemies to its faults, its faults furnished them with the means for its destruction.[13]

Burke idealizes the monarchy and is unjust to the revolutionaries. But, in doing so, he acknowledges the faults of the monarchy. Its chief fault was its 'good intention ill-directed' and its 'restless desire of governing too much'.

> The hand of authority was seen in every thing, and in every place. All, therefore, that happened amiss in the course even of domestic affairs, was attributed to the government. . . .[14]

This comment comes from *Thoughts and Details on Scarcity* (1795), Burke's economic tract opposing government interference with the economy. But here he is making a point about the causes of revolution. Other things being equal, an interventionist state is more likely than a *laissez-faire* state to be overthrown by revolution because it is held responsible for the well-being of civil society. Burke considered overgovernment to be one of the causes of the American Revolution.[15]

Although Burke believed that both oppressive and excessive government caused revolution, he did not advocate weak government. In the concluding paragraph of *Thoughts and Details on Scarcity* he declared that tyranny might make men justly wish the downfall of abused powers, but no government had ever yet perished from any other direct cause than its own weakness.[16] Burke believed in both *laissez-faire* and firm government.

> A great, enlarged, protecting, and preserving benevolence has it, not in its accidents and circumstances, but in its very essence, to exterminate vice, and disorder, and oppression from the world. Goodness spares infirmity. Nothing but weakness is tender of the crimes that connect themselves with power, in the destruction of . . . religion, laws, polity, morals, industry, liberty, and prosperity. . . .[17]

However, Burke's views on strong government were not straightforward. The passage just quoted comes from a letter of October 1790. Here is Burke in 1769.

> Particular punishments are the cure for accidental distempers in the state; they inflame rather than allay those heats which arise from the settled mismanagement of the government, or from a natural indisposition in the people. It is of the utmost moment not to make

mistakes in the use of strong measures: and firmness is then only a virtue when it accompanies the most perfect wisdom.[18]

The two passages can be interpreted so that they are mutually consistent. The first says that strong government is necessary to put down the subversion of morality. The second says that strong government must be combined with wisdom. But the second also says that punishment inflames rather than allays passions arising not only from the settled mismanagement of government, but also from a natural indisposition in the people. This implies a certain ineradicable restlessness in human nature which should be handled tactfully by government. If there is something intrinsic to human nature which is inflamed by strong government, then the case for strong government must be qualified to an important degree.

The two passages may still be held to be consistent if a distinction is made between (a) the prudent government of inevitable human weakness, and (b) the firm suppression of deliberate subversion. But the spirit of the two passages cannot be reconciled. This can be seen in the way the second passage continues.

When popular discontents have been very prevalent, it may well be affirmed and supported, that there has been generally something found amiss in the constitution, or in the conduct of the government. The people have no interest in disorder. When they do wrong, it is their error, and not their crime. But with the governing part of the state, it is far otherwise. They certainly may act ill by design, as well as by mistake.[19]

It is therefore possible to detect a shift from early Burke's distrust of, to late Burke's trust in strong government. This is reflected in emphasis from bad government to subversive conspirators as causes of disorder, but no change in theory.

Burke's view of the causes of revolution was, therefore, complex, though not systematic. Weak government might be responsible for its own downfall. Strong government might inflame unrest if not applied with great wisdom. Even the wisest governments might not be able to please the people. Inevitable human error might lead to discontent and disturbance. Sometimes Burke emphasized tyranny and stupidity as causes of popular resentment. At other times, deliberate subversion. What cannot be said is that he had no explanation of revolution. Nor did he ever explain revolution solely by conspiracy.

What, then, did he believe to be the causes of the French Revolution? His best account is to be found in his *Letter to William Elliot* (1795). On the eve of the French Revolution, he writes, Europe had never been more splendid. Yet its very prosperity contained in itself the seeds of its own danger. It caused laxity and debility in the upper class. In the rest of society it produced 'bold spirits and dark designs'.

A false philosophy passed from academics into court, and the ruling class was itself infected with the theories which led to their destruction. 'Knowledge, which in the last two centuries either did not exist at all, or existed solidly on right principles and in chosen hands, was now diffused, weakened, and perverted.'

General wealth loosened morals, relaxed vigilance, and increased presumption. When men of talent began to contemplate the distribution of the common prosperity, they compared the receipts with the merits of the recipients. 'As usual, they found their portion not equal to their estimate (or perhaps to the public estimate) of their own worth.'

When the French Revolution revealed that a struggle 'between establishment and rapacity' could be sustained, 'though but for one year, and in one place', it was clear that 'a practicable breach was made in the whole order of things and in every country'. Note the change in rhetoric. The debilitated ruling class has become establishment. The men of talent, previously charged with presumption, have become rapacity. Burke has set aside the idea that a decadent élite is being challenged by new social energy. Splendid old Europe is under attack by evil men.

'Religion, that held the materials of the fabric together, was first systematically loosened.' All other opinions, which men commonly called 'prejudices', necessarily fell with it. Property, left undefended by principles, 'became a repository of spoils to tempt cupidity, and not a magazine to furnish arms for defence'. Attacked on all sides by 'the infernal energies of talents set in action by vice and disorder', authority could not stand upon authority alone. 'Situations formerly supported persons. It now became necessary that personal qualities should support situations.' Formerly, where there was authority, wisdom and virtue were presumed. But now, 'the veil was torn', and, 'to keep off sacrilegious intrusion', it was necessary that in the sanctuary of government something should be disclosed not only venerable, but dreadful. Government was required to show itself at the same time full of virtue and full of force.[20]

The charge that religion was 'systematically' loosened does suggest the conventional idea of a conspiracy of intellectuals. Religion was undermined. As a consequence, all the other supports of the old order – opinion, property, authority – fell like dominoes.

Plamenatz was clearly mistaken when he said of Burke: 'Without saying so in so many words, he takes it for granted that the institutions of a great country like France are all compatible with one another and are also in harmony with a mutually consistent set of prejudices.'[21] On the contrary, he held that the old regime had generated a destructive class conflict. Canavan was also wrong to say that Burke attributed the Revolution to a conspiracy. He did believe that, within a complex process of social disintegration, conspirators were at work, but the conspiracy of intellectuals only took place, and could only take effect, in a society which was, as a result of factors largely independent of them, potentially or actually unstable.

The social structure of the old regime had intrinsic weaknesses. But Burke did not treat these as independent variables which explained the Revolution. They had been made by the monarchy. To strengthen itself, the monarchy had weakened every other force in society. To secure the allegiance of the nation to itself, it had dissolved all other allegiances. Thus, once the allegiance of the people to the crown was broken, 'the whole frame of the commonwealth was found in a state of disconnection'.[22]

Burke identified the classic conditions for revolution: a

weak, highly centralized state presiding over a society divided between a decadent ruling class and an aspirant powerful new class. The chief cause of the French Revolution was not the conspiracy of intellectuals, but the policy of the French monarchy. It was the monarchy that had disconnected the whole frame of the commonwealth.

Writing in 1965 'On the Etiology of Internal Wars', Harry Eckstein made this remark.

One crucial choice that needs to be made is whether to put emphasis upon characteristics of the insurgents or incumbents, upon the side that rebels or the side that is rebelled against. Not surprisingly, the existing literature concentrates very largely on the rebels, treating internal war as due mainly to changes in the non-elite strata of society to which no adequate adjustment is made by the elite. This would seem to be only natural; after all, it is the rebels who rebel. At least some writings suggest, however, that characteristics of the incumbents and the classes that are usually their props must be considered jointly with characteristics of the insurgents, indeed perhaps even emphasised more strongly.[23]

Eckstein did not cite Burke as a proponent of this view, but we have seen that he placed great emphasis on élite characteristics as causes of revolution. He also emphasised intra-élite divisions. He held that the French monarchy had created antagonism between itself and the classes that were usually its props: the nobility, the clergy and the magistracy.[24]

In view of the contrary evidence, how should we explain the conventional view that Burke could only explain revolutions by conspiracy theory? There is a strong general reason why we should expect some ambivalence and ambiguity in Burke's attitude towards sociological and conspiratorial accounts of the French Revolution. He valued, with reservations, the old regime and detested the Revolution. This moral position led him to emphasize the virtues and stability of the first and the wickedness of the second. A sociological explanation suggests the weakness and moral failings of the old order and therefore lends some justification to the Revolution. Yet his very hostility to the Revolution, and his fear that it might be imitated in England, impelled him to understand its real causes. Because of the force with which Burke expressed his moral attitude to the Revolution, many commentators have noticed his idealization of the old regime and missed the countervailing sociological analysis of it.

Burke did, of course, idealize the old regime. He also said that it *appeared* stable before the Revolution.[25] The Revolution was astonishing and unpredictable. But it was not *inexplicable*.

> Here is a state of things of which, in its totality, if history furnishes any examples at all, they are very remote and feeble. I therefore am not so ready as some are, to tax with folly or cowardice those who were not prepared to meet an evil of this nature. Even now, after the events, all the causes may be somewhat difficult to ascertain. Very many are however traceable. But these things history and books of speculation . . . did not teach men to foresee, and of course to resist.[26]

Burke may also be accused of failing to offer a scientific explanation of revolution because he used Providence as an explanatory factor. But what is most striking about Burke's resort to Providence as an explanation is its rarity. It is his way of expressing his perplexity about naturalistic causation, not of denying its possibility. To point to the occasional supernaturalistic explanation in Burke is not to show that he had no naturalistic ones. His sociology is set in a conventional Christian theological framework. It is still a sociology.

Another source of objection to reading Burke as a sociologist of revolution derives from his metaphysics in a rather different way. Burke held that a just society correspond to the nature of things which had been ordained by God. An unjust revolution was therefore unnatural and accordingly difficult to explain naturalistically. This difficulty is manifested in Burke's habit of speaking of the revolutionaries in demonological terms, which are not merely rhetorical abuse, but, in the light of Burke's metaphysics, to be read literally. '[W]hat was done in France . . . was a foul, impious, monstrous thing, wholly out of the course of moral nature.'[27]

There are therefore two supernaturalistic explanations of the French Revolution: both God and Satan may have been behind it. Burke's demonology is the link between his theology and his conspiracy theme. If the Revolution was the work of monsters, was there not a conspiracy after all? What evidence supports the view that Burke saw the Revolution in terms of conspiracy?

Among those who have attributed to Burke the view that the French Revolution was the result of a conspiracy was Alfred Cobban. He thought it strange that Burke should have 'sought to account for such a vast upheaval as the French Revolution in such a superficial manner'.[28] But he relied, for his interpretation, exclusively on one passage from one letter of Burke's: 'I charge all these disorders, not on the mob, but on the Duke of Orleans, and Mirabeau, and Barnave, and Bailly, and Lameth, and La Fayette, and the rest of that faction, who, I conceive, spent immense sums of money, and used innumerable arts, to instigate the populace throughout France to the enormities they committed.' But this passage is quite consistent with the view that, although factions may fan flames, they do not start fires. The 'enormities' this faction is charged with instigating are not the same as the 'vast upheaval' of the French Revolution. Conspiracies may cause riots, not revolutions.

This is something less than a conspiracy explanation of the French Revolution. But Burke did have, not one, but two conspiracy explanations for which the evidence is much stronger. The first is the 'conspiracy of intellectuals' thesis. In his *Remarks on the Policy of the Allies* (1793), Burke wrote:

How many could have thought, that the most complete and formidable revolution in a great empire should be made by men of letters, not as subordinate instruments and trumpeters of sedition, but as the chief contrivers and managers, and in a short time as the open administrators and sovereign rulers?[29]

This seems clear enough. Men of letters were the chief *contrivers* and *managers* of the Revolution. But which revolution? That of July 1789 or that which took place between 1789 and 1793? Is Burke accusing the men of letters of contriving the original revolt or the ensuing transformation of French society?

An answer to these questions may be found in his earlier *Letter to a Member of the National Assembly* (1791): 'I may speak it upon an assurance almost approaching to absolute knowledge, that nothing has been done that has not been contrived from the beginning, even before the states had assembled. . . . They are the same men and the same designs that they were from the first, though varied in their appearance.'[30]

Is 'contriving' conspiracy? We must now consider the most influential conspiracy passage in Burke. It comes from the *Reflections*.

The literary cabal had some years ago formed something like a regular plan for the destruction of the Christian religion. This object they pursued with a degree of zeal which hitherto had been discovered only in the propagators of some system of piety.[31]

'Cabal' is very close to 'conspiracy'. The cabal is charged with a regular plan, zealously executed, for the destruction of the Christian religion. Does this mean they caused the French Revolution?

There are good grounds for answering affirmatively. Burke believed religion to be the foundation of the state. To attack religion was to undermine the state.

On [the Christian ] religion, according to our mode, all our laws and institutions stand as upon their base. That scheme is supposed in every transaction of life; and if that were done away, every thing else, as in France, must be changed along with it. Thus, religion perishing, and with it this constitution, it is a matter of endless meditation, what order of things would follow it.[32]

This is Burke's first conspiracy explanation of the French Revolution. The literary cabal in France planned the destruction of the Christian religion. Where the Christian religion is destroyed, everything else must be changed. Did Burke hold, after all, that a conspiracy caused the French Revolution? The answer is negative if that belief is taken to mean that it was a sufficient cause of the Revolution. Burke stated elsewhere that the systematic loosening of religion was one contributory factor in a complex situation of social disintegration. The 'literary cabal' passage does not contradict this interpretation. Burke never said that the subversion of the Christian religion was a sufficient cause of the French Revolution.

In his *Appeal from the New to the Old Whigs* Burke denied that , before the Revolution, there was much dissatisfaction with the monarchy. How, then, was the Revolution to be explained? 'It was by art and impulse; it was by the sinister use made of a season of scarcity; it was under an infinitely diversified succession of wicked pretences, wholly foreign to the question of monarchy or aristocracy, that this light people were inspired with their present spirit of levelling.'[33] This is the second conspiracy explanation.

The Revolution was made by 'art' and 'impulse'. This is the key conspiracy phrase. But what art and what impulse? The 'art' is, firstly, 'the sinister use made of a season of scarcity'. 'Sinister use' is very vague. 'Season of scarcity' suggests that one of the impulses may have been the impulse of starving people to eat. This part of the second conspiracy explanation may be analyzed into two causal components: (1) hunger; (2) a very vaguely specified 'sinister' manipulation of hunger.

The second aspect of the 'art' of subversion was 'an infinitely diversified succession of wicked pretences, wholly foreign to the question of monarchy or aristocracy'. What pretences? Who led whom to do what? Apart from the Duke of Orleans passage discussed above, Burke does not indicate what he is thinking of. This is an innuendo rather than an explanation.

Thus, the second conspiracy explanation – the manipulation of the people before, during and after the meeting of the Estates-General in 1789 – though clearly offered by Burke, dissolves, on examination, into extreme vagueness. If this were Burke's only account of the French Revolution, Cobban, Plamenatz and Canavan would be right to maintain that his analysis was utterly inadequate. But it was not his only account.

Burke believed (rightly) that revolutionary conspiracies existed. He also believed (rightly) that they sometimes made an important contribution to the causes of revolution. He morally disapproved of one particular revolutionary conspiracy he believed to exist and expressed his disapproval in extremely forceful language. In this one case, his moral disapproval led him to attribute responsibility for the Revolution to the conspiracy and, consequently, to hold it to be a cause.

Yet, although Burke sometimes placed great emphasis on the conspiracy of revolutionary leaders, he never said that their conspiracy was the sole or a sufficinet cause of revolution. Burke gave a sociological account of the forces which may undermine a prosperous and seemingly stable society. In this account, conspiracy was given a place, but a secondary one. No radical and widespread grievance, no revolution. Conspirators never make revolutions out of nothing. Radical and widespread grievances may grow from the faults of governments or the fissures of developing societies. In such situations, the availability of a revolutionary ideology to the aggrieved may turn turmoil into revolt. Thus radical intellectuals play their part. Stupid and wicked rulers play theirs, too. The strains of economic progress; the development of class conflicts; the skill of rulers in managing these strains and conflicts; the skill of counter-élites in mobilizing aggrieved sections of the population – these are the chief ingredients of Burke's account of the causes of revolution. But his understanding of the processes of revolution went well beyond this.

## NOTES

1. John Plamenatz, *Man and Society* (London: Longmans, 1963), vol. 1, p. 362.
2. Francis Canavan, *The Political Reason of Edmund Burke* (Durham, North Carolina: Duke University Press, 1960), p. 71.
3. *The Works and Correspondence of Edmund Burke* (London: Rivington, 1852), vol. III, p. 77.
4. Ibid., vol. V, p. 526.
5. *The Correspondence of Edmund Burke* (Cambridge and Chicago University Presses, 1958–1970), vol. IX, p. 283; *Works and Correspondence*, vol. III, p. 219; vol. V, p. 312.
6. *Works and Correspondence*, vol. III, p. 314 (emphasis Burke's).
7. Ibid., vol. V, pp. 526–7.
8. Ibid., vol. IV, pp. 482–3.
9. Ibid., vol. III, p. 315.
10. Ibid., p. 209.

11.  Ibid., vol. VI, p. 59.

12.  Ibid., vol. IV, p. 532.

13.  Ibid., vol. V, p. 210.

14.  Ibid., pp. 210–11.

15.  Ibid., vol. III, p. 219.

16.  Ibid., vol. V, p. 211.

17.  *Correspondence*, vol. VI, pp. 148–9.

18.  *Works and Correspondence*, vol. III, p. 114.

19.  Ibid., pp. 114–15.

20.  Ibid., vol. V, p. 147.

21.  Plamenatz, p. 539.

22.  *Correspondence*, vol. VI, p. 242.

23.  Harry Eckstein, 'On the Etiology of Internal Wars', *History and Theory*, IV, 1965, p. 145.

24.  *Works and Correspondence*, vol. IV, p. 581.

25.  *The Speeches of the Right Honourable Edmund Burke* (London: Longman, Hurst, Rees, &c., 1816), vol. III, p. 480.

26.  *Works and Correspondence*, vol. V, p. 59.

27.  Ibid., vol. IV, p. 401.

28.  Alfred Cobban, *Edmund Burke and the Revolt against the Eighteenth Century* (London: Allen & Unwin, 1960), p. 120.

29.  *Works and Correspondence*, vol. V, p. 58.

30.  Ibid., vol. IV, p. 361.

31.  Edmund Burke, *Reflections on the Revolution in France* (Harmondsworth: Penguin Books, 1968), pp. 211–12.

32.  *Works and Correspondence*, vol. V, p. 489.

33.  Ibid., vol. IV, p. 423.

# 11

# The Dynamics of Revolution

Burke's contribution to the theory of revolution is not only, not even primarily, restricted to the theory of its causes. In 1964, an eminent modern theorist of revolution wrote: 'Despite the protracted normative argument between pro-revolutionaries and anti-revolutionaries, initiated by Paine and Burke, almost nothing careful and systematic has been written about the long-run social effects of internal wars. . . . But in regard to etiology, to "causes", we are absolutely inundated with print.'[1] Yet, despite the protracted theorizing about revolution since those words were written, we are still 'inundated with print' in regard to etiology, and almost nothing careful and systematic has been written about the long-run social effects of revolutions. In this situation, we should note that Burke's main contribution was precisely in this generally neglected area. That this should be so is surprising since his theory of revolution was expounded mostly in his analysis of the French Revolution, the long-run effects of which he was unable to observe. None the less, Burke was superior to most modern theorists of revolution, not only in having a theory of revolutionary consequences as well as one of the causes of revolution, but in having an integrated theory of the causes, courses and consequences of revolution.

The idea that a radical and widespread grievance is a necessary condition of revolution constitutes the main link between Burke's account of the causes of revolution and his account of its dynamics and consequences.

The concept of 'grievance' has epistemological implications, and these epistemological issues have political consequences. What is a 'grievance', a real grievance, not an illusory

one? How can we tell when we have to do with a real grievance? And who is competent to answer such questions?

What I have always thought of the matter is this – that the most poor,
illiterate, and uninformed creatures upon earth are judges of a practical oppression. It is a matter of feeling; and as such persons generally
have felt most of it, and are not of an over-lively sensibility, they are
the best judges of it. But for the real cause, or the appropriate
remedy, they ought never to be called into council about the one or
the other. They ought to be totally shut out; because their reason is
weak; because, when once roused, their passions are ungoverned;
because they want information; because the smallness of the property, which individually they possess, renders them less attentive to
the consequences of the measures they adopt in affairs of moment.[2]

The poor, then, are good judges of practical oppression, for
such oppression is a matter of feeling, and the poor have felt
most of it. But they are not good judges of the real causes of
their oppression, nor of the appropriate remedies for it, for
such judgements are matters of reason, and their reason is
weak. These judgements should be made by the 'sober,
rational, and substantial' part of the population.

In a situation of practical oppression, the crucial question is
whether the oppressed will be led by the sober, rational and
substantial, or by 'artful men', who exploit irritations of the
popular mind, presumably by identifying false causes and
inappropriate remedies.

If it is morally crucial to which of these two groups the
oppressed will turn, then it is necessary to specify the conditions under which they will seek out the one or the other.
Burke states two conditions under which the oppressed will be
likely to take the wrong, i.e. the radical turning. The first is
when the government is unsympathetic to the practical
oppression. The American Revolution was an example of such
a situation.[3]

The second is when the rational and substantial are in disarray. This to repeat, from a different perspective, a point made
in the last chapter: when the ruling class is weakened by moral
decay and/or internal conflict, the people will turn to counter-
élites for the solution to their problems.

The sober, rational and substantial are the established élites of society. Counter-élites are not sober, rational and substantial. Their social origins do not suit them to be good rulers. Lawyers are the most important, though by no means the only case. In 1775 Burke noted the popularity of legal studies in America, and went on:

> . . . when great honours and great emoluments do not win over this knowledge to the service of the state, it is a formidable adversary to government. . . . This study renders men acute, inquisitive, dexterous, prompt in attack, ready in defence, full of resources. In other countries, the people, more simple, and of a less mercurial cast, judge of an ill principle in government only by an actual grievance; here they anticipate the evil, and judge of the pressure of the grievance by the badness of the principle.[4]

Lawyers, therefore, are 'artful men' par excellence, talented, aggressive, more ideological than practical, dangerous if alienated.

The trouble with lawyers is that they are both too clever and not clever enough. They are too clever in so far as their dextrous minds delight in turning practical grievances into ideologies, thereby fanning the flames of discontent. They are not clever enough in that the talent that makes a good lawyer is insufficient to make a good ruler. Their experience is too narrow, they do not know the variety of mankind nor the complexity of public affairs.[5]

But the narrowness of lawyers, and of all other talented persons outside the established élite, does not, if they are thrown into positions of leadership during a revolution, merely lead to incompetent government. It leads to tyranny. Revolution places untried talent in power. Only experience teaches the complex difficulties of rational reform. But destruction and despotism are simple. When there are radical and widespread grievances because of the palpable defects of old establishments, and when government does not respond to the expression of such grievances, the people will turn to the radical ideologists, men of talent and energy, but without experience of government and therefore simple-minded about its problems. The result will be wholesale destruction of existing institutions. This remedy appeals strongly in the short run to the aggrieved. But it is not appropriate.[6]

Burke's view that revolutionary change necessarily led to destruction and tyranny was not the product of the French Revolution. In 1780, in his *Speech on Economical Reform*, he had said:

> . . . in hot reformations, in what men, more zealous than considerate, call *making clear work*, the whole is generally so crude, so harsh, so indigested; mixed with so much imprudence, and so much injustice; so contrary to the whole course of human nature, and human institutions, that the very people who are most eager for it are among the first to grow disgusted at what they have done.[7]

This passage applies to hasty reform, but applies *a fortiori* to revolution. Note how Burke attributes to radical reforms, and closely associates, qualities denoting incompetence and qualities denoting oppressiveness: crude and harsh; indigested, imprudent, unjust and contrary to human nature.

Radicals, Burke assumes, are 'hot' and 'zealous'. As a result, they do not consider the effects of what they do. '[W]hen people see a political object, which they ardently desire, but in one point of view, they are apt extremely to palliate, or underrate the evils which may arise in obtaining it.'[8] Such people are not likely to administer appropriate remedies to the grievances of the people.

Radicals suffer, not only from intellectual, but also from moral defects. These latter were exemplified by Rousseau. Rousseau, said Burke, displayed 'an austere virtue pursued to an unsociable fierceness'.[9] Radicals generally, he believed, hate vice too much and love men too little.[10] But Burke also believed Rousseau's virtue to be sham. This sham virtue was the model for the French revolutionaries. 'Benevolence to the whole species, and want of feeling for every individual with whom the professors come into contact, form the character of the new philosophy.'[11] Both these moral feelings enable radicals to take up the cause of the people and to go on to oppress them.

The destructiveness and oppressiveness of revolutionaries, on Burke's account, has two sources: their location in the social structure and their cultural inheritance. The two are interrelated. As social and political outsiders, they make crude and harsh judgements on existing institutions. In doing so, they use appropriate cultural weapons. Rousseau's 'austere virtue' and 'universal benevolence' are well suited to the purpose. But there is another source, equally attractive to radical ideologists, and equally dangerous. It stems from Descartes.

According to the 'false philosophy' of the French revolutionaries, says Burke, all authority must be subject to the judgement of reason. It can never be legitimated by 'prejudice'. It follows, he argues, that revolutionary regimes are no safer than their predecessors. 'By what they call reasoning without prejudice, they leave not one stone upon another in the fabric of human society. They subvert all the authority which they hold, as well as all that which they have destroyed.'[12]

In his *Preface to M. Brissot's Address to his Constituents*, Burke enlarges on how the chickens have come home to roost.

Another great lesson may be taught by this book, and by the fortune of the author, and his party: I mean a lesson drawn from the consequences of engaging in daring innovations, from a hope that we may be able to limit their mischievous operation at our pleasure, and by our policy to secure ourselves against the effect of the evil examples we hold out to the world. . . . The revolutionists who have just suffered an ignominious death, under the sentence of the revolutionary tribunal (a tribunal composed of those with whom they had triumphed in the total destruction of the ancient government), were by no means ordinary men, or without very considerable talents and resources. But with all their talents and resources, and the apparent momentary extent of their power, we see the fate of their projects, their power and their persons. We see before our eyes the absurdity of thinking to establish order upon principles of confusion, or, with the materials and instruments of rebellion, to build up a solid and stable government.[13]

Burke is here talking of the course and consequences of revolution rather than its causes. But these are consequences of one of the causes of revolution. The 'principles of confusion' undermined the old order, helped to convert grievances into revolt, and now not only produce internecine strife between revolutionary factions, but undermine the establishment of any new social order.

The rights of men, Burke maintained, and the new principles of liberty and equality, were very unhandy instruments for those who wished to establish order. 'They who were taught to find nothing to respect in the title and the virtues of Louis XVI, a prince succeeding to the throne by the fundamental laws, in the line of a succession of monarchs continued for fourteen hundred years, found nothing which could bind them to an implicit fidelity, and dutiful allegiance, to Messrs. Brissot, Vergniaud, Condorcet, Anarcharsis Clootz, and Thomas Paine.'

In this difficulty, the revolutionary leaders did as well as they could. To govern the people, they had to incline the people to obey. This end they had to accomplish by such instruments as they had in their hands. 'They were to accomplish the purposes of order, morality, and submission to the laws, from the principles of atheism, profligacy, and sedition.' Thus they began to assume the mask of an austere and rigid virtue; they declaimed against tumult and confusion; they made daily harangues on the blessings of order, discipline, quiet, and obedience to authority.[14]

This is the onset of the 'Thermidorean' phase of the revolution. The revolutionary government attempts to transmute the 'principles of confusion' into the rhetoric of order. Discipline, quiet and obedience to authority are virtues once again. But, it seems, to no avail. 'Every part of their own policy comes round, and strikes at their own power and their own lives.'[15]

But why were the ideas of the Revolution 'principles of confusion'? Why could they not legitimate the new order? Burke has two answers. Firstly, the monarchy had been legitimated by the title and virtues of Louis XVI, and by fourteen hundred years of constitutional continuity. These had proved insufficient to defend it against the new philosophy. In the place of the monarchy, we have Messrs. Brissot, Vergniaud, Condorcet, Anarcharsis Clootz, and Thomas Paine – untried outsiders. Those who had been taught to disobey the former had no reason to obey the latter.

This still does not explain why the revolutionary ideology does not legitimate the new men and their regime. To meet this objection, Burke brings forward a second argument. Age does not legitimate by itself. But it does breed expectations. It fixes rights and duties. It is a 'compass to govern us'.[16] The ancient ideology told people to obey the king. The new ideology tells them to obey the revolutionary government. But what is the moral basis of the claim made by this ideology? It is abstract. Its practical value is doubtful. Before all else, it teaches men their rights, not their duties, and least of all the duties of order, discipline, quiet, and obedience to authority.

Thus it is that, in Burke's view, revolutionary ideology leads naturally from subversion to anarchy. And, from anarchy, it leads as naturally to the rule of force.

The people of Lyons, it seems, have refused lately to pay taxes. Why should they not? . . . They may say to the assembly, Who are you, that are not our kings, nor the states we have elected, nor sit on the principles on which we elected you? And who are we, that when we see the gabelles which you have ordered to be paid, wholly shaken off, when we see the act of disobedience afterwards ratified by yourselves, who are we, that we are not to judge what taxes we ought or ought not to pay, and who are not to avail ourselves of the same powers, the validity of which you have approved in others? To this the answer is, We will send troops.[17]

Burke implies that men may obey government through love, fear, self-interest, unthinking habit, and/or speculative theory. Love tinged with fear to form 'awe' is the true basis of good government.[18] When traditional authority is destroyed, so are love and habit as the bases of political obedience. The alternatives are self-interest, speculation and naked fear.

On the scheme of this barbarous philosophy . . . laws are to be supported only by their own terrors, and by the concern, which each individual may find in them, from his own private speculations, or can spare to them from his own private interests. In the groves of *their* academy, at the end of every visto, you see nothing but the gallows.[19]

Revolution destroys that love of state which is rooted in 'prejudice'. Private speculation is an unstable basis for loyalty. Few men have a material interest in a revolutionary regime, since it destroys the wealth of the nation.[20] Only the gallows remain.

When the the people of Lyons refuse to pay taxes, Burke supposes, the response of the revolutionary government is to send troops. Burke several times emphasized the military implications of revolutionary government. As early as 1790 he wrote: 'Every thing depends upon the army in such a government as yours. . . . You see by the report of your war minister that the distribution of the army is in a great measure made with a view of internal coercion.'[21]

Later, Burke was to state even more clearly that the revolutionary regime in France was a military dictatorship.

. . . [T]hose who arbitrarily erected the new building out of the old materials of their own convention, were obliged to send for an army to support their work. . . . At length, after a terrible struggle, the troops prevailed over the citizens. . . . Twenty thousand regular troops garrison Paris. Thus a complete military government is formed. It has the strength, and it may count on the stability, of that kind of power. . . . Every other ground of stability, but from military force and terror, is clean out of the question. . . . The whole of their government, in its origination, in its continuance, in all its actions, and in all its resources, is force; and nothing but force.[22]

The revolutionary regime in France was a tyranny. The country consisted of two descriptions: oppressors and oppressed. The first controlled the state, the army, the public revenue, and the property of the nation. They could pay the poor to control the rest. The outcome was what is now called totalitarianism.

Committees, called of vigilance and safety, are every where formed; a most severe and scrutinizing inquisition, far more rigid than any thing ever known or imagined. Two persons cannot meet and confer without hazard to their liberty, and even to their lives. Numbers scarcely credible have been executed, and their property confiscated.[23]

Burke blamed the government of the old regime for divorcing the nobility from the people and thus abolishing potential leaders of resistance to the revolutionary tyranny.

Force is the only resource of the revolution. But there is another, complementary, support for revolutionary force. '[C]riminal means once tolerated are soon preferred.' Deceit and violence begin as a means to the end of public welfare, but become the end itself, public welfare becoming merely their pretext. Political violence is habit-forming.[24]

Thus revolutions necessarily entail two apparent paradoxes. The first is that their initiators are often their victims: 'those who countenance great commotions in their beginnings, are those, who in the end, smart most for them in their fortunes.'[25] The second is that the excessive desire for freedom leads to tyranny.[26] Both paradoxes are only 'apparent' for the relations of cause and effect they summarize are part of the nature of things. They are only paradoxes to those who hold simple-minded views about politics.

Burke believed that all societies and all governments have certain common requisites. They are also susceptible to certain common sources of disorder. Both sets of generalizations apply equally to traditional and revolutionary societies and governments. Both the requisites of order and the sources of disorder are rooted in certain universal features of human nature. Certain vices – such as pride, ambition, revenge, and ungoverned zeal – are the causes of the world's miseries. Religions, moral codes, ideologies, are the pretexts. The pretexts are always a specious appearance of a real good.

The instruments of great public evils are always power-holders. But you cannot cure the evil by abolishing power. You can change the names of public offices, but you cannot change the need for offices.

The danger in seeing the causes of evil in institutions rather than in appetites is that 'wickedness is inventive'. Pride, ambition, revenge, ungoverned zeal can persist through many institutional changes. Those who believe that the fundamental evils of the human condition can be remedied by the set of institutional changes called 'revolution' will become victims of the perennial vices which continue to work their way through the new institutions, uncriticized because concealed by revolutionary ideology. 'You are terrifying yourself with ghosts and apparitions, whilst your house is the haunt of robbers.' You are guillotining the ghosts of the old ruling class, whilst a new ruling class has moved into power to oppress you.[27]

The class antagonisms which helped to initiate the French Revolution also shaped its course and outcome.

[The republicans in France] have resolved . . . to reduce [the permanent landed interest] to a mere peasantry for the sustenance of the towns, and to place the true effective government in cities, among the tradesmen, bankers, and voluntary clubs of bold, presuming young persons; advocates, attorneys, notaries, managers of newspapers, and those cabals of literary men, called academies.[28]

The Revolution was one of money and ideas against land. It was a bourgeois revolution.

It was not only bourgeois in this sense. It was also bourgeois in being a war of town against country. The victors were the urban bourgeoisie. The victims were not only the landed aristocracy, but also the peasants.[29]

The French Revolution was unique. Nonetheless, it exemplified certain general political truths. It was not simply the result of a conspiracy. Nor was it inexplicable. It was produced by certain long-term social changes combined with some foolish and some wicked human choices. It had its origins in economic growth; in the growth of knowledge; in the emergence of new social classes making new claims; in the political decay of traditional ruling élites; in disunity between different sections of the traditional ruling class; in popular grievances and radical ideologies.

Burke's view of the causes, course and outcome of the Revolution was based on his view of human nature and society. In particular, it was based on the 'Hobbesian' nature of unrestrained man and the need of society for power and order. In striking contrast to Hobbes, Burke emphasized the need for traditional culture to mitigate the evils of power. Revolutions destroyed this culture. They were, therefore, carried out and maintained by unmitigated power. The chief institutional forms of this power were despotic government and the army. The principal link between cause and outcome of revolution (though not the principal cause of revolution) was subversive ideology. This helped to destroy the old order, but, if there was to be a new order, it had to be suppressed, for it was incompatible with a stable society. Causes and outcomes were also linked by class structure. Class fragmentation and conflict caused the revolution and it ended with a new class equilibrium, though an equilibrium maintained by force.

Revolution, Burke thought, had two other consequences of the first importance. The first was counter-revolution. Burke, of course, passionately advocated counter-revolution against the regime of revolutionary France. But, in his thought, counter-revolution was not only a prescription, but an empirically probable consequence of revolution. Since revolution led to destruction, anarchy and tyranny, counter-revolution was likely. Whether it occurred depended upon a number of intrinsically unpredictable factors, such as the will and unity of the deposed ruling class and its natural foreign allies. If the counter-revolution were successful, its government would necessarily have many of the same features as that of the revolution, for it would face many of the same problems. The counter-revolutionaries would not have a system to reform, but a system to begin. One thing was certain: '[T]he settlement cannot be immediate; . . . it must be preceded by some sort of power, equal at least in vigour, vigilance, promptitude, and decision, to a military government. . . .'[30]

Burke also believed that revolution bred counter-revolution in a quite different way. Revolution in one country would lead the rulers of others to suppress dissent more forcefully and to fear the effects of reform.[31]

The last consequence which Burke attributed to revolutions was more revolutions. He feared the spread of the French Revolution to Britain. But he also thought that it might spread much further afield. That revolution had shown that 'it is very possible to overturn the whole frame and order of the best constructed states, by corrupting the common people with the spoil of the superior classes'.[32] A single spark may start a prairie fire. Burke believed that the success of the American

Revolution was one of the causes of the French, for the former 'made it seem practicable to establish a republic in a great extent of country' and gave to French republicans 'a degree of strength, which required other energies than the late king possessed, to resist, or even to restrain'.[33]

Burke's theory of revolution may be severely criticized on various grounds. He was a biased and unreliable reporter of contemporary events. His general conservative politics and his unwillingness adequately to acknowledge the misery in which many people lived both in England and France is morally repugnant to even a moderate liberal and incompatible with the humanitarianism which he professed and sometimes practised. His method lacks scientific rigour. The underlying metaphysics is unoriginal and unconvincing and the epistemology at best sketchy. These lines of criticism are easy enough to substantiate, but I do not wish to add anything to what I have said in earlier chapters, but rather to take the weaknesses of the theory for granted and to explore its merits.

Burke's theory is a theory about the 'real world' of politics – and is, in this sense, an 'empirical' theory – but his view of the 'real world', or, more precisely, his view of what needed to be said about the real world, was derived explicitly from a moral theory. This moral and political theory specified proper and improper means of historical change and led him to analyze why sometimes the first was chosen and sometimes the second, and what the consequences of each choice were.

Because Burke's theory of revolution was derived from such a moral and political theory, it achieved two results which are hard to achieve with those modern scientific methods which rely on statistical generalization. Firstly, because he valued tradition, he was able to detect the world-historical significance of the French Revolution as the first great modernizing revolution. Secondly, because he valued order as the basis of progress conceived in terms of 'rational liberty', he analyzed the consequences of a radical attack on order and the relationship of those consequences to progress. Thus Burke recognized the possibility both of unique 'world-historical' events and of general laws, while retaining considerable scepticism about universal generalization. He was also able to analyze the causes, courses and consequences of revolution in a unified manner, an achievement modern theorists of revolution have found difficult to repeat.[34]

Burke's analysis is weakened by his conservative bias, not so much because he idealized the old regime (for he did not always do so), nor because he attributed revolutions to unexplained conspiracies (for he did not always do so), nor yet because he exaggerated the evil consequences of revolutions (for he was far from being wholly wrong about these), but because, although he did recognize the defects in the old regime, he underestimated the pressures for social and political change.

At this point Burke's writings on economics, social structure and electoral reform become relevant to his theory of revolution. In his economic writings, Burke was a champion of the wealth-producing bourgeoisie, but he wished to restrict the political role of this class. The central contradiction in his political theory is not, as has sometimes been supposed, between youthful radicalism and senile conservatism, for he was always a conservative reformer, but between his bourgeois conception of civil society and his aristorcratic conception of the state. The chief weakness of his political theory and, as a consequence, of his theory of revolution, was that he was a conservative utopian: he wished to conserve what could not be conserved. His theory suffers from this weakness even though he explicitly affirmed that a society must constantly change in order to conserve its fundamental principles.

## NOTES

1.   Harry Eckstein, ed., *Internal War: Problems and Approaches* (London: Collier-Macmillan, 1964), p. 28.
2.   *The Works and Correspondence of Edmund Burke* (London: Rivington, 1852), vol. IV, p. 533.
3.   Ibid., vol. III, p. 315.
4.   Ibid., p. 256.
5.   Edmund Burke, *Reflections on the Revolution in France* (Harmondsworth: Penguin Books, 1968), p. 133.
6.   Ibid., pp. 278–80.

7.   *Works and Correspondence*, vol. III, p. 353.
8.   Ibid., vol. IV, p. 406.
9.   *Annual Register*, (1759), p. 479.
10.   Peter J. Stanlis, *Edmund Burke and the Natural Law* (Ann Arbor: University of Michigan Press, 1965), p. 178.
11.   *Works and Correspondence*, vol. IV, p. 374.
12.   Ibid., p. 465.
13.   *Works and Correspondence*, vol. V, pp. 169–70.
14.   Ibid., pp. 156–7.
15.   Ibid., p. 165.
16.   *Reflections*, pp. 172–3.
17.   Ibid., p. 349.
18.   Ibid., p. 194.
19.   Ibid., pp. 171–2.
20.   Ibid., p. 353.
21.   Ibid., p. 344.
22.   *Works and Correspondence*, vol. V, pp. 463–4.
23.   Ibid., p. 27.
24.   *Reflections*, pp. 172, 176–7.
25.   *The Correspondence of Edmund Burke* (Cambridge and Chicago University Presses, 1958–1970), vol. VI, p. 103.
26.   *Reflections*, p. 261.
27.   Ibid., pp. 247–8.
28.   *Works and Correspondence*, vol. IV, p. 558.
29.   *Reflections*, p. 348.
30.   *Works and Correspondence*, vol. V, pp. 52–3.
31.   *Reflections*, p. 125.
32.   *Correspondence*, vol. VII, p. 383.
33.   *Works and Correspondence*, vol. V, p. 338.
34.   See my argument in 'Edmund Burke and the Theory of Revolution', *Political Theory*, 6, 1978, 277–97.

# 12

## Particular Revolutions and their Universal Significance

Because Burke believed both in a universal order and in the importance of particular circumstances, he may be considered to have held a general theory of revolution and to have made special analyses of individual revolutions. However, Burke never presented a systematic account of the former, which exists explicitly only as a set of principles which inform the latter. In order, therefore, to understand the theory adequately, we must examine the analysis of particular revolutions.

There is little profit in reading Burke's accounts of particular revolutions from motives of historical scholarship. It is not that these accounts have been superseded by modern scholarship. It is that they never were scholarship. Their interest, particular though they are, is theoretical.

Burke's reflections on particular revolutions raise two theoretical points which we have not considered so far. The first is that revolutions may be classified into different types with great moral and historical implications. The second is that a revolution may be theoretically important, not because it is an example of an important general truth, but because it is a unique exception to previously established general truths. These two points are fused in Burke's analysis of the French Revolution, for he placed it in a class of its own, and this uniqueness was, for him, of momentous significance.

The French Revolution, according to Burke, was 'the greatest moral earthquake that ever convulsed and shattered this globe of ours'.[1] 'Moral earthquake' is a striking conception to encounter in Burke, for he was generally concerned to distinguish between moral and physical processes. Since, in recent political science, there has been some debate about the theoretical status of Great Revolutions,[2] it is worth examining what Burke thought was great about the French Revolution. Firstly, it was a moral revolution, that is, a radical change in values. Secondly, if it was like an earthquake, it was violent, sudden, unexpected and destructive. A Great Revolution, then, is one that embodies and brings about a radical change in values, destroys fundamental institutions, and has far-reaching subversive effects. 'It looks to me', Burke wrote in the *Reflections*, 'as if I were in a great crisis, not of the affairs of France alone, but of all Europe, perhaps of more than Europe.'[3] Two years later (1792) he was convinced that it was 'the most important crisis that ever existed in the world'.[4]

Everything in the French Revolution, Burke maintained, supposed 'a total revolution in all the principles of reason, prudence, and moral feeling'.[5] It was a revolution in manners, and upon manners the laws depended.[6] 'Before this of France', he wrote in 1796, 'the annals of all time have not furnished an instance of a *complete* revolution. That revolution seems to have extended even to the constitution of the mind of man.'[7] The French revolutionaries were waging war against 'the ancient, civil, moral, and political order of Europe'.[8]

The French Revolution was also an unprecedented attack on property. If the counter-revolution were not successful, Burke declared, it was certain that 'property, and along with property, government, must fall, (in the same manner in which they have both fallen in France) in every state in Europe'.[9]

In the face of this crisis of European civilization, Burke drew, not only on his moral, sociological and political theory to understand it, but also on his view of cosmic order.

I defy the most refining ingenuity to invent any other cause for the total departure of the Jacobin republic from every one of the ideas and usages, religious, legal, moral, or social, of this civilised world, and for tearing herself from its communion with such studied violence, but from a formed resolution of keeping no terms with that world. It has not been, as has been falsely and insidiously represented, that these miscreants had only broke with their own government. They made a schism with the whole universe, and that schism extended to almost every thing great and small.[10]

Yet, even though the Revolution was uniquely evil, it was possible that Providence had decreed it to be the beginning of a new order in France, even throughout Europe, and beyond.[11]

What was the nature of this new order? On 9 February 1790 Burke gave this view.

In the last age we were in danger of being entangled by the example of France in the net of a relentless despotism. . . . Our present danger. . . is, with regard to government, a danger from anarchy: a danger of being led, through an admiration of successful fraud and violence, to an imitation of the excesses of an irrational, unprincipled, proscribing, confiscating, plundering, ferocious, bloody, and tyrannical democracy. On the side of religion, the danger of their example is no longer from intolerance, but from atheism. . . .[12]

Burke is upset. But through his emotional language one can perceive a not unreasonable historical analysis. In the short term: chaos and tyranny. In the long term: democracy, secularization, and greater state control of property. This is to modernize Burke, but the modernization transmutes what is there.

The new order which the Revolution was establishing was as unprecedented as the Revolution itself. It was a tyranny, but of an entirely new kind. It was 'of all governments the most absolute, despotic, and effective, that has hitherto appeared on earth'. Never were the views and politics of any government pursued with half the regularity, system, and method that obtained in revolutionary France.[13]

Burke called the revolutionary government 'absolute', thereby trying to turn the tables on his radical opponents who justified the Revolution as the overthrow of absolutism. But it was not merely 'absolute' but 'the most absolute . . . that has hitherto appeared on earth': a world–historical regress. But it was also regular, systematic and methodical: it had some important qualities of good government, but those associated with order, not liberty.

Burke was impressed with the superior efficiency of the rational, centralized state to that of the traditionalist type. The latter he described as formed without system, existing by habit, and confused with the multitude and the perplexity of its pursuits. The aims of the French revolutionaries were wicked, impious and oppressive. But they were 'spirited and daring'. Their government was systematic. It was simple in its principle. It had unity and consistency to perfection. The state was all-powerful. It ruled everything by force. This procedure had its advantages. 'They have found the short cut to the productions of nature, while others, in pursuit of them, are obliged to wind through the labyrinth of a very intricate state of society.' They could command the product of labour. They could command the labourer himself. Revolutionary France was too strong for most of the states of Europe, 'constituted as they are, and proceeding as they proceed'.

Material resources never have supplied, nor ever can supply, the want of unity of design, and constancy in pursuit. But unity in design, and perseverance and boldness in pursuit, have never wanted resources, and never will. We have not considered as we ought the dreadful energy of a state, in which the property has nothing to do with the government.[14]

Revolutionary France might have achieved military and economic efficiency, but it could never become a system of rational liberty. In the *Reflections* Burke had allowed that, in principle, 'that which in the first instance is prejudicial may be excellent in its remoter operation; and its excellence may arise even from the ill effects it produces in the beginning'.[15] But he never used this principle to predict a happy outcome for the French Revolution. In the same work he declared: 'Whether the system, if it deserves such a name, now built on the ruins of [the] ancient monarchy, will be able to give a better account of the population and wealth of the country, which it has taken under its care, is a matter very doubtful.' He thought that France would not improve by its change, and that it would be a long time before it could 'recover in any degree the effects of this philosophic revolution'.[16] In his *Appeal from the New to the Old Whigs* (1791) he wrote that the present state of things in France was not a transient evil, productive of a lasting good, but an evil which would produce future, and possibly worse evils. It was not 'an undigested, imperfect, and crude scheme of liberty' which might gradually be mellowed and ripen into an orderly and social freedom. It was 'so fundamentally wrong, as to be utterly incapable of correcting itself by any length of time. . . .'[17]

The French Revolution was unprecedented because it constituted an abrupt regress from civilization to barbarism. This was the before/after dimension of its importance. There was also an inside/outside dimension. The Revolution was world-historical because it threatened to affect the history of the world. The revolutionaries 'meditated war against all other governments; and proposed systematically to excite in them all the very worst kind of seditions, in order to lead them to their common destruction . . . [and] for the sake of putting themselves at the head of a confederation of republics as wild and as mischievous as their own'.[18]

What had caused this unprecedented revolution? What was the nature of the regime that had succumbed to it? If the Revolution was uniquely destructive and evil, must there not have been something uniquely defective in the old regime? On one occasion, in 1793, Burke suggested that it was one of the 'best constructed states'.[19] In the *Reflections* he implied that it had 'a mixed and tempered government', a monarchy 'directed by laws, controlled and balanced by the great hereditary wealth and hereditary dignity of a nation; and both again controlled by a judicious check from the reason and feeling of the people at large acting by a suitable and permanent organ'.[20] The French constitution was a good one.[21]

But in the *Reflections* he also wrote this.

Your government in France, though usually, and I think justly, reputed the best of the unqualified monarchies, was still full of abuses. These abuses accumulated in a length of time, as they must accumulate in every monarchy not under the constant inspection of a popular representative.[22]

However, he was sure that the old regime had been reformable and revolution unnecessary. Privileges had been discontinued, but not lost to memory. The constitution was in disrepair, but not destroyed. The French had the elements of a constitution 'very nearly as good as could be wished'.[23]

The old regime was not only reformable; it was reforming.

The government was earnestly seeking to improve the prosperity of the country. It was fighting abuses. Even the unlimited power of the sovereign over his subjects, 'inconsistent, as undoubtedly it was, with law and liberty', was become more and more mitigated in practice. 'So far from refusing itself to reformation, that government was open, with a censurable degree of facility, to all sorts of projects and projectors on the subject. Rather too much countenance was given to the spirit of innovation, which soon was turned against those who fostered it, and ended in their ruin.'[24]

Burke was not consistent. The monarchy was 'directed by laws', yet the power of the monarch was inconsistent with law and liberty. In his *Speech on the Army Estimates*, 1790, one of his fiercest denunciations of the Revolution, he called the old regime a 'relentless despotism'.[25]

Whatever Burke's view of the government of pre-revolutionary France, he considered its social order an integral part of European civilization. It had built great cities; amassed great wealth; built spacious roads and fine bridges; extended communications through canals; constructed 'stupendous' ports and harbours; developed an impressive navy for war and trade; made skilful fortifications; secured itself against its enemies; cultivated almost all its territory; offered many of the finest products to the world; established great institutions of charity; brought the arts to a high state of accomplishment; bred many outstanding warriors, statesmen, lawyers, theologians, philosophers, critics, historians, antiquaries, poets and orators. Burke concluded:

. . . I behold in all this something which awes and commands the imagination, which checks the mind on the brink of precipitate and indiscriminate censure, and which demands, that we should very seriously examine, what and how great are the latent vices that could authorise us at once to level so spacious a fabric with the ground. I do not recognise, in this view of things, the despotism of Turkey. Nor do I discern the character of a government, that has been, on the whole, so oppressive, or so corrupt, or so negligent, as to be utterly unfit for all reformation.[26]

The old regime was despotic but reformable. Despotism was

not the cause of the Revolution. A few nobles were unruly. The people were gullible and some were very poor, but they were not dissatisfied with the power of the Crown. At the beginning of 1789, there was a great cry for reform, none for revolution.[27]

Why did the Revolution happen? There were conspirators, but there were many forces for the conspirators to mobilize. There were a few rebellious nobles. The people were restless. There was a 'season of scarcity'. The government was weak and wavered.[28]

Did the people support the old order? If they did, how did they come under the sway of the conspirators? Burke claimed that the latter deceived the people with false promises, bribed them with the confiscated property of the rich and terrorized them with military force. But he was troubled by the apparent popular support for the Revolution. He explained – or evaded explaining – the transfer of popular loyalty from Crown to Revolution by characterizing the French people as 'light'.

On 12 November 1789 he wrote: 'The National Assembly is nothing more than an organ of the will of the burghers of Paris; and they are so, because the feelings of the burghers of Paris do not differ much from those of the generality of the French nation.'[29] In January 1790 he said: 'On comparing the whole of fact, of public document, and of what can be discerned of the general temper of the French people, I perfectly agree with you that there is very little likelihood of the old government's regaining its former authority.'[30] But by October 1790 his view had changed: 'France continues under its first stupefaction and the terror of its first suprise: for by surprise that great kingdom was taken, as if it were a little fort garrisoned by invalids.'[31]

There were deeper causes of the Revolution. The ruling class was corrupted by luxury and novel ideas. It lost its will to rule as certain 'men of letters' were peddling radical political theories. In this situation, could the Revolution have yet been avoided with a better government and, in particular, a better king?

'You know, Sir,' Burke wrote in March 1791, 'that no party can act without a resolute, vigorous, zealous, and enterprising chief. The chief of every monarchical party must be the monarch himself.'[32]

In 1780 Burke called Louis XVI a very great man.[33] In the *Reflections* he described him as 'a mild and lawful monarch', the acts of whose reign 'were a series of concessions to his subjects, who was willing to relax his authority, to remit his prerogatives, to call his people to a share of freedom, not known, perhaps not desired by their ancestors'.[34] However, he had left his virtues unguarded by caution; because he was not taught that, where power is concerned, he who will confer benefits must take security against ingratitude.[35]

In a letter of 12 November 1789 he wrote: 'There seems no energy in the French monarchy able to revive the royal authority. . . . The King is heavy, inert, inexperienced, timid, without resources, even if he were not a prisoner. . . .' And in another, of March 1791: 'You have a well intentioned and virtuous prince – but minds like his, bred with no other view than to a safe and languid domination, are not made for breaking their prisons, terrifying their enemies and animating their friends.'[36]

But this was not the worst that Burke had to say about Louis. In the letter of 12 November 1789 he declared that the chief supports of the monarchy, the nobility and the clergy, were extinguished, 'and extinguished by the ill-judged acts of the Crown itself'. The monarchy was responsible for nothing less than the disconnection of the whole frame of the commonwealth.[37]

In his *Thoughts on French Affairs* (1791) Burke wrote that Louis was 'deluded to his ruin' by his desire to humble and reduce his nobility, clergy, and magistracy. Presumably, Burke supposed, he did not mean wholly to eradicate those bodies as the Revolution had done. None the less, with his own hand 'Louis XVI pulled down the pillars which upheld his own throne; and this he did, because he could not bear the inconveniences which are attached to everything human; because he found himself cooped up, and in durance, by those limits which nature prescribes to desire and imagination; and was taught to consider as low and degrading that mutual dependence which Providence has ordained that all men should have on one another'.[38] Burke not only accused Louis of bringing about the Revolution. He charged him with some of the most serious errors he attributed to the revolutionaries: failure to recognize the necessary limits of human capacities; excessive indulgence of both desire and imagination; going against nature; and defying the decrees of Providence.

Monarchies, Burke thought, were prone to division between the monarch and the rest of the ruling class: 'kings . . . are very easily alienated from all the higher orders of their subjects. . . . It is with persons of condition that sovereigns chiefly come into contact. It is from them that they generally experience opposition to their will.'[39]

It was Louis' virtue that he was a reforming monarch. But his reforms were, at least in part, motivated by his desire to win the support of the common people in his struggle against the upper classes, a move which led to his ruin.[40] And the 'false philosophy' of the times had insinuated its way into the court itself, with disastrous consequences. The king's ministers were so infected with 'the contagion of project and system . . . that they publicly advertised for plans and schemes of government, as if they were to provide for the rebuilding of a hospital that had burned down'. This unchained the fury of rash speculation amongst a people too apt to be guided by a heated imagination and a wild spirit of adventure.[41]

Burke censured not only the king and his ministers. He found a source of the Revolution in the 'whole official system, particularly in the diplomatic part'. The diplomats condemned their government for the decay of French influence in other lands. From quarrelling with the government, they began to complain of monarchy itself, as a system of government too inconstant for a 'regular plan of national aggrandisement'. Thus the diplomats saw their way forward through a republic.[42]

Outside the state apparatus, all was far from well with the ruling class. Burke denied, in the *Reflections*, that the nobility had 'any considerable share' in the oppression of the people. However, he believed them to be 'not without considerable faults and errors'.

Habitual dissoluteness of manners continued beyond the pardonable period of life, was more common amongst them than it is with us; and it reigned with the less hope of remedy, though possibly with something of less mischief, by being covered with more exterior decorum. They countenanced too much that licentious philosophy which has helped to bring on their ruin. There was another error amongst them more fatal. Those of the commons, who approached to or exceeded many of the nobility in point of wealth, were not fully admitted to the rank and estimation which wealth, in reason and good policy, ought to bestow in every country; though I think not equally with that of other nobility. The two kinds of aristocracy were too punctiliously kept asunder; less so, however, than in Germany or some other nations.

This separation was 'one principal cause of the destruction of the old nobility'. Burke added that it did not justify revolution. It had been a reformable abuse.[43].

This was Burke's portrait of the substantial part of the population in disarray. Who were the revolutionaries? Burke had two kinds of answer: the conspiratorial and the sociological. The conspiratorial answer was that the Revolution was led by ambitious men who bribed and deceived the poor into plundering the rich. 'It is fatally known, that the great object of the Jacobin system is to excite the lowest description of the people to range themselves under ambitious men, for the pillage and destruction of the more eminent orders and classes of the community.'[44]

The sociological answer is the thesis of the bourgeois revolution. In the *Reflections* Burke noted that the Assembly was largely made up of lawyers, 'not of distinguished magistrates, . . . not of leading advocates, . . . not renowned professors in universities; but . . . of the inferior, unlearned, mechanical, merely instrumental members of the profession'. The general composition was of 'obscure provincial advocates, of stewards of petty local jurisdictions, country attornies, notaries, and the whole train of the ministers of municipal litigation, the fomentors and conductors of the petty war of village vexation'.

In addition, there was 'an handful of country clowns' and 'not a greater number of traders, who, though somewhat more instructed, and more conspicuous in the order of society, had never known any thing beyond their counting-house'. There was also a considerable number of doctors and 'dealers in stocks and funds, who must be eager, at any expense, to change their ideal paper wealth for the more solid substance of land'.[45]

Money was a crucial factor in the Revolution. The nobility was separated from the wealthy commons. 'By the vast debt of France a great monied interest had insensibly grown up, and with it a great power.' Various customs and laws had kept the landed and monied interests more separated in France, and the owners of the two forms of property 'not so well disposed to each other' as in England. 'In this state of real, though not always perceived warfare between the noble ancient landed interest, and the new monied interest, the greatest because the most applicable strength was in the hands of the latter.'[46]

The new money had a definite class spirit. 'The monied interest is in its nature more ready for any adventure; and its possessors more disposed to new enterprises of any kind. Being of recent acquisition, it falls in more naturally with any novelties. It is therefore the kind of wealth which will be resorted to by all who wish for change.'[47]

There was a close connection between the spirit of risk characteristic of the monied interest and the boldness of intellectual speculators. Risk was the spirit of the French Revolution. 'Your legislators, in every thing new, are the very first who have founded a commonwealth upon gaming, and infused this spirit into it as its vital breath. The great object in these politics is to metamorphose France, from a great kingdom into one great play-table; to turn its inhabitants into a nation of gamesters; to make speculation as extensive as life; to mix it with all its concerns; and to divert the whole of the hopes and fears of the people from their usual channels, into the impulses, passions, and superstitions of those who live on chances.'[48]

Burke was especially concerned with the fluctuating value of money. To bring this about was to play dice with every man's life. It meant disorder and injustice. But all would not be victims equally. 'The truly melancholy part of the policy of systematically making a nation of gamesters is this; that though all are forced to play, few can understand the game; and fewer still are in a condition to avail themselves of the knowledge. The many must be the dupes of the few who conduct the machine of these speculations.'[49] In particular, the country will be the dupe of the town. Where the value of money is uncertain, the peasant will be reluctant to sell at the town market. The towns will be short of food. The townspeople will be inflamed. The peasants will resist. There is potential civil war. And potential tyranny over the peasants.

Money can become revolutionary because there is a real, not merely a semantic connection between financial, intellectual and political speculation.

There is also a time of insecurity, when interest of all sorts become objects of speculation. Then it is, that their very attachment to wealth and importance will induce certain persons of opulence to list themselves, and even to take a lead with the party which they think most likely to prevail, in order to obtain to themselves consideration in some new order or disorder of things. . . . Those, who speculate on change, always make a great number among people of rank and fortune, as well as amongst the low and the indigent.[50]

With the French Revolution, all was new. The old order had not only its characteristic form of hierarchy, but its characteristic forms of conspiracy and subversion. Oppressive monarchs, ambitious nobles, restless masses; these were the traditional ingredients of disorder. But the old order was passing away and, with it, the old sources of disorder. The *middle classes* (Burke's term) were now greater than ever before.

Like whatever is the most effectively rich and great in society, these classes became the seat of all the active politics; and the preponderating weight to decide on them. . . . There were all the talents which assert their pretensions, and are impatient of the place which settled society prescribes to them. These descriptions had got between the great and the populace; and the influence on the lower classes was with them. Without the great, the first movements in this revolution could not, perhaps, have been given. But the spirit of ambition, now for the first time connected with the spirit of speculation, was not be restrained at will.[51]

The Revolution was made by the middle classes, especially the speculators, and it would benefit the middle classes, especially the speculators. 'Those whose operations can take from, or add ten per cent to, the possessions of every man in France, must be the masters of every man in France. The whole of the power obtained by this revolution will settle in the towns among the burghers, and the monied directors who lead them.'[52]

The power of the urban bourgeoisie was also based on organization and communication. 'The correspondence of the monied and the mercantile world, the literary intercourse of academies, but, above all, the press of which they [the middle class] had in a manner entire possession, made a kind of electric communication every where.'[53] The habits of burghers, their occupations, their diversions, continually brought them into contact. 'Their virtues and their vices are sociable; they are always in garrison; and they come embodied and half disciplined into the hands of those who mean to form them for civil, or for military action.'[54]

The opposite was true of the countryman. The very nature of country life, the nature of landed property, their occupations and their pleasures rendered combination and organization impossible among country people They could assemble, arm, act only with the utmost difficulty and with the greatest expense. If they could commence, they could not sustain their efforts. They could not proceed systematically.[55]

If the Revolution were successful, therefore, France would be governed by 'the agitators in corporations, by societies in the towns formed of directors of assignats, and trustees for the sale of church lands, attornies, agents, money-jobbers, speculators, and adventurers, composing an ignoble oligarchy founded on the destruction of the crown, the church, the nobility, and the people'. This would be the upshot of 'all the deceitful dreams and visions of the equality and the rights of men'.[56]

The transfer of power to a new kind of property was also a moral revoluton. The new rulers were 'sophisters' and 'jobbers' who considered national reputation as the credit of the *caisse d'escompte*. They would care more about a fall of a quarter per cent in the value of *assignats* than the destruction of their country.[57]

Burke's critique of what he called 'Jacobinism' is a classic conservative critique of political radicalism.

What is Jacobinism? It is an attempt . . . to eradicate prejudice out of the minds of men, for the purpose of putting all power and authority into the hands of the persons capable of occasionally enlightening the minds of the people. For this purpose the Jacobins have resolved to destroy the whole frame and fabric of the old societies of the world, and to regenerate them after their fashion. . . . As the grand prejudice, and that which holds all the other prejudices together, the first, last, and middle object of their hostility, is religion.[58]

But Jacobinism not only destroyed true religion. It was itself a new, false religion, 'the new fanatical religion . . . of the rights of man'.[59] This religious transformation was the essence of the French Revolution.

Burke held that certain ideas are alluring because they appear enlightened, humane, progressive and liberating, but analysis and historical experience shows that, if implemented, they have consequences which have the opposite properties. Burke expressed this paradoxical truth by playing with such words as 'superstition', 'prejudice' and 'enlightened'. For instance, in the *Reflections* he wrote:

The age has not yet the complete benefit of that diffusion of knowledge that has undermined superstition and error; and the king of France wants another object or two, to consign to oblivion, in consideration of all the good which is to arise from his own sufferings, and the patriotic crimes of an enlightened age. Although this work of our new light and knowledge, did not go to the length, that in all probability it was intended it should be carried; yet I must think, that such treatment of any human creatures must be shocking to any but those who are made for accomplishing revolutions.[60]

By emphasizing the 'enlightened' character of the revolutionaries, Burke sought to draw attention to the gap between their liberal claims and their tyrannical achievements.

It is a vulgar error to suppose that Burke was guilty of inconsistency because he supported the 1689 and Amercian revolutions and opposed the French. It is a vulgar error partly because he supported the American revolution with extreme caution (he supported the American *cause* rather than the American *revolution*). It is also a vulgar error because, in his views of these three revolutions, Burke maintained the same set of general principles. In his attitude towards 1689 and 1776, he was never a radical. Since all three revolutions are often considered to be 'world-historical', we should examine why Burke thought the first two to be fundamentally different from that of France.

King James II, the British Government in its treatment of America, and the French revolutionaries had, according to Burke, one important feature in common: they were all innovators. The revolutionaries of 1689 charged King James with the subversion of the Protestant church and state, and of their fundamental laws and liberties. The Revolution was made to preserve the 'ancient indisputable laws and liberties' of the people. Indeed, although Burke referred to 1689 as 'the glorious event commonly called the Revolution in England', he went on to say: 'What we did was in truth and substance, and in a constitutional light, a revolution, not made, but prevented. . . . In the stable, fundamental parts of our Constitution we made no revolution. . . .'[61]

Similarly, he declared, in his *Speech on American Taxation* (1774), that British taxation of the American colonies was an oppressive innovation. He urged the Government to 'oppose the ancient policy and practice of the empire as ramparts against the speculations of innovators on both sides of the question'.[62] In the *Appeal from the New to the Old Whigs* (1791) he explicitly compared the American Revolution to 1689.

He considered the Americans as standing at that time, and in that controversy, as England did to King James II, in 1688. He believed, that they had taken up arms from one motive only; that is, our attempting to tax them without their consent; to tax them for the purposes of maintaining civil and military establishments. If this attempt of ours could have been practically established, he thought, with them, that their assemblies would become totally useless; that, under the system of policy which was then pursued, the Americans could have no sort of security for their laws or liberties. . . .[63]

Burke's radical distinction between defensive and innovative revolutions is historically dubious. He made his case for the conservative character of 1689 by treating it in isolation from earlier upheavals in seventeenth-century England, thereby evading the issue as to what role political radicalism had played in establishing the constitution he was committed to defend. With respect to America, he did not ignore the part played by abstract ideas in the Revolution, but chose to regard them as marginal to the real issues. If the facts were as Burke stated them, the reasons he gave for his distinction were consistent: necessary revolution in defence of ancient liberties against tyrannical innovation is approved; unnecessary revolution against reformable government on the speculative hope of improving innovation is condemned. But the distinction rested upon several doubtful factual assumptions: that the *ancien régime* was reformable without revolution; that speculative predominated over real grievances in the French Revolution; that the operative ruling ideology of both England and America in their recent history had been conservative rather than innovative; that political radicalism and speculative ideas had played no significant role in the creation of the British Constitution of 1689 or in the American Revolution.

How useful today is Burke's distinction between defensive and innovative revolutions? Since most modern revolutions have taken place in 'underdeveloped' countries, and since 'development' is one of their chief aims, they are clearly innovative. Burke's distinction draws our attention to the fact that they have typically been, if not a defence, then a counter-attack against that particular form of political innovation known as imperialism. The traditional has been invaded by the tyrannical. In Marxist theory, anti-imperialist revolutions are generally 'progressive'. Burke, not Marx, helps us to note the element of *recovered* national or ethnic dignity in these revolutions. If it seems far-fetched to suggest that Burke can help us understand the anti-imperialist revolutions of our time, we should remember that much of his work was devoted to a thorough-going critique of British imperial policies in Ireland, America and India on the ground that they deprived the native inhabitants of their traditional rights.

Probably only highly innovative revolutions can be world-historical. World history is the history of innovation. We must all obey the great law of change, Burke said. He fought as desperately as vainly against the possibility that this law might be embodied in a radically new development. He looked into the future and feared that it might work.

## NOTES

1. John. C. Weston, Jr., 'Edmund Burke's View of History', *The Review of Politics*, 23, 1961, p. 225.
2. Harry Eckstein, 'On the Etiology of Internal Wars', *History and Theory*, IV, 1965, pp. 134–5.
3. Edmund Burke, *Reflections on the Revolution in France* (Harmondsworth: Penguin Books, 1968), p. 92.
4. *The Correspondence of Edmund Burke* (Chicago and Cambridge University Presses, 1958–1970), vol. VII, p. 218.
5. *The Works and Correspondence of Edmund Burke* (London: Rivington, 1852), vol. V, p. 424.
6. Ibid., pp. 300–1.
7. Ibid., p. 216 (emphasis Burke's).
8. Ibid., p. 322.
9. *Correspondence*, vol. VII, pp. 387–8.
10. *Works and Correspondecne*, vol. V, p. 306.
11. Ibid., vol. IV, p. 591.
12. Edmund Burke, *The Writings and Speeches of Edmund Burke* (1898–9), vol. III, p. 218.
13. *Works and Correspondence*, vol. V, p. 461.
14. Ibid., pp. 340–1.
15. *Reflections*, p. 152.
16. Ibid., p. 237.
17. *Works and Correspondence*, vol. IV, p. 401.
18. Ibid., pp. 402–3.

19.  *Correspondence*, vol. VII, pp. 387–8.
20.  *Reflections*, pp. 227–8.
21.  *Writings and Speeches*, vol. III, p. 220; *Works and Correspondence*, vol. IV, p. 389.
22.  *Reflections*, p. 230.
23.  Ibid., pp 121–2.
24.  Ibid., pp. 236–7.
25.  *Writings and Speeches*, vol. III, p. 218; *The Speeches of the Right Honourable Edmund Burke* (London: Longman, Hurst, Rees, &c., 1816), vol. IV, p. 63.
26.  *Reflections*, pp. 235–6.
27.  *Works and Correspondence*, vol. IV, p. 423; *Reflections*, pp. 230–1.
28.  *Works and Correspondence*, vol. IV, pp. 423, 473.
29.  *Correspondence*, vol. VI, p. 36.
30.  Ibid., p. 79.
31.  Ibid., p. 141.
32.  Ibid., p. 241.
33.  *Works and Correspondence*, vol. III, pp. 349–50.
34.  *Reflections*, pp. 126, 177.
35.  *Works and Correspondence*, vol. IV, p. 490.
36.  *Correspondence*, vol. VI, pp. 36, 241.
37.  Ibid., p. 241.
38.  *Works and Correspondence*, vol. IV, p. 582.
39.  Ibid., p. 581.
40.  Ibid.
41.  Ibid., p. 383.
42.  *Works and Correspondence*, vol. V, pp. 338–9.
43.  *Reflections*, pp. 244–5.
44.  *Works and Correspondence*, vol. V, p. 121.
45.  *Reflections*, pp. 129–32.
46.  Ibid., pp. 209–11.
47.  Ibid., p. 211.
48.  Ibid., pp. 309–10.
49.  Ibid., pp. 310–11.
50.  *Works and Correspondence*, vol. IV, p. 484.
51.  Ibid., vol. V, pp. 343–4.
52.  *Reflections*, p. 311.
53.  *Works and Correspondence*, vol. V, p. 343.
54.  *Reflections*, pp. 312–13.
55.  Ibid., pp. 311–12.
56.  Ibid., p. 313.

57. *Correspondence*, vol. VI, pp. 212–13.
58. Ibid., vol. VIII, pp. 129–30.
59. *Works and Correspondence*, vol. VI, p. 59.
60. *Reflections*, pp. 166–8.
61. *Reflections*, pp. 112–13, 117; *Writings and Speeches*, vol. III, pp. 225–6.
62. *Works and Correspondence*, vol. III, pp. 194, 218–20.
63. Ibid., vol. IV, pp. 419–20.

# 13

# The Critique of Political Radicalism

Edmund Burke constructed a classic conservative critique of political radicalism. The chief immediate object of his attack was the radicalism of late eighteenth-century France and England. But he appealed to general principles which, though expressed in the language and with the concepts of his own time, are sufficiently similar to widely-held conservative ideas of today that we may and should assess their value. Today's radicals are not Burke's radicals and vary greatly in their beliefs. But Burke's radicals were never the real radicals of his own time. Nowhere in his works can we find a scrupulous account of the ideas or actions of any particular radical thinker or politician. Burke attacked certain abstract radical ideas by means of certain abstract conservative arguments. These abstract ideas may be held by radicals in different times and places, facing different concrete problems.

To the proposal that we should evaluate Burke's critique of radicalism it may be objected that, since he appealed to 'natural feeling' and rejected systematic argument, he protected himself, many would say illegitimately, from systematic rational criticism. I have shown, however, that he did not reject reason nor the idea that politics should be rational.

Burke not only at times expressed a preference for intuition over ratiocination but also advocated pragmatism against theory. Theory, he said, was speculative, not real. Theory was too broad and too deep. The real problems of society were particular and their remedies must therefore also be particular. A theoretical approach to social problems led to the characteristic defects and dangers of radicalism: solutions too remote from reality and too big for the problems. But, although he did not present his ideas systematically and was far from consistent, he did have a theory of politics and of political radicalism. This political theory was based upon the metaphysical doctrine that nature was order. This doctrine had two meanings. Nature ordained stability: good order is the foundation of all good things. Nature is also regular. Thus politics is governed by discoverable laws. Because stability is natural, revolution is against nature. But, though revolution is (morally) unnatural, it is still governed by nature's laws. These dictate that revolution leads to anarchy, which in turn must lead to tyranny. Thus, for all his pragmatism, Burke proposed a law of revolution for us to assess, a law both general and normative, a law derived from a highly articulated political theory.

Burke's metaphysics is banal and unpersuasive. His epistemology carries much more force. The project of revolution, he argues, presupposes a degree of reliable social knowledge which no individual or faction can reasonably claim. The radical is, not as a matter of contingent psychological fact, but in his essence intellectually arrogant. As a theorist he thinks big. As a radical, he applies his big theories without adequate knowledge of the probable consequences of his actions and with little understanding of the inadequacy of his knowledge. The identification of practical grievances or real abuses in government is easy. They are always there and plain enough. The cure of grievances and the correction of abuses is often possible and always desirable when possible. But the radical who attempts the reconstruction of society cannot achieve his goal. Where abuses are clear and great, and grievances strongly felt, destruction of old institutions may not be difficult. But building new order out of the chaos of destruction is a formidable task. Tyranny is the short cut. Thus, the necessary relation between radical politics and tyranny is not only metaphysical, it derives from the sociological consequences of acting politically upon weak theories and a poor theory about the practical possibilities of theory.

This is perhaps Burke's strongest argument. Few would deny that social knowledge is highly uncertain. The conclusion that we should change social institutions with caution appears to follow. The radical claims that he has great tasks to perform but he lacks the technique to perform them.

The argument is strong but not conclusive. Burke himself recognized its weak point. His fallibilist case against radicalism, like the very similar case that has been made by conservatives many times, presupposes a certain view of the relation between the radical and his political problems. It sees the radical confronting injustice in society. He theorises the causes and the cures. He concludes that the injustice is not an accident lying on the surface of society, to be removed by a well-aimed reformist blow, but is rooted in the foundations of the existing social form. The remedy, therefore, must be to remove, not merely the injustice, but the social form which necessarily produced it. But this objective, says the conservative, is impossible on the epistemological grounds already given.

But the radical does not always, perhaps does not typically, confront a stable society with an accidental blemish. He faces a society already in disorder, a society whose rulers cannot solve the problems before them. Burke did not believe that revolutions were caused by conspiracies of radical intellectuals. Rather, they were caused by the mistakes, stupidity, arrogance and oppression of rulers, and by the strains produced by social and economic development. In such a situation, radicals might make bad worse. But societies may disintegrate from their internal contradictions. Particular radical solutions may be ill-conceived and lead to new oppression. But in some circumstances no moderate solution may work. Caution may become a speculative ideal, not a practical method.

Because Burke held this view of the causes of revolution, he acknowledged that revolution might be justified by necessity. Whether any particular revolution is justified by necessity can only be answered by analysis of the particular circumstances. But, even when the circumstances have been analyzed, conservatives and radicals will not agree. Where radical action has been taken, the conservative will argue that less ambitious solutions would have produced better results. Not only will the two not have the same idea of 'better', but the conservative case rests upon a counterfactual claim that if conservative solution $x$ had been tried then beneficial result $y$ would have ensued. This claim presupposes precisely the kind of knowledge of social cause and effect which the conservative criticizes the radical for claiming. Thus, the fallibilist case againt radicalism is not conclusive. Conservatives are fallible, too. And the mistakes they make may also be big ones.

Burke held that radicals were doomed not merely to failure but to achieve the opposite of what they intended. If this argument were correct, it would be decisive. As Burke put it himself: 'Proceeding, therefore, as we are obliged to proceed, that is upon an hypothesis that we address rational men, can false political principles be more effectually exposed, than by demonstrating that they lead to consequences directly inconsistent with, and subversive of, the arrangements grounded upon them?' In the case of the French Revolution, he maintained that the revolutionaries proclaimed and then trampled on the rights of man. They promised freedom and happiness but delivered tyranny and misery. This was not due to bad luck nor merely to bad judgement. It was in the nature of things. The promise of radical emancipation from evil is an illusion which, if acted on, necessarily leads to radical evil.

Radical ideals, Burke freely acknowledges, are, in the abstract, extremely appealing. But abstract ideals are not only an inadequate substitute for practical remedies, they often mask vicious intent. Those who seek the support of others to further their own ambitions will state their aims in terms of the interests of those others, not of themselves. Thus, their ideals will appear altruistic and noble. The results may not match the stated aims because the stated aims were never the real aims. To modernize the point: would-be dictators will manipulate popular-democratic symbols to secure popular support for their ambitions.

But this is an argument against fake not genuine radicalism. Burke was concerned to emphasize, however, that the people may easily mistake the one for the other. None the less, his case against radicalism does not rest on the assumption that radicals are insincere. True radicalism is as dangerous as false. Radicals believe that existing society is fundamentally unjust and that the society they aspire to is very fine. Slow and cautious reform seems to them a sort of toleration of the intolerable. Justice demands impatience with injustice. But impatience is not wise. Nor is it just. Impatience imbued with a sense of justice becomes fanaticism. And fanaticism is a tyrant.

Burke was the first of a long line of conservative thinkers who have seen political radicalism as a sort of fanatical secular religion. One of the stigmata of fanaticism is manichaeanism: dividing the world into the just and the unjust, the saved and the damned. This manichaeanism seems reasonable when the just are 'the people', the overwhelming majority, and the unjust their oppressors. But the radical is not humble before the popular will. He has a theory of the popular interest. He has a mission to bring the people happiness. And if the people take a different view of the means to their own happiness, the radical leader, the just man, feels constrained to bring them to a true consciousness of their own interest, by force if necessary.

There was, Burke thought, a deep cause of a difference of view between radicals and the people whose interests they claimed to represent about the sources of general happiness. Radicals wish to change society fundamentally and fast. The majority, even if sorely abused, has a vested interest in society. Society guarantees a certain minimum, however low. Even if it be indeed low, there is a degree of security in it. People adjust to difficult circumstances, even if they wish they were better. They know what to expect and can plan their lives accordingly. The radical promises something much better. But he creates disorder and with disorder not even the minimum is guaranteed, there is no security, and the future is uncertain. Stable societies, even if unjust, provide security, which is an important source of happiness. Radicals offer promises of great benefits and the probability of actual chaos. The people wisely distrust their radical saviours. Radicals trust themselves too much and therefore come to distrust the people it is their mission to help.

Revolutions achieve the opposite of what they intend because what they intend – radical freedom, equality, democracy and perfect justice – cannot be achieved and because they offer the people, in the name of freedom and democracy, what the people prudently decline. Consequently, radicals must force through the impossible and the unpopular. The result can only

be the negation of the freedom, equality, democracy and justice that they promised.

There is much truth in all this. The vocation of the radical
and that of the democrat are often heard to reconcile. The
people are, of course, sometimes radical, so that radical and
popular aims coincide. But the alliance is unstable. Theories of
'false consciousness' at best explain why the problem exists,
they do not provide a solution. The 'radical' Burke here
attacks is an abstraction: an extreme case rather than an ideal
type. Not all radicals are fanatics. Some restrain their pursuit
of justice when it clashes with democracy and liberty. Respect
for the popular will and self-criticism are neither impossible
nor unknown among radicals. Nevertheless, such self-
restraint is a restraint upon radicalism: the more restrained the
seeker after justice, the less radical he is. Except in times of
unusual popular radicalism, a certain tension must exist between radical means and radical ends.

Radicalism is not necessarily incompatible with freedom
and democracy. Indeed, in any unfree and undemocratic society, freedom and democracy entail a radicalism of ends. But
radicalism of means, fundamental change fast, is undoubtedly
despotic in tendency.

Burke warns the democratic radical that democratic radicalism of means may well be self-contradictory. The radical
may reply, with the argument already canvassed, that, in situations of social disintegration, there may be no non-radical
solutions and, even if radicalism be an evil, a choice of the
least evil is the best available option. He may also reply that, if
radicalism may lead to despotism, conservatism may conserve
it.

Burke opposed despotism but saw justifiable political
change as the specific remedy of particular grievances and
abuses. 'I would not exclude alteration neither; but even when
I changed, it should be to preserve. I should be led to my
remedy by a great grievance.' Safe politics is slow, cautious
and dull. This is not an easy course. The virtue of moderation
requires a deep courage to be temperate when the multitude
impatiently condemns you. Radicalism is more exciting.
Self-restraint is necessary to resist the temptation of political

adventure and instant popularity. Hang on to the real good you have and improve it. Resist the blandishments of speculative blessings. Only the real can be good. What the radical promises is not real.

But what if the defect is radical? If moderation is complicity with despotism? If the multitude is impatient because the abuse is indeed intolerable? Reality is then evil, not imperfect good. Radicalism is not adventurism but realism. If radicals are often caught in a contradiction between their aims and their achievements, so was Burke. Time and again, he exposed the British Government as despotic, at home and abroad, but he continued to advocate a piecemeal, patient reform which was hardly adequate to the objectives he set it. Burke's gradualist approach to slavery entailed complicity with despotism. So did his toleration of a society in which the wealthy fed their dogs and horses with the food which should have nourished the children of the poor. Burke acknowledged this difficulty for gradualism. In desperation, he appealed from real misery to abstract laws of nature.

Burke still deserves our attention, therefore, because his arguments can be generalized and, when generalized, put hard, though not unanswerable questions to radicals. I have also sought to show that his understanding of the French Revolution in particular and of revolutionary dynamics in general has been widely misunderstood and, as a consequence, underestimated by scholars. Burke was a much better sociologist of revolution than is usually recognized. He had an implicit general theory of revolution which is superior to many recent theories of revolution in two important respects. Firstly, he had an integrated theory of the causes, processes and consequences of revolution while most modern theory is confined mainly to the causes and has little to say about the consequences. Secondly, he integrated empirical and normative theory while modern theorists tend to separate the two and largely ignore the latter.[1]

Edmund Burke teaches that the business of political radicals – the uprooting of established political and social institutions – may lead to quite unexpected and undesired consequences, involving great human suffering. He excoriated radicals for dogmatism and frivolous adventurism. He called for realism, pragmatism and respect for persons. 'I must see with my own eyes, I must, in a manner, touch with my own hands, not only the fixed, but the momentary circumstances, before I could venture to suggest any political project whatsoever. . . . I must see all the aids, and all the obstacles. I must see the means of correcting the plan, where correctives would be wanted. I must see the things; I must see the men.' 'No man carries further than I do the policy of making government pleasing to the people. But the widest range of this politic complaisance is confined within the limits of justice. . . . I never will act the tyrant for their amusement. If they will mix malice in their sports, I shall never consent to throw them any living, sentient creature whatsoever, no not so much as a kitling, to torment.' He often did not practise what he preached. He was not always humane. He was often dogmatic. He understood less than he thought he did. But he did understand that what appears to be good will may be evil will. He understood that good will may motivate acts with evil consequences. That identifying and damning evil is easy, while making good is hard and usually slow. That our fond desires cannot alter the nature of things, by contending against which what have we got, or shall ever get, but defeat and shame?

Radicals, especially Marxists, often pride themselves on their realism. Conservatives teach that realists are conservatives. Radical projects usually fail and often lead to disaster. Radicals are self-righteous and intellectually arrogant. There seems to me enough truth in this for the theory underlying it to be considered seriously. But, because conservatives hold that radical projects are utopian and dangerous, they are inclined to minimize existing misery or attribute it to necessary laws. The first position belies their claim to realism and the second their critique of abstract dogma. Thus the debate between conservatives and radicals remains inconclusive. Burke is still worth our attention because his is a classic statement of conservatism. It has the classic strengths and weaknesses of that position. He offered eighteenth-century solutions to eighteenth-century problems. But those problems belong to a family whose descendents live still among us. We still do not have very good solutions. We must therefore come to grips with his.


## NOTE

1. See Michael Freeman, 'Edmund Burke and the Theory of Revolution', *Political Theory*, 6, 1978, pp. 277–97, and Ted Robert Gurr, 'Burke and the Modern Theory of Revolution: A Reply to Freeman', ibid., pp. 298 et seq. For very recent, and more convincing theorizing about revolution, see S. N. Eisenstadt, *Revolution and the Transformation of Societies* (London: Collier Macmillan, 1978) and Theda Skocpol, *States and Social Revolutions* (Cambridge: Cambridge University Press, 1979).

# Index